A GLASGOW GANG OBSERVED

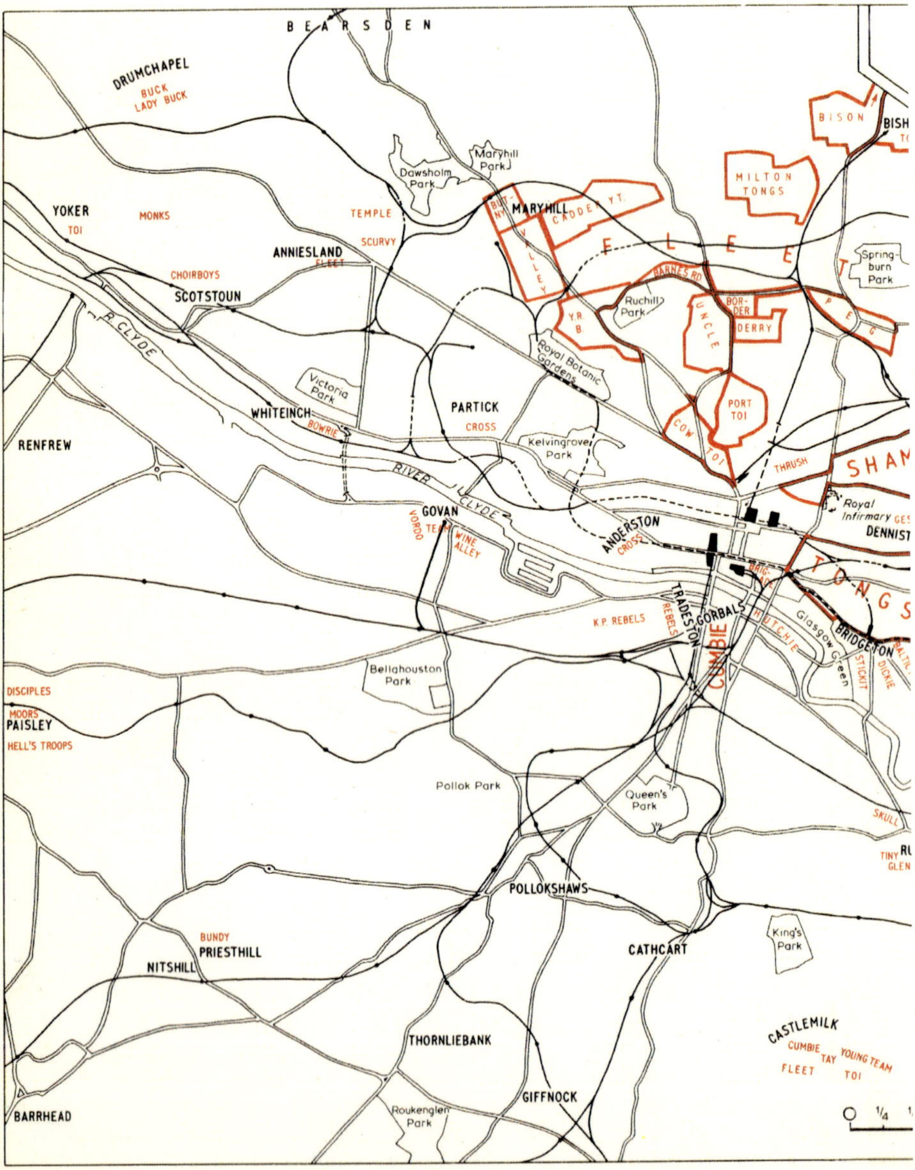

BEARSDEN
DRUMCHAPEL
BUCK
LADY BUCK
YOKER
TOI
MONKS
TEMPLE
SCURVY
ANNIESLAND
FLEET
CHOIRBOYS
SCOTSTOUN
R. CLYDE
Maryhill Park
Dawsholm Park
MARYHILL
CADDER Y.T.
VALLEY
BISON
MILTON TONGS
F L E E T
Springburn Park
BARNES RD
Ruchill Park
Y.R. B.
UNCLE
BORDER
DERRY
PEG
Royal Botanic Gardens
Victoria Park
WHITEINCH
BOWRIE
RENFREW
PARTICK
CROSS
Kelvingrove Park
PORT TOI
COW TOI
THRUSH
RIVER CLYDE
GOVAN
VORDO
TEAM
WINE ALLEY
Royal Infirmary
ANDERSTON
CROSS
TONGS
TRADESTON
REBELS
K.P. REBELS
GORBALS
CUMBIE
HUTCHIE
Glasgow Green
BRIDGETON
STICKIT
DICKIE
Bellahouston Park
DISCIPLES
MOORS
PAISLEY
HELL'S TROOPS
Pollok Park
Queen's Park
SKULL
TINY GLEN
POLLOKSHAWS
King's Park
BUNDY
PRIESTHILL
NITSHILL
CATHCART
CASTLEMILK
CUMBIE
TAY
YOUNG TEAM
FLEET
TOI
THORNLIEBANK
GIFFNOCK
BARRHEAD
Roukenglen Park
0 1/4

MAP OF GLASGOW GANGS
NAMES AND TERRITORIES OF GANGS KNOWN TO
THE YOUNG TEAM, 1966–1967

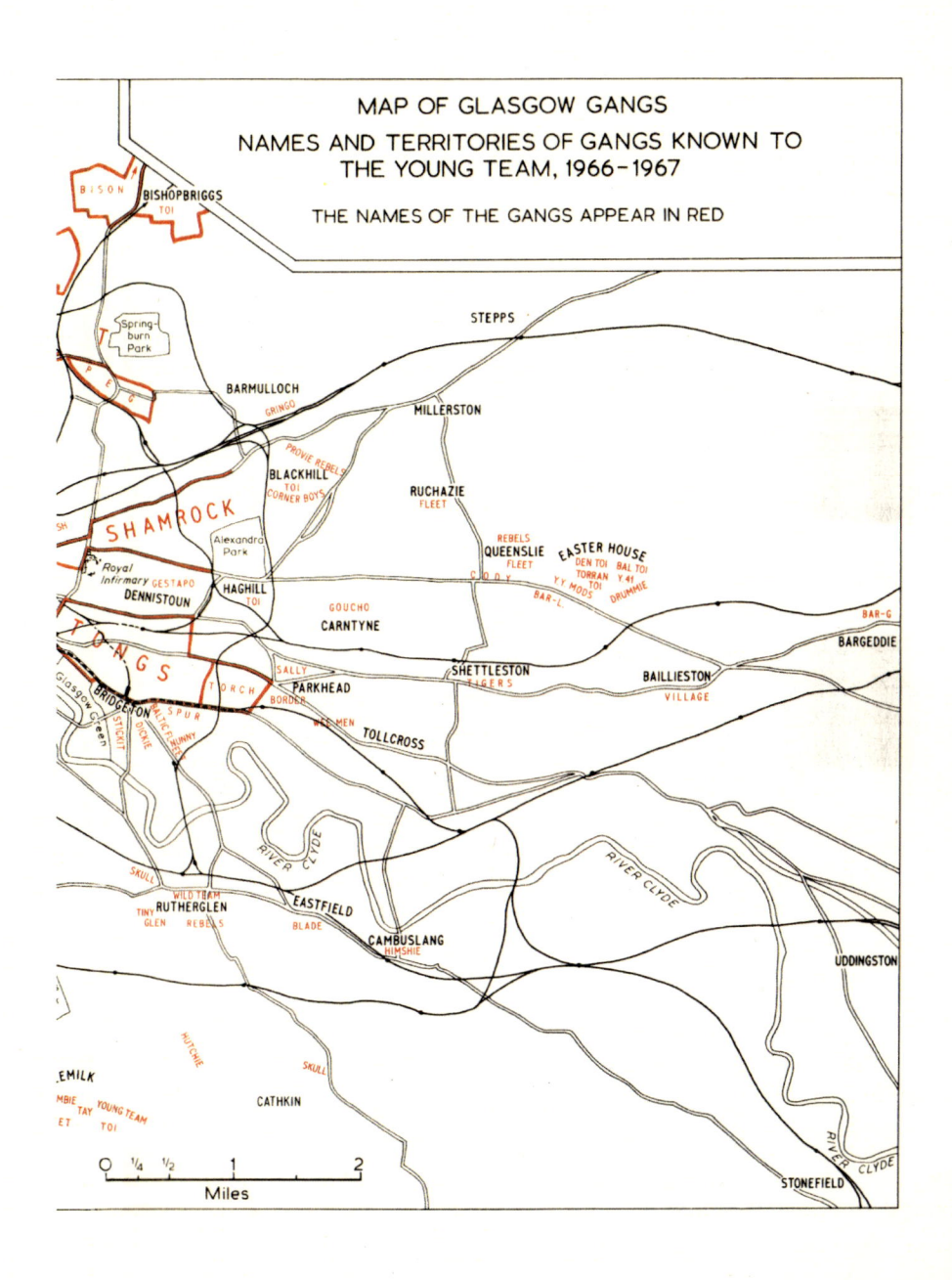

THE NAMES OF THE GANGS APPEAR IN RED

A GLASGOW GANG OBSERVED
JAMES PATRICK

Neil Wilson Publishing • Glasgow

to the boys of ...
who never say no

First published in 1973 by Eyre Methuen, London.

This edition published by
Neil Wilson Publishing
www.nwp.co.uk

© James Patrick 1973, 2012, 2013

Second edition published 2012
Third edition published 2013

The author has established his moral right to be
identified as the Author of this work.

A catalogue record for this book is available
from the British Library.

ISBN: 978-1-906000-38-7
Ebook ISBN: 978-1-906000-39-4

Printed and bound in the EU

Contents

Preface to 1973 edition xi
Preface to 2013 edition xiii
1 Entrée 1
2 The background 5
3 The first night 14
4 I meet the King 24
5 The in-group 32
6 On a Sunday afternoon 44
7 The relevant murders 50
8 Saturday afternoon and Monday evening 59
9 'Jist dossin' aw day' 65
10 Uzz Gemmies 69
11 A pause for reflection 77
12 Birds, birds, birds ... 86
13 Gallous gear, brilliant patter and the writing on the wall 97
14 Malkies, goofies and the busies 104
15 Tim 113
16 Exit 116
17 Epilogue 123
18 Housing and gangs in Glasgow 128
19 British research into gangs 137
20 American research into gangs 152
21 Treatment and prevention 185
Glossary 204
Annotations 213
Bibliography 217
Index 229

Preface to 1973 edition

THIS BOOK HAS been written for the general reader rather than for the criminologist, the clinical psychologist, or the specialist in the sociology of deviance, because I believe the problem described is of more than academic importance. It does not purport to be an authoritative or exhaustive treatise on Glasgow's juvenile gangs, but is a descriptive account of a participant observation study of one such gang which I met on 12 occasions between October 1966 and January 1967.

In all I spent just under 120 hours in the field; and as my involvement with the gang deepened, so the hours lengthened until towards the end of January I was in the company of the gang during one weekend from seven o'clock on Friday evening until six on Sunday morning.

I have deliberately allowed some years to pass between the completion of the fieldwork and publication. The main reasons for the delay have been my interest in self-preservation, my desire to protect the members of the gang, and my fear of exacerbating the gang situation in Glasgow which was receiving nationwide attention in 1968 and 1969. Reasons of personal safety also dictate the use of a pseudonym.

What follows is not a study of Glasgow, or of Glasgow youth in general, or of a particular community within the city. It is a small-scale piece of research which is in no way a statistical survey and so the conclusions may well be of a restricted character. My aim has been unashamedly exploratory – to present a brief glimpse of the reality which engages Glasgow gang boys, 'to comprehend and to illuminate their view and to interpret the world as it appears to them.' (Cf. Matza, 1969, p.25)

I have not been able to include – for legal reasons – a full account of my relationships with the gang or with the police. As a result, a discussion of the ethical and methodological problems associated with participant observation has been postponed to such time as a complete record of events can be given.

It remains for me to acknowledge my indebtedness to a variety of people, especially James McMeekin and Max Paterson for professional and personal advice. Stan Cohen and David Downes kindly read the more analytical chapters which were improved by their suggestions. I should also like to thank Charles McKay and Leonard Turpie for the various forms of help they gave me.

James Patrick, August, 1972

Acknowledgement

The lyrics to 'Deadend Street' by Ray Davies which appear on pages 93-4 are © Warner/Chappell Music, Inc., Sony/ATV Music Publishing LLC, Universal Music Publishing Group.

The Young Team, 1966-7

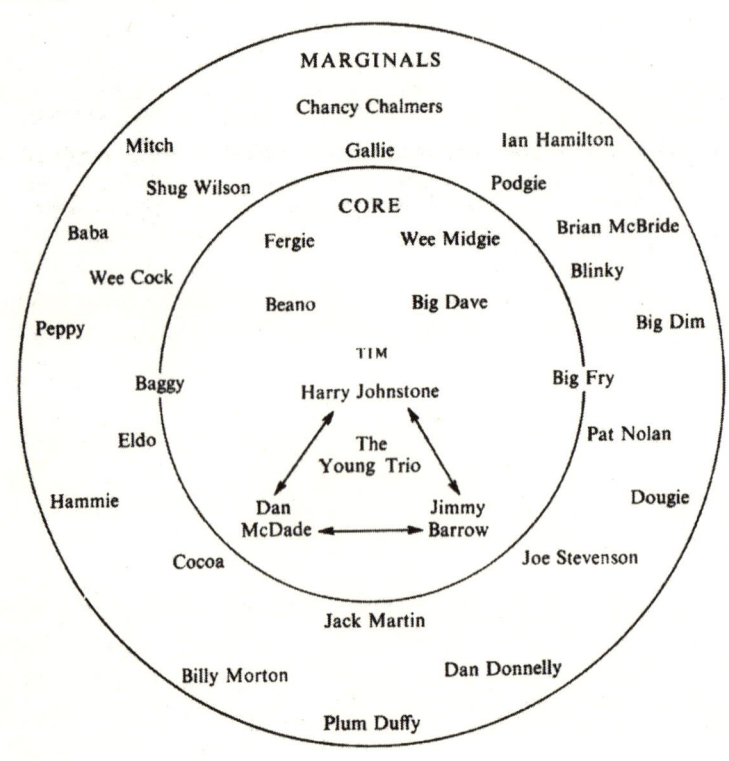

```
                    MARGINALS
                  Chancy Chalmers
        Mitch        Gallie         Ian Hamilton
          Shug Wilson         Podgie
                      CORE          Brian McBride
     Baba      Fergie    Wee Midgie
                                       Blinky
       Wee Cock
                  Beano    Big Dave          Big Dim
    Peppy
                       TIM
              Baggy   Harry Johnstone   Big Fry
       Eldo              The
                      Young Trio            Pat Nolan
                   Dan  ←→  Jimmy
                   McDade   Barrow       Dougie
    Hammie
                                     Joe Stevenson
              Cocoa
                       Jack Martin
              Billy Morton      Dan Donnelly
                       Plum Duffy
```

xii

Preface to 2013 edition

THIS BOOK BEGAN life as a thesis for the University of Glasgow, although not one which initially it was keen to accept. As I explain in the text, I was originally invited to join the gang by Tim Malloy, the pseudonym I gave to a boy in an Approved School where I was working as a newly qualified teacher. I wanted to understand why boys on 'leave' from the school for a weekend, instead of demonstrating their ability to keep on the right side of the law, often returned to the school with further serious charges against them which increased their period of detention. Tim, for his part, was just as keen to show me that I, as a young, middle-class Glaswegian who had been brought up only a mile from him, might as well have come from the moon, so little did I understand his life.

In addition to working in the Approved School, I was simultaneously studying for a higher degree and began casting around for a suitable subject for a thesis. So when the tutor gave each student in the class a 5x3-inch index card on which to commit our first thoughts on the title and topic of our proposed theses, I wrote: 'A participant observation study of a Glasgow gang.' Three years later I submitted my thesis, having not heard from my supervisor in the meantime: that's what passed for higher degree supervision in those days, although I did receive useful advice from other members of staff when I was preparing the text for publication.

Within a few weeks of submitting the work, however, I was contacted by the Head of Department who explained that my thesis would not be accepted: it was, apparently, too much of 'a hot potato' and could I please think of another topic and submit a different thesis. I firmly declined to do so, arguing instead that my topic was an appropriate subject for a higher degree and that the difficulties that arose from its controversial subject matter could be dealt with.

The upshot was that a special sub-committee was convened under the Chairmanship of the Clerk to the Senate to investigate and report. I was invited to appear before this sub-committee and, appreciating the force of the legal dictum that anyone who speaks in his own defence has a knave for an adviser and a fool for a client, I approached a personal friend, Jim McMeekin, a solicitor, to act on my behalf. He was able to persuade the assembled professors that the thesis was neither libellous nor did it present any other legal difficulty; understandably, the university was anxious to be reassured on these points.

Moreover, no objection had been raised when I had registered the title of the thesis three years previously and that I had in the interval invested considerable time and energy in completing the task; further, Jim asked rhetorically, was the University proposing to argue that it could not accept a thesis on a topic of such pressing concern to the city?

After a short adjournment, Jim and I were informed that the thesis would be accepted and examined, but access to it would be restricted, with those wishing to read it having to acquire written permission from the department in question. I formed the impression that the university was as concerned to avoid any attention from the tabloid press, as it was to be reassured that the thesis did not present any legal problems.

The thesis was then examined successfully but I decided to postpone publication for five years, principally because I wanted to give the main characters the time to become adults and to settle into secure jobs and relationships before they read about their exploits as 16-year-olds. Most did exactly that, but a few went on to commit some very serious, violent offences which carried with them long terms of imprisonment. And far from wanting to be protected by pseudonyms and by the omission of any identifying material, all those I contacted before publication wanted to appear under their real names and in colour photographs.

Having recently re-read the book after many years, I cannot resist adding two reflections. I want both to strengthen one argument about the police and to correct what I now consider to be an imbalance in the chapters where I tried to place the gang I studied into a wider social context.

Faced with large numbers of adolescent boys at street corners who claimed to 'rule the pitch', some sections of the police force responded, at that time, just like a gang whose masculinity had been publicly challenged. They met violence with violence, arriving suddenly in overwhelming numbers and striking out indiscriminately with their batons, fists and feet until the corner was cleared. This created a deep sense of injustice among the boys who wanted the police to obey the law even if they themselves broke it whenever it pleased them to do so. The beatings meted out by the police also stiffened the boys' resolve to strike back in the only way they had found to be effective, namely, by singling out, wherever they could, a policeman patrolling on his own, whom they would then attack with ferocity. And so the cycle of violence continued as the police in their turn sought vengeance for what they considered to be a cowardly assault on one of their colleagues.

In the absence of a sociological imagination which a department of sociology at Glasgow University could have provided me with, but none existed in the mid-1960s, I called the final chapter 'Treatment and Prevention', which suggests to me now an overly individualistic, psychological and medical approach to the problems described. Certainly I gave appropriate prominence in the text to Glasgow's slum housing and to its long history of violence, and gang violence at that. But what now seems to me to be missing is sufficient recognition of the continuing structural position of all working-class adolescents, male and female, not only in Glasgow but throughout the UK; especially those who are born into multi-deprived families and overcrowded, 'sink' estates, who receive an inferior education to match all their other deprivations, and who move in and out of the most menial jobs without training or prospects, if they land a job of any kind.

In the 40 years since this book was first published there have been riots from time to time in Liverpool, Birmingham, Manchester, Bradford, Newcastle and most recently in London during the summer of 2011, when those who had nothing to lose showed their contempt for the forces of law and order. Government after government has repeatedly shown themselves incapable of a co-ordinated response commensurate with the scale and nature of these problems. In this regard the central message of *A Glasgow Gang Observed* remains as relevant as ever: riots will recur and we will continue to suffer from the depredations of those without a stake in this society until we give them what we want for our own children, namely: a high quality education and vocational training, leading to a job and a home, worthy of a human being.

James Patrick
November 2012

1
Entrée

I WAS DRESSED in a midnight-blue suit, with a 12-inch middle vent, three-inch flaps over the side pockets and a light blue handkerchief with a white polka dot (to match my tie) in the top pocket. My hair, which I had allowed to grow long, was newly washed and combed into a parting just to the left of centre. My nails I had cut down as far as possible, leaving them ragged and dirty. I approached the gang of boys standing outside the pub and Tim, my contact, came forward to meet me, his cheeks red with embarrassment.

'Hello, sur, Ah never thoat ye wid come.'

Fortunately, the others had not heard the slip which almost ruined all my preparations. I had not planned to join a juvenile gang; I had been invited. For two years I had been working in one of Scotland's approved schools during my vacations from Glasgow University and Jordanhill College of Education. As a result I applied for a full-time post as a teacher, was accepted and started work in August 1966. During the Easter and Summer holidays of that year I had met Tim, who had been committed to the school some months previously. Thanks to some common interests, we quickly became friends; a friendship which was resumed when I returned to the school. In discussion with the boys the topic of gangs and gang-warfare constantly cropped up. One particular conversation in the middle of July I remember well. A group of boys were lying sun-bathing in the yard during their lunch-hour. I was sitting on a bench among them, criticising boys who got into trouble while on leave. Tim, who had been on the edge of the group and lying face downwards on the ground, suddenly jumped up and asked me what I knew about boys on leave and how they spent their time. The honest answer was very little, nothing at all in fact. At this point the signal for the end of lunch-break was given and, as the boys put on their vests and shirts and walked over to their 'line', Tim sidled up to me and asked me to come out with him and see for myself.

This combination of invitation and challenge worried me during the holiday I had before taking up my permanent appointment. While I knew from records that Tim was a gang member, with an older brother serving a sentence for murder, the realization of what an opportunity was being offered me, coupled with a general feeling of well-being after three weeks in Italy, made me resolve to accept Tim's suggestion. The very fact that Tim wanted someone in authority to see 'whit the score wis' intrigued me. On my return I made use of every possible occasion to discuss privately with Tim the most suitable time for me to meet him while he was on leave, the type of clothes I should wear, the bond of silence and loyalty which would have to exist between us, etc. At first Tim thought that I should be introduced to his mates as an approved school teacher but I soon pointed out the dangers and difficulties of that arrangement. For a start, I would then have been unlikely to see typical behaviour. It was slowly dawning on me that the best solution to the problem would be for me to become a participant observer.

I realised, however, that this method of approach presented its own problems, chief of which was to what extent I should participate. My greatest worry was that incidents might be staged for my benefit, that Tim's behaviour might be radically altered, for better or worse, by my presence. Tim's willingness to introduce me to the gang solved the problem of obtaining entree. But from then on I would have to play it by ear. I spent the month of September thinking and planning, as the tan on my face slowly disappeared to leave me as pale as Tim and the others. I consulted no one during this period as to what my role should be, my main reasons being a need for total secrecy and a fear of being stopped. Privately I came to the conclusion that I must be a passive participant – a conclusion that became increasingly difficult to abide by, as I shall explain later. I had read, but not fully appreciated, Michael Young's thoughts on the 'Interpenetration of observer and observed' in his book *Innovation and Research in Education*. A sentence of his was to remain in my mind: 'The main problem, and excitement, of the social sciences is how to cope with the involvement of observer in observed ... '. Not only had I to recognise the fact that I was bound to change what I was observing just by observing it, but I had also to contend with the problems of role confusion. The situation of my being a middle-class teacher during the week and a member of a juvenile gang at the weekend produced a very real conflict for me. In fact it was the internal struggle between identification with the boys and abhorrence of their violence that finally forced me to quit.

To overcome the problem of background, I decided to present myself as Tim's 'haufer' (i.e. his best friend in the approved school), who was out on leave at the same time, and, 'havin' nae people' (i.e. relatives), had been befriended by Tim. This proved to be a simple but effective answer to questions about where I lived.

A third problem was that of language. Born and bred in Glasgow, I thought myself *au fait* with the local dialect and after two years of part-time work with these boys I considered myself reasonably familiar with their slang – another serious mistake as it turned out. So confused was I on the first night that I had to 'play daft' to avoid too many questions and also to enable me to concentrate on what was being said.

Entrée

The plan was to meet Tim on the Saturday evening of his next weekend leave. Boys from Glasgow and the surrounding area were allowed home for a weekend once a month and for Sunday leave in the middle of the month.[1] I began to concentrate on making my physical appearance acceptable to the group. I was prepared to give my age as 17, although this point was never questioned. In fact I was able to pass myself off as a mate of a 15-year-old boy; my exact age remained indeterminate but apparently acceptable. Clothes were another major difficulty. I was already aware of the importance attached to them by gang members in the school and so, after discussion with Tim, I bought the suit I have described in the first paragraph. Even here I made two mistakes. Firstly, I bought the suit outright with cash instead of paying it up, thus attracting both attention to myself in the shop and disbelief in the gang when I innocently mentioned the fact. Secondly, during my first night out with the gang, I fastened the middle button of my jacket as I am accustomed to do. Tim was quick to spot the mistake. The boys in the gang fastened only the top button; with this arrangement they can stand with their hands in their trouser pockets and their jackets buttoned – 'ra gallous[2] wae'.

One point of cardinal importance remains to be explained: namely, how an approved school teacher could develop such a close relationship with a pupil. I was the youngest member of the staff and looked it, and this as much as anything else made my relations with the boys easier and more informal. A common set of interests football, swimming and pop music – helped to further my connection with Tim. He for his part showed an intense curiosity about my home, family and middle-class background and I was equally curious about him. Our conversations during the evenings and weekends when I was on duty, plus the camaraderie engendered by a week's camping with a group of boys including Tim, seemed to ensure a closer relationship than usual between teacher and pupil in a normal day school. But the bond of loyalty thus forged was soon to be tempered in far more testing circumstances.

Finally, Tim and I came to an understanding that, whatever happened, nothing would be disclosed by either of us to other members of the staff or to anybody else. This was seen by both of us as a necessary precaution for our own protection. Tim kept his part of the bargain throughout the four-month period I was involved with the gang (from October 1966 to January 1967) and continues to keep it. I have given a fictitious name to every single character in this book, and any material of an incidental nature which would make participants traceable will be slightly altered or omitted. This leads me to a discussion of the legal advice I have received. Some abridgements have necessarily been made. Unhappily for society, no character in this book is fictional. And, while using pseudonyms, I have retained nicknames of a type likely to be repeated in other gangs throughout the city. I propose to describe the general area in which I worked, to list the gangs in that area, but I shall not identify the name of the gang I joined. Wherever possible, I shall let events and characters speak for themselves. There were 12 outings in all and the first few will be recounted in detail. Then, instead of a blow-for-blow account in strict chronological order of every time I met the gang, key events and representative situations will be described.

But allowing the characters to speak for themselves presents two final problems – those of obscenity and unintelligibility. I must warn the reader that some of the phrases used, apart from predictable swearing and blaspheming, are extremely crude and are only included to convey a total picture of conversations I heard. The second difficulty is more intractable. Whole pages may at first glance appear to be extracts from *Oor Wullie* or *The Broons* (characters in strip cartoons of Glasgow life), but such is the dialect. A glossary is included as an appendix to the book to enable the reader to translate the main text into English.

On the Friday night as I left school, I reminded Tim for the last time that I was coming purely as an observer. At first he had been amused and delighted at my acceptance of his offer; latterly, as I made detailed preparations with him, his attitude became one more of incredulity. I now understand why.

2
The background

BEFORE I TAKE up the thread of the narrative, several general points remain to be made. Readers should, I feel, be in the possession of the same information as I had at the outset both about Tim himself what I knew of him and his background from school records – and about gangs in Glasgow, and, more particularly, the area I was about to enter.

Tim was born in November 1950 and admitted to the approved school in December 1965 at the age of 15. Seven days after his first appearance in the school he absconded with three other boys, returning voluntarily the following day at the instigation of his brothers. Shortly afterwards he was examined on diagnostic tests in English and Arithmetic, his results showing him to be in no way educationally retarded. Tim was also invited to write a composition on his home and he was allowed 30 minutes for the exercise:

> My name is Tim Malloy. I live at 71 High Street, Glasgow, NW. I am the youngest of a family of NINE – 4 Brothers, 4 Sisters. I live with my mother and father. I went to St Enoch's school but I did not get on very well with any of the teachers. My last year especially I was never at school because I was expelled for arguing with a teacher. I had a very good life at home and got practically everything I wanted until my brother got Arrested for Murder. FROM JANUARY TO MAY and after that everything quieten down and everything at home went great again [sic].

I would now like to summarise and at times quote directly from such documents as Tim's probation and school reports to convey the extent of the information with which an approved school was supplied. We read that Tim's previous convictions began at the age of 13 when he was put on probation for theft. A year later, he reappeared in court, was again found guilty of theft and was fined one pound, but was admonished on a charge of attempted housebreaking with intent. Still aged 14, he served 28 days detention for two charges of assault and breach of the peace. Within days of his release he was charged with the offences which caused him to be sent to an approved school – assault and attempted theft, assault and robbery, and assault. No details were provided with regard to any of these charges.

Tim's religious persuasion, like that of his parents, was set down as

Roman Catholic, but their connection with the church was described as nominal. Tim's father had been unemployed for many years through ill health, his mother was a housewife, and both of them were dependent on national assistance. Their character was cryptically given as 'good so far as known'. The four girls in the Malloy family were all married and living in their own homes. The eldest boy, William, aged 24, was serving a life sentence for murder, the second boy, Peter, three years imprisonment for assault, and a third brother, Michael, 12 months for assault. John, the brother closest in age to Tim, being at that time 16, was reported to be unemployed, on probation, and living in his parents' home. Mr and Mrs Malloy rented a three-apartment Corporation flat at five pounds a month, which was said to be in good condition, comfortably furnished, but situated in a highly delinquent neighbourhood. Although Tim had spent three years at St Enoch's junior secondary,[3] all the headmaster could find to write about his educational achievement was that his progress in general and practical subjects was fair, that his IQ was 105, and that he had been absent for almost one third of his second year at school. Of Tim's character and behaviour at St Enoch's, the headmaster wrote:

> Resents discipline, sullen and socially rebellious. This boy has recently suffered extreme emotional stress. His nervous response has been one of fury. He threatens older boys with backing of force from gang. Subject to flashes of unreasoning temper. Does not respond to any offer of help or kindness.

Tim was described by the probation officer as:

> ... an averaged-sized 14-year-old boy of stocky build with straight, mid-brown hair (worn in a fringe), good fairly even teeth, broad features and a fresh, healthy complexion. His finger nails are very badly bitten. He is of good appearance and deportment and mixes easily with other boys but is anxious to be accepted as a dominant figure in the group. He does his best to convince others that he is a 'hard man' and he is quite prepared to bully weaker boys. He is an active, agile lad who enjoys participation in recreational activities though he prefers informal or unorganised pursuits.
>
> Malloy is a sullen lad, suspicious of authority, and he has inherited the reputation of his older brothers as being troublesome and rowdy in the neighbourhood. Whereas he can be a difficult boy, he is also capable of being respectful and has some common sense. It is probable that he is a very disturbed lad who has been unable to cope

with the domestic trouble caused by his other brothers' actions. The eldest was before the High Court on a charge of Murder.

Two weeks before his brother's trial, Malloy's behaviour became such that the headmaster decided that it would be better if Malloy stayed away from school for a few weeks. After the trial the parents were informed that Malloy should return to school but he remained away until the resumption of the school in August.

Malloy's attendance since the beginning of the August term has been 29 out of a possible 146. Although part of this term was spent in the remand home it reflects a most unsatisfactory attitude to school and authority. On several occasions when he did attend, Malloy was sent home from school because of his aggressive behaviour and undisciplined manner.

In the Malloy family there exists an aggressive attitude towards the police whom they regard as victimising them. Mother shares this view and it is probable that Malloy has been caught up in this attitude. One of the difficulties in preparing a report on this lad is that his sullen, reticent attitude results in him giving away little of his true personality.

At that time my information about gangs was supplied by the daily press, a diet supplemented by conversations with the boys and members of the staff. Looking back, I now find it extremely difficult to give an accurate account of how much I knew then. Names like the Calton Tongs, the Gorbals Cumbie (from Cumberland Street), the Maryhill Fleet, the Possilpark Uncle (coined from the television show *The Man from Uncle*) and perhaps one or two others were familiar to me. Weapons, I knew, were used occasionally, clothes were a matter for detailed discussion, and girls were involved somehow. I had read (like most Glaswegians) the stop-press in the Sunday newspapers which began: *Boy stabbed. Last night a gang of teenage hoodlums ... .* This, I think I can say honestly, was the extent of my knowledge.

The press and the city generally had slowly become aware of the gang problem. News stories on juvenile violence began to appear in the late 50s and early 60s, but it wasn't until 1965 that the trickle of news items on gangs began to swell into a flood. In March of that year, newspaper headlines proclaimed: *The Gangs are Back!* As the vandalism, the slashings, the 'group disorders' (to use the term favoured by the police) mounted, articles on causation, diagnosis and therapy kept pace with the growing interest in the problem. The organising secretary of youth clubs in the area explained the phenomenon as follows: 'It's the spring, you know. They don't come out on the dark nights. They are too timid.'

In January 1966, some of the tenants of the Easterhouse housing estate formed citizen action groups and vigilante organisations. The Lord Provost of Glasgow seemed to be more than favourably disposed to the idea but it was soon scotched by the senior magistrate of the city, who realised that anyone who took the law into his own hands could only be treated like any other transgressor of the law. The idea of vigilantes died an early death.

In February of the same year a group of over 40 shopkeepers and businessmen petitioned their local Member of Parliament, asking him to take the necessary steps to protect their property and themselves from the gangs. In response to the increasing demand for action, an anti-teenage gang committee was formed, headed by the Lord Provost and the Chief Constable.

By May 1966, the national television and radio networks had taken up the story and phrases like 'a stabbing is no longer news in Glasgow' (on the *Twenty-Four Hours* television programme) caused a furore. In the same month, the crime figures for Glasgow in 1965 were released and revealed that over 850 people had been arrested for carrying an offensive weapon, that over 1,500 people had been arrested for breach of the peace and just slightly less for disorderly behaviour. In the local municipal elections in May the self-styled Progressive Party made the return of the birch one of the main planks in their election campaign.

As the year progressed, attitudes hardened and a chief inspector from Glasgow speaking at a police conference was quoted as saying: 'I have mentioned the word vandal. But this, like juvenile delinquent is a modern term. We in the police service prefer the original expression – "hooligan" and "thug". Whatever one calls them, I don't think a weed by any other name is less troublesome.' Later in the same speech, the following passage occurred: 'Police officers are, thank goodness, human beings. They display a great deal of restraint. But how much longer they can hold themselves in check is another question. If the courts will not use the teeth provided for them, the police may decide to do the biting.'

Predictably, it was left to a local politician to utter the hackneyed exaggeration: 'the authorities have allowed a situation to develop where if truth be known people cannot walk along the streets.' Such was the atmosphere in the city when I undertook this piece of work.

Two final points before I resume the main story: to make the narrative more comprehensible, there is on the endpapers a map of Glasgow, divided up into gang territories as they were in 1966. Special attention has been paid to the north-west side of the city. Instead of the one gang name, the Maryhill Fleet, I discovered that there were no less than 20 of various sizes and importance within the area or its surroundings. These were: the Maryhill Fleet, the Butny, the Valley, the YRB (Young Rolland Boys from Rolland Street), the Barnes Road, the Young Cadder Team, the Peg (from Springburn), the Border and the Uncle (both from Possilpark, as was the Young Deny, a Protestant Orange group), the Port Toi (from Port Dundas), the Cowcaddens Toi, the Milton Tongs,[4] the Bishopbriggs Bison and the Bishopbriggs Toi, the Drumchapel Buck, the Blue Angels, the Mummies, the 365; and no doubt others exist of which I know nothing. Each of these gangs had a clearly marked out territory, as I have indicated on the map.

It was one of the above gangs, henceforth known as The Young Team, which I joined. Interestingly enough, the boys themselves never used the word 'gang', always 'team'.

To convey some idea of the immensity of this problem in Glasgow and of Glasgow's effect on the rest of Scotland, I have produced a list of all the gang names which I heard during my four month period of involvement: the Shamrock (a predominantly Catholic gang from Townhead and Garngad, otherwise known as the Toon Tongs); the Thrush (also from Townhead, the name signifying the deadly rival organisation to *The Man from Uncle*); the Blackhill Toi and the Corner Boys, also from Blackhill; the Provie Rebels from Provanmill; the Gringo from Barmulloch; the Fleet from Ruchazie; the Queenslie Rebels, the Queenslie Fleet and the Cody from the Queenslie Industrial Estate (the latter name being formed, according to one theory, from the first letters of the exhortation 'Come On, Die Young!' – an alternative explanation to this premature death wish has been suggested to me in that the letters stand for the phrase 'Cowards Only Die Young' which is more in keeping with the typical bravado of the gang boy); the Bar L from Barlanark; the YY Mods (Young, Young), the Young 41, the Torran Toi from Torran Road, the Den Toi, the Bal Toi from Baldovan Crescent, and the Drummie, all from Easterhouse; the Bar G from Bargeddie and the Village from Bailleston; the Tigers from Shettleston; the Goucho from Carntyne; the Wee Men from Tollcross and the Border, a gang squeezed between the Wee Men and the Torch from Parkhead, where the Sally from Salamanca Street are a minor gang; the Tongs and the San Toi from Calton (the former growing in importance as the latter declined); the Haghill Toi from the place of the same name and the Gestapo from Dennistoun; the Brigton Derry, the Spur, the Baltic Fleet (from Baltic Street), the Nunnie, the Dickie and the Stickit, all from Bridgeton ; the Skull (the name chosen by a gang in Cathcart also), the Wild Team, the Tiny Glen, and the Rutherglen Rebels from Rutherglen; the Blade from Eastfield; the Himshie from Cambuslang; the Cumbie from Cumberland Street in the Gorbals; the Hutchie from Hutchesontown (there is another Hutchie gang in Polmadie – perhaps families moved from the older district to the new estate); the Rebels, from both Tradeston and Kinning Park, the latter being known mainly by the initials KPR. The Bridgegate district has a gang called the Brigade, a shortened and altered form of the full name. The Anderston and Partick Cross take their name from the respective road junctions. The Govan Team, the Vordo and the Wine Alley all come from Govan and the Bundy from Priesthill. Whiteinch has the Bowrie, Anniesland the Fleet, the Scurvy and the Temple (the last from the Temple district). Scotstoun has the religious-sounding Choirboys and Monks, Yoker has its Toi and still further to the west is the DRS, namely, the Dumbarton Riot Squad. The new housing estate of Drumchapel has the Buck, who were said to have a female contingent called the Lady Buck. Finally, the housing estate of Castlemilk is a good example of how the names of major gangs in the central areas are transported to new environments: the Castlemilk Cumbie, the Castle-milk Fleet, the Castlemilk Toi, and the Castlemilk Young Team are all to the fore, as is the Tay, a gang based on a local street name. Other gang names which I heard of from Tim's conversation after I had withdrawn from the gang were the Star from Garthamlock, the Wimpey from Dalmuir, and the Kinning Park Stud.

The following gang names, more quaint and historical, were mentioned in derisory terms by the Glasgow gang boys:

Edinburgh:	The Jacobites, the Burdiehouse Toi and the Leith Walk Mob.
Dundee:	The Huns, the Shimy, the Cats, the Hatchet and the Cosmo.
Girvan:	The Saxons.
Greenock:	The Young Strone (from the housing estate of the same name).
Paisley:	The Disciples, the Moors and Hell's Troops.
Hamilton:	The Kydds and Hell's Angels.
Motherwell:	The Motherwell Cross and the Slash.
Coatbridge:	The Rio and the Dykes.
Airdrie:	The Bush Boys.
Falkirk:	The Chunky.

A list of 24 gangs in Glasgow in the 1920s and 30s is given in the Glasgow *Evening Citizen* (19 January 1955). It reads as follows:

Antique Mob, from Shettleston; Beehive Gang, from Gorbals; Black Diamond Boys, from South-side; Black Muffler, from Clydebank; Black Star, from Calton; Butny Boys, from Maryhill; Calton Entry Mob, from Tollcross; Cheeky Forty, from Roystonhill; Cowboys, from Dennistoun, Dirty Dozen,

The background

from South-side; Hammer Boys, from South-side; Kellybow, from Govan; Kent Star, from Calton; Liberty Boys, from South-side; Norman Conks, from Bridgeton; Redskins, from South-side; Romeo Boys, from East End; Sally Boys, from East End; San Toy, from Calton; Stickers, from South-side; Stickit Boys, from Bridgeton; The Billy Boys, from Bridgeton; The Derry Boys, from Bridgeton; The Nunnie Boys, from Nuneaton Street.

Those names that have survived the 30-year period would appear to be the Nunnie, the San Toy, the Sally Boys, the Stickit, and of course the Butny Boys.

The inclusion of such a list should not brand me as an alarmist, for many of these so-called gangs are no more than spontaneous and essentially harmless friendship groups of adolescent boys meeting irregularly on street corners. Others are the names of gangs which have had their heyday, are now moribund, and live on in folklore only. Still others are of a volatile and transitory nature who 'appear and disappear like midges on a summer's night'.[5] This leaves a number of noteworthy gangs, varying in size and importance, whose presence is all too real. The truth lies somewhere between the two extremes: on the one hand, there is the folly of exaggerating the number and the influence of the gangs; on the other, the equally dangerous error of underestimating the extent of gang culture within the city.

Before I give my own impression of Maryhill, the neighbourhood where I carried out this investigation, I shall quote from an article in the *Glasgow Herald* (for 27 January 1968):

> Within the present confines of Glasgow there are the remains of the villages engulfed by the city in its extremely rapid expansion since 1830. Some villages remain in name only, such as Gorbals, Anderston, Partick and Maryhill. The trouble is that the growth of Glasgow has dehumanised many of these villages. The spread of the tenements swallowed up street after street, regardless of whether this was the main street of the village, and equally regardless of the buildings, the church, the castle or the prison which had to be destroyed to make space for them. In Glasgow at present there are many ordinary tenemented streets, no different from the countless others, which at one time were the main streets of villages ...
>
> The beautiful and romantic Kelvin is now overgrown with weeds and surrounded by rubbish. The neat village has a trunk road running through its centre. The old houses overlooking the main street are blacked, bricked up and ruinous. The canal is concealed behind walls and hoardings, and the view over to the hills is obscured by dingy street lights and disfigured by waste and derelict ground.

Unfortunately this book contains no detailed ecological study of Maryhill. But according to one leading American theory of delinquency, adolescent gang warfare is most likely to arise in disorganised slums, characterised by high rates of mobility, and 'populated in part by failures in the conventional world ... [and] the outcasts of the criminal world'. (Cloward and Ohlin, 1960, p.173.) Certainly, adult crime in Maryhill appeared to be unorganised and petty, but I would speculate that the neighbourhood was far more integrated and cohesive than the theory would lead us to expect. A statistical attempt to show whether the areas in Scotland with the highest rates for violence were also those where there had been the largest shifts in population proved to be negative (Shields and Duncan, 1964, pp.52ff.); and the Chicago slum studied by Gerald Suttles (1968, p.231) contained no 'urban rabble prone to riot, pillage, disorder, and crime', but over 30 boys' street corner groups who formed an integral part of an ordered and intricately organised social structure.

My own recollections of the neighbourhood are predominantly of black streets lit by pale orange lighting and strewn with broken glass, empty beer cans, half bricks and at times broken-down furniture. Where any wooden fences round gardens remain, they are no better than dirty sticks protruding from the ground at all angles. The small patches of grass in front of houses have long since been trampled into mud. And these are the newer pre-war houses I am describing and not the leprous tenements closer to the centre of the city.

Maryhill Road runs from the old village of the same name down towards St George's Cross, Cowcaddens, and the centre of Glasgow. Some gang members lived in this more central area in grim, squalid tenements, most of which have since been knocked down as unfit for human habitation. It was these buildings with their acrid smell of damp, disease and urine which never failed to produce nausea in me. The blast of foul air hit you as you entered the close and jumped over pools of tainted water. I once went to the toilet at the stair head in one of these insanitary abominations; having had a lot to drink, I overcame my disgust of the noisome odour. But not even the pressure of a full bladder could force me to stay in a closet with rats scurrying out from behind the toilet bowl.

At night, I noted that the side streets of the area were heavily parked with coal lorries, cement mixers and road haulage vans. One of the characteristic features of the area was the sight of children of both sexes playing in the streets at ten, 11 and even 12 o'clock at night. Some of these children, I estimated, could have been no more than five or six. They rolled in the sand left at the side of the street by road menders and tossed rubble at each other. Their older companions of nine and ten extinguished the lights in the red warning lamps

The background

and tinkered with the machinery lying around. When the night watchmen shooed them away, they ran down to and across the canal and up to exclusive middle-class Kelvindale to play at bouncing off the thick privet hedges which protect the gardens. The solid wooden sleepers which had been driven into the ground to fence off the canal now lay uprooted, leaving enough room for a cart and horse to approach the water, never mind a child.

At 11 o'clock at night only the fish and chip shops and the dirty book shops are open. All around, the rag and scrap metal merchants, the supermarkets, the laundromats, the Orange Lodges and the Catholic churches, the cash and carry stores, the cafés, the billiard halls, the public houses at street corners, and the bingo halls are bolted and barred. The local Labour Party office is flanked by a licensed betting office on one side and a public house on the other. Small groups of boys lounge about close mouths, smoking, talking, and watching prostitutes arrive back from the centre of the city with their clients.

Most lampposts, shop fronts, telephone boxes, hoardings, closes, walls, bus shelters (and even the interiors of buses) are daubed and disfigured with gang slogans and boys' names. Not even the entrance to the local police station is free of these scrawlings. One new estate, surrounded by a high wall, in the centre of the area, seems to escape the general depredations. There the buildings are spotless, the grass is given leave to grow, and gives hope for the future.

Before midnight small queues form at the main meeting points in the district to buy the morning paper. At our corner stands a frail, wrinkled, old newspaper seller in cloth cap, muffler, and heavy coat, with a Corporation transport bus conductor's money bag slung round his shoulder. Not only is the old man bespectacled and toothless, he also has a cleft palate. Young boys startle him by finding imaginary weapons behind his back. He breaks out in excited, nervous swearing: 'Ya bathtarding thuckers!' Suddenly, all around are smitten with cleft palates and echo and mimic the old man's speech impediment.

3
The first night

TIM HAD TOLD me that on Saturday nights the boys normally met between six and eight at a pub close to the centre of the city. I had heard its name before and knew it to be on one of the main approach roads from the north-west side of the city. The arrangement with Tim was that I would see him around seven o'clock; an arrangement which I kept, to Tim's obvious astonishment. Despite all my planning, despite all our detailed discussions and last-minute reminders, he had remained unconvinced of my intentions.

The boys had just decided to move into the pub as I approached them, this being one of the reasons why they did not hear Tim's opening remark. As we in turn entered the pub I saw that Tim was wearing the weekend clothes he kept at the approved school: a casual shirt with large brown and yellow diamonds as the pattern, grey-checked trousers, black shoes. In addition, he now had on a black leather shortie coat which he realised would have been stolen if left at the approved school. Tim had been released on leave from school at about ten o'clock that morning, had travelled home and gone straight to bed, only getting up in time to go out for the evening.

Inside the pub, the gang broke into little groups of three or four and drinks were ordered. 'Baggy', a large fat boy who was dressed, I was happy to see, in the same style as myself (apart from his pink and black striped socks), ordered pints of beer for himself, Tim and me. Even on the following day I found difficulty in recording the first few minutes of this meeting - a failure of memory due, I think, to my nervousness. However, within a short time it was established that I was an approved school boy, a fellow inmate of Tim's and a housebreaker. I saw from Baggy's face that this last claim had been a mistake. On our return to the school, Tim told me that the gang, although convicted numerous times for shop-breaking, had never broken into a home: 'It's yir ain people - people jist like yersel'.' Tim's own conviction for attempted housebreaking with intent seemed to belie this protestation, or so I thought until I learned that under the law of Scotland 'housebreaking' covers the forced entry of 'any roofed building', i.e. shops, factories, garages, as well as private houses. I gave my own first name, thinking that this was the safest approach; Tim never quite became accustomed to addressing me in this way, though latterly he seemed to derive much enjoyment from the exercise. I confessed to be 'dain' ma Hoosey' (serving my time at an approved school) 'fur screwin' hooses' (housebreaking). Baggy 'wis in the mulk', working for

The first night

Scottish Farmers; his round lasted from 5.30 to 10.30 every morning, leaving him free for the rest of the day. For this he earned 'eleven poun' – no' bad for a seventeen-year-auld.'

Tim spent his time answering shouts of welcome from boys already ensconced around the bar and from those who were still arriving. He was adding little to our conversation, perhaps out of embarrassment. I, for my part, wanted to say as little as possible and avoid answering questions, as both the answer and the accent it was delivered in were liable to be wrong. Happily, Baggy liked talking and I asked questions or nodded approval where appropriate. I learned that he had spent one year in the Merchant Navy, but had not been permitted to go ashore when off the coast of South Africa because he had 'nae papirs'. Baggy was bitterly resentful about this, though I didn't fully understand the point. No chance was given me to inquire further, as Baggy turned with relish to a description of the sword which he kept down the sidepanels of a scooter he had bought for £20 from a boy in the Maryhill Fleet. Here we went off at a tangent again. This time I missed the point of the story about the boy, whose name I have forgotten, but whose father was a bookmaker, able to make a gift of an Austin Mini to his son. Baggy was obviously envious; suddenly he dropped this subject and instead told me how he had been able to afford the scooter. He had stolen 'trannies' (transistor radios) and hub caps from cars outside the main hotels in Glasgow, turning the collection into money through dealing with a 'punter' at Charing Cross.

This word I remembered to ask Tim about. Although in the context the meaning of 'punter' was clear enough, on that first night I was often completely at a loss as to what was being talked about. The fact that I was able to clarify difficulties or obtain more information from Tim in school, proved invaluable. Otherwise I doubt if I could have continued. Tim, I was well aware, had given me minimal information about the gang prior to my first outing, but after that he could not have been more helpful. For instance, Tim told me later that the word 'punter' was 'a normal man where you live who never gets caught,' to whom you took stolen goods and traded them in for guns, 'blades', or money. 'Ye can even take a packet of Persil tae them and get somethin' oan it.' Tim then told me that one of his older brothers, Pete, had 'done a joab', a wages snatch for a bookmaker in return for a gun, an Italian biretta. Another brother, Mick, had been so jealous that he had 'gone doon tae the coffee stall at Charing Cross and asked fur a punter.' A man had then left and later reappeared with someone who told him what kind of a gun he had and what price it was. In this manner, Mick had acquired a sawn-off double-barrelled shotgun. One other item of knowledge I was to pick up myself about punters: they were the people who sold bottles of wine at extortionate prices on Sundays when all other sources of supply were closed. The word was also generalised to mean a member of a 'team' or gang, as in the much used phrase 'Ya Cumbie punter'.

Meanwhile, I was listening to Baggy's description of the battle with the Milton Tongs at the Bishopbriggs Bowling Centre. Running out of the building, he had taken his sword from the scooter, cut one boy and the rest had scattered. 'A bunch o' crap-bags, thae Milton Tongs.' At this point, Pat Nolan entered the pub, saw Tim and came to join us, insisting on buying drinks all round. Pints of lager, heavy beer and bottles of Newcastle Brown were ordered. Pat was about five feet four, slightly built, with protruding teeth. What he lacked in height he made up for in noise. Within minutes, we heard that during the week he had been 'up fur R and D' (charged with riot and disorderly behaviour). The fine had been £50. With the actions of a cashier slapping money down, he reconstructed the scene: 'Wallop! Wallop! Pied.' During the laughter, he saw two men entering the bar who looked to me like Indian students. Tim whispered to me, 'Watch Pat. He hates thae Pakies. Watch him stare at them.' Pat shouted something which I didn't catch to the other boys in the room, who all turned and began to stare at the new entrants. Sensing the atmosphere, the two young men withdrew as Pat and the other boys exploded with laughter. This incident led Pat to reminisce about 'the big darkie in the Calton Tongs, a big Pakie he wis – thoat he wis a gemmie – came doon Maryhill hissel' and wis ripped' – by Tim's elder brother Mick.

Now Tim began pointing out boys in the pub to me: ' "Big Hauf" the boay wi' glessies and his front teeth missin',' had taken on the two McCormick brothers and 'chibbed' them. 'Peam' used to live in Maryhill before his family flitted to Drumchapel, but he still travelled into town to meet the boys every Saturday night. Frank Murphy, a boy with a crewcut and a large ugly scar stretching from the tip of his chin to his ear, was the centre of attraction. He had, I was told, 59 stitches on the side of his face; he had been 'ripped' only a few weeks ago: 'It wis in the papirs.' Then my attention was directed to Tommie McConnell whose claim to fame was that he had punched a boy through the window of a large department store in town. During this identification parade I was becoming increasingly aware that I would have to excuse myself for a trip to the toilet, and so, using the approved school jargon (which I had already noticed was acceptable), I claimed to be 'burstin' for the can.'

As I walked off I heard an old-age pensioner asking for a pint of beer and a packet of nuts. This prompted Pat to remark: 'Nice to see y'ir still gettin' yir nuts.' More laughter. In the toilet I read a large spray-painted slogan:

The first night

>Wild
>Young
>Catholic
>Team
>Rules
>OK

Around this notice gang members had appended their signatures, e.g. Mad Harry, Fry, Jim, Mad Mex etc.

I re-entered the bar in time to see a labourer, while stretching for his drink, nudge Pat accidentally in the back. Pat immediately challenged him and his mate to a fight. I had noticed the two navvies earlier, standing beside us in the pub, two hefty six-footers in gumboots and donkey jackets. As voices began to rise, the boys in the pub (and there were roughly 30 of them there, with more next door in the singing lounge with their girlfriends) began to encircle them. Pat put his left hand into his top right-hand inside pocket where 'chibs' or weapons were normally carried. 'If you bring that oot, y'ir deid,' shouted one of the workmen. 'Wee Midgie', whose hair looked as if it lived up to the sobriquet, and who was standing behind the two labourers, struck them over the head with a full lemonade bottle. As the men fell, Pat and Baggy kicked them mercilessly in the face and stomach while Tim lifted an empty bottle of Newcastle Brown Ale and cracked it over their heads. To protect the workmen from further injuries I ran forward, grabbed Tim and pushed him out of the door and into the street where we raced for a good few hundred yards with Pat, Baggy and Wee Midgie following closely behind. 'Run like fuck!' someone was shouting, and I obeyed.

We were now walking up Sauchiehall Street listening to Pat criticizing himself for having started the fight. 'Ah should hiv' ma heid examined. Startin' aw that an' me up in court oan Wednesday an' aw.' By now it was nearly ten o'clock and Baggy suggested going to the Granada Dance Hall. As we were about to go in, Tim and Baggy changed their minds, Tim claiming that he wanted to return home 'to pit a shirt oan'. We agreed to meet inside later on. Pat and I then filled up membership forms, Pat ostentatiously paid over the 14 shillings and we were in. Immediately Pat began playing the role of a policeman, which he did surprisingly well for a boy just over five feet in height. He strutted through the café-bar and over to the cloakrooms where he picked a fight with a girl directly in front of him in the queue. As she handed over her coat, he was poking her on the arm and instructing her to be 'oan yir merry wae. Its polis that's orderin' ye.' She walked off for a few yards and then turned and yelled, 'Y'ir too fuckin' wee fur polis.' Entering into the spirit of things, I replied: 'We're speshuls.' (Glaswegians have a distinctive way of saying 'special'.) This seemed to calm everybody down, so Pat and I went to the toilets. Now we had become members of the Calton Tongs, with Pat screaming 'Tongs! Tongs!' at the top of his voice. Pat pushed a small boy back into the toilet as we entered. The boy was hardly four-foot-ten in height, looked barely 14, but was startlingly good-looking in his mod suit. Again Pat was quarrelling, this time about what gang the boy belonged to. His hand was moving to his inside pocket but in the street I had learned that he 'wisnae kerryin'.' At this point an old man, obviously the toilet attendant, came in and smoothed things over: 'He's only a boay.' Pat turned, raced up the stairs, and burst on to the dance floor.

The girls looked superb in the half light, their very young faces heavily painted and their eyes black with mascara. Some wore lime green trouser-suits, others daring backless dresses. Their skirts and 'sexy wee black froaks' were all very short. Pat commented, as he pushed forward and was pushed back by the girls, that some dresses were so low: 'Ye can see their breakfasts.' In the corner of the room, in the corridors, and even on the steps leading down to the gents' toilet, some fierce 'winchin'' was in progress. Pat continued shoving, with me following in his wake until we were in the second of the two small dancefloors. Approaching the band, Pat pushed against two men who were standing listening to the music. In fact three powerfully built individuals turned round and demanded of the diminutive Pat: 'Who the fuck are you pushin'?' 'Ah'm pushin' you, thug face,' came the reply. As he pretended to reach for his forgotten weapon, Pat was punched by the first bouncer and then by all three. He fell to the floor as the dancers, who swiftly included myself, dispersed. He was kicked repeatedly, the force of the kicks moving his body towards the door. As he clasped his stomach and blood came from his mouth, girls in the room began shouting: 'Leave him alane. It's wee Pat Nolan.' As if all was normal, the group – I almost betrayed my age by calling it 'the band' – continued to play their version of the Four Tops record 'Reach Out', a song always to be associated in my mind with this incident. The biggest of the bouncers returned with blood stains on his frilly evening shirt and because he seemed to be looking for me, I made my way discreetly to the door. Once out in the open air, I looked around for Pat but seeing no one I decided to go home. I had had enough for one night.

In recounting the events of that evening without too much interruption for explanation, I have in fact omitted large sections of the conversation I heard back in the pub. One important occurrence I must now mention. When boys entered the pub and came up to greet Tim, they slipped either ten shilling notes or half-crowns or pints of beer into his hand. More than once I was offered money, too, but Tim saved me the embarrassment of taking it by saying that I was in no need of it as the school provided pocket money for 'homeless and friendless' boys. Two boys also came round collecting contributions to a fund which had been started to raise ten pounds bail money for two of their number who had been 'lifted' the night before for fighting the Cowcaddens Toi. Everybody earning money was expected to contribute.

Rhyming slang proved to be one of my major difficulties. One phrase had me completely baffled: 'It's jist yir Donald.' Here, as so often in rhyming slang, there was not only the rhyme to contend with but an abbreviation as well. The full phrase would have been 'Donald Duck' (luck). It was this second jump which obscured the meaning. If I had not been able to consult Tim, this might have remained a mystery.[6] But in general I had simply to think quickly to discover the rhyme. When I had claimed to be 'dain' ma Hoosie for HB', Baggy had replied: 'Ya tea-leaf ye!'[7] My asking Pat to repeat one of his sentences made him inquire after my hearing: 'Are ye corn-beef?' (i.e. deef, i.e. deaf). Again, Pat had turned to a working man standing in the bar, and, referring to his denim jacket and trousers, had remarked: 'Ah fancy yir tin flute. I'll soon hiv' wan masel'.' By this he meant that he might shortly be wearing the uniform of Polmont borstal.

I had remained in the pub for almost three hours during which the boys avidly discussed gang gossip: which boys from which gangs had been arrested, on what charges, and what the sentences had been. Something approaching an interim report was being delivered to Tim, who I realised was 'the leader-aff' of this particular gang, a factor which no doubt eased my own entree. Boys approached him bearing the news of who had 'chibbed' whom, where and how. The welter of detail and the combination of language and accent made it impossible to remember all that was said. A recurrent phrase, used by Tim and the others at the end of an item of gang news, was 'It wis in the papirs.' This was evidently very important.

After the more recent events had been described, past exploits were relived in all their detail. One of the outstanding events in the history of the gang appeared to be a battle with the Calton Tongs in George Square. According to Tim over a hundred of his boys (most of them with girlfriends) had been sitting around the square waiting for the one-am bus. Seven or eight boys crossing the road began shouting: 'Tongs! Tongs! Ya Bass!' At this, the 'hundred' Maryhill boys had risen, drawn their blades, and attacked. One of the Tongs, according to my informant, was stabbed 'seventeen times'. Amid the screams of terror from the ordinary citizens of Glasgow, the police riot squad (pronounced so as to rhyme with 'pad') had arrived and 28 'of oor boays wis huckled. It wis only when the busies came that oor boays guyed the course. It wis great, man.'

From this major exploit, which I was to hear of again, the conversation turned to lesser, more personal triumphs. Tim told of dealing with one or two members of what were relatively unimportant gangs like the Partick Cross. Or Pat talked of assaulting, with two other boys, a 'screw' in Maryhill, who had evidently been knocked to the ground where he had lain still, protecting his face from the kicks aimed at it. With typical exaggeration Tim bragged: 'We've chibbed aboot seven polis.'

On we went to a discussion of the Mummies, a sinister group I had heard of in the approved school but of whom no mention had been made in the press as yet. Now I discovered that not even the gang knew exactly who they were, although they operated in their area very close to the junior secondary school, which most of them had attended. The Mummies, with faces and hands swathed in bandages, toured the district in a small van into which they enticed young boys and girls, who were then assaulted with weapons. The verdict of the gang was that 'they must be mental tae dae it tae weans. Shit-bags the lot o' them, clawin' wee lassies intae a van an' chibbin' them.'

Next I listened to a eulogy of Tim's immediate elder brother, John. At present in Polmont borstal, his greatest feat in Tim's eyes was his theft of swords, knives and a double-edged battle axe from an antique shop in the city. 'The blades he thieved, he selt tae the ither boays in the team.' This reminded Pat Nolan of the day John had attacked his teacher with a brick and, on being sent to the headmaster, had proceeded to belabour him as well, thus guaranteeing his expulsion. Tim then recollected that his own class had become infamous in his day and added that every boy in it had since become a feared gang member. Baggy had attended the equivalent Protestant school and yet was still a member of the Catholic gang – my first intimation of how unimportant religion was to these boys in deciding what 'team' they belonged to. Though he had spent three years at this school, Baggy couldn't remember its name, or rather he couldn't pronounce it correctly. But what he could remember was that the teachers 'were for ever wavin' the belt at ye, belt-happy they wur, goin' up and doon in the class, slappin' ye wi' it fur nuthin'.' One teacher had been particularly prone to this type of behaviour, as Baggy described it: 'Wan day I hid enough o' it. As he came by, he hut me wi' it an' Ah grabbed it. "Aw! Fuck this," Ah says and goat intae him wi' his ain belt.' The first wave of laughter was dying when he added: 'Ah goat expelled an' aw.'

Pat then recalled that Tim had stabbed a boy from his own class. Tim took up the story, gave the boy's name, and explained the circumstances; an explanation which, I was uncomfortably aware, was aimed at me. In the past they had been 'great mates but noo he's a member o' the Toi; he wisnae a Maryhill boay; he came fae anither pitch.' After the stabbing, Pat continued,

The first night

Tim had closed his lock-back razor [8] and handed it to his 'bird' who had hidden it in her handbag.

Someone then suggested the story, which I was invited to believe, of the Mad Mexican, who had been arrested while 'gettin' intae two blokes wi' the butt of his gun' and who had shot a policeman in the ear to make good his escape. Such an incident, I felt, would have been reported in the papers and discussed widely; I had heard nothing of it but diplomatically remained silent about my reservations. Subsequent research has proved the story to be totally without foundation. The Mad Mexican was obviously a figure of some authority, only to be spoken of in the same breath as the King, Dick Stevenson. When Maryhill was up in arms (the phrase to be taken literally), and all the smaller gangs, including Tim's, joined together to 'hander' the Fleet, then the King came into his own. No one could 'touch' Dick, I was told; he was undisputed leader, with the Mad Mexican deputizing for him during his absences in borstal. He was 'the gemmiest boay in Glesga, the first wan tae go right ahead wi' aw thae mugs.'

The praise continued for quite some time, in the middle of which Pat in an aside said that Dick at one point in his career had been sent to 'my' approved school. It was mainly due to Dick and what he meant to the gang situation in Maryhill that Tim was able to boast: 'We run the toon. Thae Buck are scared tae come in. They stay oot in Drumchapel.' In the golden age of the gang, in the days when Dick was not being continually arrested, there had been a scooter squad, 30 or 40 strong, which formed the vanguard while dozens of boys had followed behind. The description brought to my mind an image of tanks and infantrymen at the end of the First World War. The boys had all dressed alike to heighten the effect, in a uniform of sandals, red socks, white trousers, a red polo-neck casual, with a white cardigan or jersey. 'It looked great, man. Thoosans o' boays aw dressed the same,' commented Tim.

The above was all I was able to record late that night and during the following day. So much more was presented too obscurely or too quickly for accurate recall. Three general points struck me. Firstly, I hadn't realised that the boys would know the members of other gangs by name. The leaders of all the major gangs throughout the city, and not just those closest to Maryhill, were well known. Meetings in remand homes, borstals and approved schools explained much of this familiarity.

A second point made its impression on me right from the beginning. Gangs appeared to me to be based on territory. Boys belonged to the Valley, for example, because they lived in that area. Later on, I discovered that this district, of which Gairbraid Avenue was the centre, had always been so called and that the gang from that area took its name from 'the Valley', i.e. the geographical fact that the avenue winds down between two steep embankments to the River Kelvin. In the 1930s, the gang from Gairbraid Avenue had also been called 'The Valley'. Similarly, the area immediately west of the Valley was called 'The Butny', where Baggy came from. Much later, by consulting Alexander Thomson's *Random Notes on Maryhill*, I discovered that this area, one of the earliest parts of Maryhill, began as a row of houses which 'went by the name of "Botany".' Built at the beginning of the 18th century, this row housed the first school in Maryhill, known locally as the 'Botany School'. The row was pulled down and cleared away in 1890 and yet the name has lived on to the present time. Why the name 'Botany' should be used I have been unable to discover. So many buildings in this district were now either derelict or in the process of being demolished that there were too few boys available to constitute a gang. Consequently they had attached themselves to the nearest gang. The 'Possil Uncle' was based on Possilpark, the young Cadder Team on the area of the same name, and the Barnes Road and the Young Rolland Boys were centred on their respective streets. All these 'teams' belonged to the larger grouping called Maryhill, where the main gang was the Maryhill Fleet. But two of the smaller gangs mentioned above, the Barnes Road and the YRB, had broken away from this set-up and had become the sworn enemy of the rest.

Such was the fame and the power of the Maryhill Fleet that not only did the smaller gangs like the Valley, the Butny, the Uncle and the Young Cadder Team look to the Fleet for protection and support, but boys also came from Anniesland and even Helensburgh, a journey of 22 miles, to join. As long as they eschewed membership of their local gang (a serious risk to take), and proved themselves loyal and active members of the Fleet, they were accepted. The greatest scorn and indeed hatred was reserved for 'the mixer', the boy who was a member of two or more gangs or who flitted from gang to gang.

For him no punishment could be severe enough, and, after being stabbed, such a boy would become an outcast.

One final matter remains to be clarified. The older-looking boys standing around the bar did not belong to Tim's gang. They were the lieutenants of Dick Stevenson and all were members of the Fleet. The smaller gang which Tim 'led aff' and to which Pat, Baggy, and Midgie belonged, was only one of the five such which 'handered' the Fleet, thus swelling their numbers on important occasions when the 'chips wir doon'. All four boys were adamant about one thing, namely, that they were more aggressive than the Fleet. Tim's claim was: 'We're gemmier than them. We're the wans that start it an' they move in efter.' The others agreed wholeheartedly; the smaller gangs with the much younger boys provoked trouble and, when fighting broke out, the major gang in the area was challenged to assert its supremacy, which it did by taking part.

Before I am accused of being too credulous, let me say that the stories I have told are simply reported verbatim or as close to that as memory permits. It does not follow that I consider them to be accurate; I do, however, believe them to be indicative of general attitudes.

4
I meet the King

AT SCHOOL ASSEMBLY on Monday morning I caught Tim's eye and we nodded knowingly to each other. As soon as we were alone together, I bombarded him with questions and so cleared up many puzzling remarks. He, in turn, informed me of the aftermath of Pat's beating at the hands of the dance hall bouncers. Pat had limped back down the road in the direction of the pub, had met both Fleet and Young Team members, and told his story. Word was sent to Maryhill to Tim Malloy and to Dick Stevenson. Within an hour, 'more than a hundred boys' had assembled in Sauchiehall Street. Those who were already in town had gained entrance to the Granada. When the main party arrived outside and started to hurl full cans of beer and bricks through the windows, those inside began to smash chairs and draw weapons. The bouncers, under attack from two fronts, were overwhelmed. The main doors were rushed and entrance gained. With girls screaming and pouring out of the building, and the battered and bleeding bouncers locking themselves in the manager's office, the gang commenced a programme of systematic destruction. Every chair and table, every bottle of lemonade and glass, every window, light and balustrade was smashed. Gang slogans were daubed on the walls with spray-paint and only the wail of the sirens of the approaching police cars brought the 'party', as Tim called it, to a halt. Not one boy was arrested for the damage. The police arrived too late.

Two tasks occupied my time during the following days: I collected information on Dick Stevenson and Frank Murphy, and I reflected on my situation. The first task was the easier solved; I consulted the school files for references to Dick. His record of offences began only days after his tenth birthday when he was put on probation for two years for theft. At the age of ten and a half he served 28 days detention for theft. The following year he was fined one pound, again for theft, and, after three more breaches of probation, he was committed to a junior approved school, where his stay was lengthened to two years and four months because he had broken into several houses while an absconder from the school. He was released at the age of 13 but before his 14th birthday he had served two sentences of detention, each of 28 days – for theft. Dick continued to appear in court to face new charges on the same type of offence until he was eventually sent to an intermediate approved school where he was admitted in August 1962, at the age of 14.

The probation report further informs us that Dick's parents, like Tim's,

I meet the King

are 'nominal' Roman Catholics. His father was an unemployed labourer, his mother a housewife with five children, all seven living in two rooms of a slum tenement for which Glasgow Corporation charged them £3 14s. 2d. a month. With regard to the quality of family relationships, the report commented:

> Stevenson frankly admits to liking only his mother and has no feelings or affection for any other member of the family. He does not appear to be too perturbed or concerned about the possibility of returning to an approved school, as he is not too happy at home.

The educational information which arrived at the approved school with the boy runs to all of 40 words, including name, address etc. Dick's school work is described as poor, his IQ is given as 80, and his attendance 'very regular'. As to his character and conduct at school, the report stated: 'Behaves well in class without bother. Known to be a ring-leader in after-school escapades. Good appearance.' This was all the headmaster knew, or perhaps all he was prepared to communicate, about a boy who was to cause such havoc in the streets of Glasgow.

The probation report offered this summary of Dick at the age of 14:

> He is a selfish boy, quick-tempered and aggressive in his attitude to other boys. Discipline he dislikes and his general attitude is one of passive resistance. He is a plausible rogue and is prepared to lie in the face of irrefutable evidence. Of low average intelligence, his educational age is about ten years. He is lazy and spends considerable energy dodging work of any kind. There are no signs of remorse about Stevenson, adult advice is scorned by him, and he has no intention of changing his ways.

One month after his admission to the school, the boy absconded. For fully three months he was at large until he was returned to the school by the Maryhill police who charged him with shoplifting. He had been arrested while breaking into a chemist's shop 'to steal perfume for his girlfriend'. At the time he was found to have four pounds in his pocket. In court the boy was admonished and returned to the intermediate approved school. My connection with the school had not yet begun, but the records do contain the following report written by a social welfare officer on Dick's behaviour in the school:

> Since his entry into the school this lad gradually established himself as a ringleader and a bully *of the first order*. His vicious temper, which

lost him his privileges on many occasions, his *vile* behaviour towards the weaker boys stamped him as being a *careerist* ... his career – Habitual Criminal. Very little good can be said of this boy. The *main case was* his low mental intelligence. He was *thick-headed* to the extent that his behaviour was on a par with his intelligence and therefore his distinguishing right from wrong was non-existent. It was his code of living, irrespective of consequences. He had started on the well-trodden path of crime – and unfortunately he has shown that he is unwilling or incapable of accepting help towards rehabilitation.

The words are emphasised just as they appear in the original, which is in my opinion, more informative about the character of the author than that of the subject. The officer in question has since left the approved school service.

In August 1963, after exactly one year in this approved school, Dick was released on licence for two years. The stated aim of the school was to train and socially rehabilitate young offenders; the only apparent changes in Dick, however, were an increase in weight and a gain in height. For, on licence, his offences continued. Within a month of his release he had lost the job the school had found for him and he remained unemployed until November when he was found guilty of breach of the peace and sentenced to 28 days detention. Shortly after his release he was charged with housebreaking, and was remanded in custody until his trial; but he escaped from the remand home and committed further offences. With seven charges for theft of motor cars and one charge for housebreaking to add to the original offence, Dick pleaded guilty to all of them, and was not surprisingly committed to a senior approved school – within four months of being released from the intermediate school (and even one of these months he had spent in detention).

After two months in the senior approved school, Dick absconded; he was later arrested, charged with housebreaking with intent and remanded in custody. He again engineered his escape from the remand home, was subsequently charged with further housebreaking offences, and, following his plea of guilty to all charges, he was committed to borstal.

In the language of the gang Dick had, by the age of 16, 'done his thruple', namely, junior, intermediate and senior approved school. Besides this he had served four sentences of 28 days detention, the first at the age of ten. And from that age on, until his committal to borstal six years later, he had been convicted more than 25 times. Society can hardly claim that it had not been given sufficient warning about Dick Stevenson.

In addition to learning about Dick Stevenson I was able to check on the injuries suffered by Frank Murphy, one of the boys in the pub on Saturday evening. I had been told that Frank had been attacked only a few weeks ago. In fact, when I tracked down the newspaper comment on the incident, it transpired that the court case had been held more than six months previously, and that the attack itself had taken place more than a year ago. Three members of the Barnes Road gang were given maximum sentences of two years to be served in a young offenders institute. Two of the accused boys were 17 years of age, the other 18. The leader of the trio wielded a razor while the other two had punched and kicked Frank Murphy as he lay on the ground. The leader's nickname was given, significantly, as 'Big Sick'. The three boys had been part of a group, whose size was estimated by observers to be over 30, and who were armed with knives, razors, sticks and a hatchet. The hatchet was found on one boy who had an arm in plaster.

The gang had been terrorizing a local fairground and, in a mob, had set upon Frank who was slashed across the face and disfigured for life. 'His injuries,' the court report continues, 'consist of a deep slash running across his left cheek, another cut which severed his ear, and a third on his neck which required fifty-nine stitches.' When Frank was giving evidence he failed to identify any of his attackers. His cross-examination by counsel for the accused has all the elements of a macabre farce:

> *Counsel*: Does the name 'Fleet' mean anything to you?
> *Frank Murphy*: No.
> *Counsel* : Where do the Fleet come from?
> *Frank Murphy*: Maryhill.
> *Counsel* : Where do you come from?
> *Frank Murphy*: Possilpark.
> *Counsel* : Isn't the only reason that you thought you were going to 'get a doing' was because you were standing up in a provocative manner shouting 'Fleet'?
> *Frank Murphy*: No.

One of the accused claimed that, since the original incident, the victim's brother had held a knife at his throat, 'but he didnae get me'. Frank's elder brother was alleged to have shouted: 'Does it take a team to get my brother?' The case for the defence collapsed, however, when Big Sick boasted in the witness box that the attack was 'the biggest rippin' Ah've done'.

Apart from finding out about Dick Stevenson and Frank Murphy, the other problem, which I mentioned at the beginning of this chapter, was what my position now was. My biggest fright came when one pupil asked me: 'Sur, wir you doon the Granada oan Setirday?' That other boys from the same approved school, out on leave on the same weekend, should go to the same dance hall, I had thought of but dismissed from my mind as too coincidental. The 'you-must-be-joking, *down-where?*' type of answer seemed to satisfy my questioner, but in future I would have to be far more careful. The list of all boys going on leave with Tim would have to be scrutinised to avoid repeating this mistake. Besides, two labourers had been seriously assaulted, one member of the gang had been badly beaten up, or 'messed up somethin' awful' in Tim's words, and one dance hall had been wrecked – all in the space of a few hours. The three incidents had been caused by Pat, certainly not by Tim, although he had eagerly thrown himself into the action once it had begun. This fact comforted me; I had been afraid that Tim might have been tempted to show off in front of me. Instead I saw that my presence had subdued him somewhat. Pat, I felt sure, had no knowledge of my real identity. In retrospect, that first night, though violent, had been immensely informative. I resolved to continue.

This time, two weeks later, the arrangement was to meet at 'the Means Test' (i.e. the Ministry of Social Security) at six pm. I duly appeared, dressed as before. We were now meeting in the gang's own territory, at an earlier hour, and close to Tim's own home. The plan was to await the arrival of the other boys and then travel down to the same pub as a fortnight before. This invitation I considered an advance, a mark of Tim's growing confidence in me. I was stationed at the selected spot before the appointed hour. Time passed and no one arrived. At seven o'clock I began to feel that all my plans were coming to naught. Then Baggy turned up with a small, stockily-built boy in tow. The newcomer, Archie Murray, wore a stylish brown suit which sported pocket-flaps which must have been all of three and a half inches. Archie's most striking feature was long, black sideburns which stretched to a point lower than his ear lobes.

We moved over to an Austin Mini parked in the main street and travelled down to the pub. Once inside, Archie insisted on buying the first round of pints of beer, as he was only staying for a short time. He was a metal sorter, who worked in Bridgeton, and who was 'goin' oot wi' ra boss's daughter.' He was certainly dressed for the occasion with his sparkling white shirt and highly polished shoes. The over-all effect was one of flashy neatness, an effect which was spoiled by a quarter-inch band of dirt under each finger nail. The information he volunteered was that he 'used tae jump aboot wi' the Fleet' but now was 'goin' wi' a bird, serious like.' He was nineteen years old and had been a member of the Young Fleet at the time of the scooter squad. His scooter had involved him in trouble – a whole series of traffic offences – but he had no other type of charge against him. He had since broken away successfully from the gang and yet still remained on friendly terms with the active members. After his one pint, he nodded over to Big Hauf, Peam, Frank Murphy and all the others of the 'heavy team' who were present, and left. One last point I noticed about him. On the left side of his face near his ear he had a scar, which the sideburn only partially covered. Here was a current hair style which also served the demands of vanity.

With Archie gone, and still no Tim, Baggy and I fell to talking. Earlier, I had spotted that Baggy was wearing the same black and pink striped socks. Indeed I noticed that he wore them every time I met him over the four-month period. Within a few minutes he had told me that he had 'loast his joab fur thievin' mulk' and selling it to other customers. For the present, he was therefore 'on ra buroo'. I changed the subject to Tim and his failure to appear. Baggy had seen him in the late afternoon 'up ra road wi' his bruthers an' he said he wis comin' doon the toon.' Things had been quiet the past fortnight, Baggy informed me. Pat Nolan had received a £25 fine on the Wednesday after his battering and considered himself to have escaped lightly. Yet his face had been so badly marked that he hadn't shown himself since that night.

By nine o'clock the pub had filled up and most of the boys I had seen on the previous occasion were present again. One or two nodded to me and I nodded back. Baggy began describing how Frank Murphy had acquired the 59 stitches in his face, only this time 'à la Baggy', the wound had required no less than 65 stitches. Despite plastic surgery, the wound was still deep, jagged and ugly. Having read the newspapers' version of the assault, I listened eagerly to see if Baggy had anything to add to what I already knew. Baggy's story was that Frank had been set upon by a rival gang, the Barnes Road, while out walking with his girlfriend. He had not only been slashed with an open razor, he had been 'ripped', the difference being that in the second case, the blade of the razor is turned in the wound. On top of that, when he fell to the ground, his attackers had kicked his face in a deliberate attempt to split the wound wide open. That night, Frank's elder brother had alerted Dick Stevenson, and with 'over a hundred boys' they had charged into the main quadrangle in Barnes Road. Dick had been armed with a gun and had shot wildly in the air, screaming at the opposition to come out and fight. Not surprisingly, the district had remained deserted and the Fleet and other supporting gangs including Tim's eventually had to withdraw. Baggy's summing up was: 'Aw ye hear up Maryhill is "Dick Stevenson this an' Dick Stevenson that". He's mad, man, but some fighter.'

At this point Baggy himself left without saying where he was going. Tim had still not shown up. Now I was really on my own, on the fringe of the major gang. I retired to a seat to make myself less conspicuous and watched them talk and argue. One fact struck me forcibly; nearly every boy, and certainly Tim, was a nail-biter. On numerous occasions, I saw boys telling a story with one hand deep inside their mouths all the while, biting and gouging until the blood came. Others remarked on this habit of Tim's. Introducing myself to Pat, that first night out, I had claimed to be Tim's 'haufer' at the school. I should have known better. Only boys who smoked 'halved' their tobacco (or 'shag') and, as Pat quickly pointed out: 'Tim disnae smoke – he bites his nails instead.'

In half an hour the bar would be closed. I decided to continue waiting for Tim until ten pm and was rewarded for my patience. For suddenly the word went round the bar: 'The King's in – Dick's here.' The 'leader-aff' of the whole district had arrived. A slightly-built boy, no taller than five-feet-eight, was being pointed out even by some of the barmen. He was dressed in a light-grey suit of the latest fashion, white shirt, and a red tie with a white polka dot and matching handkerchief. His long fair hair was well groomed, parted just to the left of centre and combed down over his ears. Behind him walked a much taller boy, who looked stronger, with broad shoulders and deep chest, wearing a light-blue suit and a black casual. In their tour of the bar, Dick led the way, shaking hands with everyone and smiling; Bob (whose name I learned later) followed behind at a respectful distance, for all the world like the Duke of Edinburgh. Dick had a few words to say to all the members of his gang, refused drink after drink, and accepted the deference of boys and young men much broader and taller than himself. Within 20 minutes they had toured the bar and gone.

I found it impossible to estimate the significance of this visit. Was he naming the rendezvous for later on that night, or was he simply exhorting his followers and reassuring himself of their loyalty? Dick had looked me over while talking to some of his boys close by, but had not spoken to me. Without Tim or Baggy, I was virtually an outsider in this company. After Dick's departure, the boys seemed to me to be planning and arranging schemes, but this is only a surmise on my part. Whatever they were doing, the circles they were standing in were far too large (maybe up to ten boys) for me to join in and find out. I remained uncomfortably on my own.

At ten past ten, i.e. closing time in Scotland, the gang left, wandered slowly up to the centre of town in small groups, mixed with the crowd, and were lost to me. One small group walked into a café and sat down and began ordering food. I came to the conclusion that the evening's activities were at an end, and returned home. There I recorded at the end of my report that I considered the evening a flop. 'After such a promising start, I thought I had become one of the group, but now without Tim I am excluded. Obviously group membership is not to be won as easily as this. Perhaps I am putting too much of a strain on Tim – or too much of a curb on his actions. The loyalty and the deception I am expecting of him is colossal.' I remember being thoroughly disheartened; it looked as if my plans were crashing to the ground. Looking back now, I can see that this occasion was of value. I had kept in touch with events in the gang, I had seen the King and he me, and Baggy and Archie had provided me with more background information. Still, I was keen to hear from Tim the reasons for his failure to put in an appearance.

5
The in-group

I HAD NOT long to wait. On Monday, Tim seemed to be avoiding me, but at lunchtime, in a deserted corridor, I was able to pin him down.

'Didn't see you on Saturday, Tim.'

'Naw, sorry sur. Ye see ma brither Mick wis huckled fur fightin'. His mate wanted tae chib me - stuck a knife in ma heid but it didnae cut me right - and Mick goat stuck intae him.'

This had all taken place in the late afternoon, and Tim had spent the evening enlisting the support of his brother-in-law who, he was quick to tell me, owned a garage. The man had married one of Tim's elder sisters and his money and status were a constant source of pride to the whole family. It was he who had engaged a leading Glasgow solicitor to defend the eldest Malloy on his murder charge and had paid handsomely for the privilege. Tim added thousands of pounds to the bill each time 1 heard him relate the story. For this latest episode Mick was later to be fined £70 and there was another lawyer's fee to be settled in addition. I gathered, though I was not explicitly told, that the brother-in-law had understandably needed some persuasion this time. Tim had been involved in the arrangements for contacting the lawyer, obtaining bail for Mick, and he himself had been interviewed by the police about the fight in the afternoon.

I told Tim that it had been a quiet evening, enlivened only by the entrance of Dick Stevenson. The mere mention of the King was sufficient for Tim to embark on a series of stories about him. He became the standard topic of conversation between us over the next few days. Tim's main contention with regard to Dick was that he had never been given a chance. Up to the present he had 'done his three hoosies' (junior, intermediate and senior approved schools), and he had 'done his borstal, and his borstal recall'; he had served prison sentences of four months and six months (the latter he had just completed), and he was only 18. According to Tim, he would never leave the gang, the very vitality of which depended on him. 'Ra Fleet feel awae tae nuthin' when he wis inside-but every time he comes oot, the boays come up again.' I asked Tim whether he was troubled at the prospect of following in Dick's footsteps through senior school to borstal and prison. 'Ah'm no' bothered - Ah'll take ma chances.' He was proud of the fact that, despite myriad battles, Dick's face remained unmarked. Pressed on this point, he conceded that he was worried about his own good looks being spoiled. He straightaway recalled that

Frank Murphy (the boy with 59 stitches) had been given a handkerchief by his bird to hide his face. Tim thought this a great joke.

The tales surrounding Dick were horrific. Once the gang had been attacking two policemen. Dick had drawn a knife and charged; some of the boys had been reluctant to follow. As the first few grappled with the police, Dick had screamed at the others: 'Get intae thae busies.' Tim's comment was that the boys had to perform as commanded, otherwise 'he wid hiv cut their heids aff.'

In the dance hall I had visited, Dick was once being annoyed by one of his own gang who, fearless in drink, was taunting him in public. 'Come oan, show's yir blade.' Dick's answer was not long in coming. 'Here it's,' he replied. Taking out a flick-knife, he plunged it into the boy's side, just beneath his heart, and left it there. The victim had staggered into the toilet and collapsed. No charge was ever made; the boy recovered in hospital without entertaining the thought of 'grassing'.

Pat Nolan told me a story which struck me at the time as the most exaggerated of all their legends about Dick, and yet it communicates something of the awe in which he was held. Recently, he claimed, Dick had broken into Army barracks and stolen submachine guns and other military equipment. Shortly after this theft, he had been challenged to fight by two men he had insulted and mocked in a pub. As they were preparing to fight, Dick had taken something out of his pocket and handed it to one of his boys saying, 'If I'm no' gettin' the best o' it, pap this haun'-grenade in.' Of course, as soon as Dick moved forward and tackled one of the men, his boys had recognised their cue and had pitched in.

Tim's conclusion was that the boy was 'mental', and his claim that Dick had 'done mair time inside than oot', was almost true. Because the police were 'aye diggin' him up' he no longer carried a 'chib', leaving this task to Bob or one of his other 'lieutenants', the latter word being mine not theirs.

But my main concern was Tim and his Young Team, and so far I had learned far more about the Fleet and Dick Stevenson. The opportunity presented itself in my third outing to meet far more members of Tim's gang. As usual, we had arranged to meet on a Saturday night at the pub near town. At the last minute Tim changed the venue, mentioning a pub in his own territory. I had suspected that the town pub was really the meeting place of the Fleet, as members of the Young Team on both occasions had been outnumbered by roughly ten to one. My suspicions were confirmed. The Young Team generally met earlier in the evening shortly after opening time at five o'clock at a pub in the centre of their own area. It was only later at night that they travelled into town, looking in at the other bar if they felt like it.

This time when I arrived, Tim and company were already settled down with pints. The décor was modern, tartan carpets covered the floors, and the Public Bar was well supplied with comfortable leather chairs. There were dartboards, a TV set, dominoes etc., and from the gantry, a photograph of Benny Lynch, the famous Glasgow flyweight champion, overlooked the proceedings. This was no sawdust pit, but a well-appointed working-man's pub, marred solely by the Young Team's slogans which covered both the front door and the toilet. Of the seven boys sitting around the table, only one looked old enough to be legally admitted. Yet they were served not only in this pub, but in any we entered. As Tim remarked to me later: 'They wouldnae dare refuse ye.'

Once in Cowcaddens, when we were deep in Toi country, or Toi land as it was sarcastically called, we turned into a pub and Tim's cousin, Nicky, the youngest-looking, ordered drinks. The barman replied: 'Away an' sit in the coarner an' send wan o' yir big mates ower.' Both customers and managers kept a careful watch for 'the licence busies', i.e. policemen in plain clothes who made periodic checks on the ages of customers. On more than one occasion, a barman had come over to them, ostensibly to clean the tables, but in reality to warn the smaller boys. Tim also confessed that his Ma had often seen him drinking in pubs, but had turned a blind eye.

As no introductions, formal or otherwise, were made, it took me all evening to assimilate the boys' names. Again, I encountered the difficulty of understanding the conversation; anyone who has heard Glasgow approved school boys talking together will appreciate my problem. Slowly I learned that the boys were Nicky Bennett (Tim's cousin, also called 'Beano'), 'Fergie', Dave Malloy (no relation of Tim's), Harry Johnstone, Dan McDade and Jimmy Barrow.

I remember asking Beano if he was actually Tim's cousin. His reply, in a voice which had still to break, indicated that he had no clear idea of the relationship between them. Beano lived in Cowcaddens and one would have expected him to be a member of the Cowcaddens Toi or of the Port Toi, as his home was close to Port Dundas. But his family connection with Tim brought him into Maryhill and made him a member of the Young Team. He was not long in boasting that he was the boy who toured Cowcaddens adding to the gang slogans sprayed on the walls by the TOI the letters LET. All thought this monstrously funny. Apart from his glossy black hair, which flowed over his collar at the back, but was closely cropped at the front, he was easily recognised by a thin vertical scar running down the side of his face from his eye to his chin. Tim's comment was: 'It makes him look great, man – a wee baby face an' a big scar.' His elder brother had struck him with a hatchet. 'They wir wee at the time. He wis four or somethin'. It wis an accident.'

Fergie was the same height as myself, with cropped hair – 'that's the *real style.*' He worked as an apprentice slater, stealing large quantities of slates from his employer and selling them at £18 a thousand. His great boast was that he had never been chibbed and more than that, he had never been caught by the police, 'no' fur nuthin',' although he had taken a leading part in the gang's activities for years. 'Fergie wid never fight me,' claimed Tim; the reason for this was no doubt fear of Tim's elder brothers. This, I felt, was true although Mick was the only brother Tim had at home at this time. As I sat down, Tim was triumphantly narrating how he had attacked Fergie's elder brother, Bertie Ferguson, who was a member of the Fleet and a friend of Mick's. Bertie, by all accounts including Tim's, would have swept the floor with him. but Mick had stepped in and challenged Bertie to a 'square-go'. 'Mick murdered him, man', Tim recalled in exaggeration, exulting both in the discomfiture of his friend Fergie and in the physical prowess of the Malloy family.

Dave Malloy was the oldest of the group, perhaps 18 or 19. Later I discovered he was a Protestant, but this was of no importance; he came from the same district as the others, and so joined the Young Team. He was of a suitable age and ferocity to join the Fleet as Tim's brother Mick had done and as his brother John was shortly to do after his release from borstal. Yet Dave stayed with the Young Team out of an interest in and affection for Tim. Fergie told me that Dave was at Tim's beck and call. Tim himself described the relationship in the following words: 'Big Dave wid dae anythin' fur me.' This claim had been tested at a dance hall where Tim had turned to Dave and pointed to a bystander: 'Ah don't fancy the look o' his puss. Go ower an' stab him fur me.' Dave had duly carried out the request. Dave himself told me that he was staying with Fergie; in fact, he had lived in the Ferguson household for 18 months. Fergie subsequently explained why: 'He his no Ma or Da - well, his Ma lives doon Possil but he never sees her.' The furthest house in Possilpark was not three miles from where we were sitting. Meanwhile, Dave had been 'bummin' away' as usual about how many blokes he had chibbed. He was taken to task by Harry Johnstone: 'How did ye no bum y:r way oot o' court?' General laughter.

Harry Johnstone, Dan McDade, and Jimmy Barrow together formed 'The Young Trio, OK', a slogan I was to see decorating walls, lampposts, and closemouths all over the district. They were a small splinter group, with a common interest in music. Harry played the mouth-organ and the other two the guitar. Harry had a horizontal scar on his right cheek, Jimmy fiery red hair and a serious squint in one eye, and Dan a face badly scarred by acne. By general agreement Dan was the maddest of them all, but the competition was steep. Tim's opinion of him was that 'he his nae heart - wid dae his granny in.' Later that night, Harry was hit on the head with a bottle. Even with the blood flowing very freely down his forehead, he refused to go to hospital. 'Ah don't believe in them – they gee ye big jags an' aw that.' His hair still matted with blood, he went up to his assailant's home. The culprit's father answered the door and Harry slashed him with a butcher's knife: 'Ah've left him wi' a big groovy.' As the boy himself came running out, Dan stuck a broken wine bottle into his face.

Thanks to some diligent research on the part of colleagues within the approved school service, I was able much later to track down some background information on Jimmy Barrow. When Jimmy was committed to an intermediate approved school for the first time at the age of 14, he already had five previous convictions and had been on probation for a year. The report submitted by his school could hardly have been shorter. It states that the boy in his second year of secondary schooling was only present for the first six months, and even then he only attended 92 times out of a possible 147. His mental capacity is given as '92, below average'. Progress in general subjects and in practical work is recorded as poor. No further comment of any kind is made.

The Barrow family consisted of father and mother, a girl of 18 employed in a factory, Jimmy, and a young boy often still at school. All five had been living in one room for years, but the parents had recently split up. The separation was said by Mrs Barrow to be the result of accommodation difficulties; however, Mr Barrow for the previous nine months had been making no contribution towards the maintenance of the family.

Jimmy's period within the approved school was scarcely trouble free. Within days of being admitted he absconded twice, and on the second occasion he was charged with housebreaking and with breaking into a cinema; in Court he was admonished and returned to the school. Six months later he failed to return from leave and was subsequently charged with housebreaking. Being recommitted to the intermediate approved school, he absconded four times within three weeks, at the end of which time he had three more charges of housebreaking to answer. A month later he appeared at Glasgow Sheriff Court and was there committed to a senior approved school. Jimmy had just been released from this senior school when I met him. The only personal information I could obtain from the first approved school was that 'James Barrow is a tall, truculent lad who appears to be weak willed and easily led.'

But to return to the pub, Tim was giving me an account of an incident over a year ago concerning Jimmy Barrow. Despite his red hair, he was reputed to be the quietest of the group, if the word quiet is appropriate at all in the context. There had been a small crowd of boys and girls at the corner, leaning up against the walls and closed shop fronts. The group had become alive to the fact that Jimmy wasn't participating to any great extent in the conversation. In a sentence which served as a timely warning to me, Tim had blurted out: 'He's a queer hawk – an' Ah *hate* somewan in a company who disnae say nuthin'.' (This facet of Tim I had already noticed in group counselling meetings at the approved school. At the first one he attended he suddenly exploded, 'Mon, eh? Some'dy talk. Ah cannae bear these silences.') The boys had pounced on Jimmy and removed his trousers, leaving him to run about in his underpants while his trousers were thrown from boy to boy.[9] Eventually, one of the girls had lent him her coat to cover himself. 'He wis nearly greetin'.' 'How wis Ah?' asked Jimmy. 'Aye, ye wir,' contradicted his mates.

This affair reminded Harry of John Malloy's game of running across the street and kissing girls he didn't know – all to the great amusement of the gallery at the corner. 'The birds goat big riddies, man – it was brilliant!' Some reference was made at this point to 'Hammie' who was 'dain' his borstal for thievin'.' Tim mentioned in an aside to me that 'Hammie used to lead aff the Young Team.' I asked how Hammie had been caught, sensing an atmosphere of absent friends every time his name was mentioned. He had been in a shop where the man ahead of him in the queue had placed two pounds on the counter to pay for goods. Hammie had picked up the money, put it in his pocket, and was walking away when he was 'nabbed'. 'Fancy gettin' yir borstal fur two poun',' was the group's feeling.

One of my toughest tasks was indeed the limitation placed upon my speech. At times I wanted either to joke, or to object to the violence, or to circumscribe their gross and manifest exaggerations, but I had to remember my observer status and refrain from saying anything evaluative or directive. To avoid being considered 'a queer-hawk' or a 'bent-shot' (homosexual), I had to chip in to the conversation every so often. To draw attention from any errors I might make, I took to swearing. My rule of speech became one of 'When in doubt, say "fuck".'

The decision was now made to collect girlfriends, and meet at 'the dancin'.' I went with Tim, Dave and Fergie, who were all reminiscing about the time the assembled Young Team had travelled across to Saracen Cross in Possilpark in as many as 12 to 15 taxis. 'It wis some sight. Aw thae taxis in a big line-up.' (The phrase 'line-up' provoked considerable laughter from the other two, as it was normally used to describe the queue of boys waiting to have sexual intercourse in one of the 'gang bangs'.) 'We came pourin' oot, aw jazzed up in wir tin flutes, aw drunk and blocked up wi' the goofies. Great, man.' Our entrance that evening was to be far more modest, however – by Corporation transport bus. On the way to the bus stop, Tim had nipped up a close to collect his bird, Maureen. She stayed in a block of reasonably new

Corporation flats, whose only disfigurement was the ubiquitous gang slogan. While we waited, Dave described Maureen's elder sister, Margaret, who was 'hooked on the goofies. Like the other birds what takes dexedrine, she disnae know whit she's dain'.' Tim returned alone, no mention was made of the missing girlfriend by the others, so on we walked.

Fergie was the next to leave. He muttered something about picking up his girl 'Frana', whom he had 'been goin' wi' fur ten month'. As soon as he was out of hearing range, Tim opened up on the subject of Fergie. Tim had been the recipient of the confidence that Fergie, who was one year older, was in love. 'Aw, naw!' Tim snorted in a mixture of contempt and embarrassment. Fergie had claimed to be on the point of getting married and giving up the team. In the midst of derisive laughter, Fergie had continued in an attempt to save face: 'An' am goaney give up stabbin'. Ah've promised the bird. Noo Ah'm only goaney rip them.' This time the laughter had been approving.

We reached Saracen Cross which was crowded with young people, predominantly girls. The three of us were to 'chat up' partners and then continue to the dance hall. But Tim was prevented from moving forward by the approach of two policemen, one of whom shouted across at him: 'So fuckin' Malloy is oot again? Is yir fuckin' brothers still in fuckin' prison?' Tim's answers also made liberal use of Glasgow's favourite adjective. The second policeman turned to Dave and me, and, noticing the marks on Dave's face he began: 'So ye goat fuckin' scratched, tryin' tae get yir fuckin' hole.' I was asked if I was with the other two, to which I replied: 'Yes'. Tim became enraged at this word. 'Button it, ya tramp ye,' he screamed at me. Afterwards I was to hear that only 'fuckin' snobs say "yes" – whit's wrang wi' "aye"?' I dealt better with the second question from the policeman about my name, having been instructed many times 'on geein' a falser.' The aim was to pronounce a name, an obscenity and an insult all in the same breath to divert attention from the alias. 'James fuckin' Patrick, ya bam-pot ye', had the anticipated effect. The first policeman leaned across and, prodding me in the stomach and chest with his fist to emphasise each word, he insisted: 'Weil, get aff this fuckin' Cross, or Ah'll fuckin' book ye.'

With the usual source of partners thus denied us, we travelled into town, Tim incensed at the 'right showin'-up' the police and I had accorded him, and entered a small dance hall at six shillings a head. We were promised that on our next visit we would be given a membership card which would reduce the cost to three shillings. Tim and Dave couldn't remember how often they had been thus cheated and so complained at being charged six shillings. One of the difficulties was recollecting which false name they had previously given. I was unable to appreciate Dave's problem fully, when I saw that the height of his imagination was 'James Smith, Maryhill Road.' However, he and Tim availed themselves of one of the club's services. On entry we had been searched by bouncers. Tim had surrendered a hatchet, and Dave a bayonet in return for which they were given cloakroom tickets. One half of the ticket was licked and placed on the weapon, the attendant saying: 'I'll pit these in the coarner an' ye can get them as ye go oot.' I was irresistibly reminded of the tough cattlemen in the Wild West who were forced by the sheriff to hang up their guns before entering the saloon. Moving into the dance hall, Tim remarked on the fatuity of the procedure, for simultaneously he produced a slim open razor from his jacket pocket.

We were joined inside by Beano, who pointed out to me the woman who ran the Club, Stella by name, and a 'big darlin' by reputation. She was a good-looking, 40-year-old blonde whose standard reply to young boys inviting her to dance was 'Run away, sonny. I wis dancin' when you were still shitin' green.' The girls present, I soon discovered, were here to dance and talking was not encouraged. At first, the boys danced only with girls from Maryhill. Most continued to dance only with these girls, but Tim and Dave began daring each other to go further afield. Time passed and the Young Team began to swell in numbers. Fergie, Jimmy, Dan and Harry were all present and so were Baggy, Midgie and others. The dance hall was situated right in the centre of town, and not on the borders of Maryhill as was the first one I had visited. Members of gangs from all over the city were pointed out to me, and soon accusations were flying that the Cumbie and the Barnes Road were carrying blades, which had allegedly been smuggled in by their girlfriends. I sensed trouble and before long it had erupted.

At the end of a dance, as couples left the floor, 'Wee Sheldon' of the Barnes Road butted 'Gallie' Gallacher in the face. Within seconds, the floor was cleared to reveal both boys rolling over and over on the ground. Tim led the charge, yelling 'Young Team! Young Team!' He was the first to reach the two struggling bodies; he kicked Sheldon's belly and face. Now boys were running from all parts of the hall and adding to the fracas. The band played on as a gang of bouncers descended on the brawling mob and began throwing them out two and three at a time. But before order was restored, two of the bouncers had blood streaming from their faces and I saw one large coloured boy 'stickin' the nut' (i.e. his forehead) into the back of one attendant's head. The man fell forward into the path of a few boys from the Young Team who were making for the exit. Beano later described what happened next: 'We did a Mexican dance oan his face. Everybody started playin' fitba' wi' his heid.'

Outside the fighting continued. Those without 'malkies' had gone round the back of the building and were now reappearing, some with milk and 'ginger' (lemonade) bottles in their hands, others with bricks, and one boy was clutching the leg of an old chair. The Young Team regrouped on the opposite side of the street and the Barnes Road at the entrance to the club. Weapons had neither been flourished nor used inside the hall, but now that the ritual taunts had begun they were suddenly brought out. Tim was screaming again and again, 'Young Team! Are ye goin' ahead, mugs?' Though already brandishing his open razor, he also grabbed a wine bottle, broke it on the wall (thus cutting his hand badly), and charged across the street. The arrival at this point of the riot squad led to further confusion, with boys running in all directions to escape. The street was now full of people, since the club had disgorged most of its members eager to see the outcome of the fight.

The Barnes Road were surely home by this time, running as they were far ahead of any possible pursuit. Tim and a small coterie around him were also far from the scene, chasing the others through the streets with weapons drawn. The police began rounding up all those left behind, among whom I stupidly found myself. Moira McManus, with whom I had danced previously, took my arm and together we walked past the police. This was a service which any girl from Maryhill provided for any boy from that area to save him from arrest. 'You're wi' me,' she said, 'and gee me yir chib an' I'll slip it intae ma handbag.' Not to appear too unmanly, I claimed to have lost my non-existent weapon in the general melee. All boys on their own were now being frisked by the police.

Walking arm-in-arm with Moira (not hand-in-hand, which I remember feeling would have been more natural for me), was beginning to restore my confidence, when two members of the Barnes Road, who must have doubled back, lurched from a close and stopped us. It was Moira who had been recognised and she in turn recognised one of them as a boy with whom she had been at school. I noticed that the taller of the two had a blade of some kind hidden up the sleeve of his jacket. The cross-questioning began:

'Are youse in this Young Team?'

'Ah'm no' wi' any team, boays,' I pleaded. 'Ah'm jist gettin' ma bird up the road. Whit's the score, oaneywae?'

In reply, the taller boy slid the blade into his hand; I could now see that it was a sharpened tail-comb.

'Shut it, ya half-wit,' he said. Obviously they were unimpressed with my story; perhaps they had positively connected me with the Young Team. They were in an ugly mood and smelled heavily of alcohol. I took no chances and ran. They pounded after me, leaving Moira on her own. I had only begun to draw away from them when I stumbled over some obstruction which sent me sprawling over the pavement. As I fell, I sensed figures closing in on me and

I realised that I had been tripped by a foot sticking out of a close. Thinking I was caught and about to be stabbed, I did as I had been instructed by Tim. I curled myself into a ball, almost in the foetal position, with my hands covering my face and my back exposed. 'Right, get up,' someone ordered. Before I could carry out the command, I was dragged to my feet by a policeman in plain clothes who was searching my suit for weapons. Hearing him mention to his mate that I was 'clean', I moved away from the wall against which they had propped me, and began dusting down my clothes.

As I was being questioned, Moira appeared to rescue me once more. I gave my name to the police loudly and clearly because I did not know whether she would remember it or not. The police turned to her and she corroborated my story that I had been in the dance hall when the trouble started; at which point, she went on, I had walked along the road with her until we were stopped by two young boys. Moira refused to give the name of the boy she had recognised, and the police, dismissing us, said: 'Ye can thank yir lucky stars; we almost goat ye fur mobbin' an' riotin'.' It occurred to me during the rest of our uneventful walk to the Young Team's corner that the police, while making for the dance-club, had dropped off a few men on the approach roads. In fact, both gangs had to travel along Maryhill Road to get back to their respective areas. Tim later claimed that a running fight had continued until they reached Bilsland Drive. I also heard him assert without being contradicted that his weapon had been an air rifle. The open razor and the broken wine bottle he had carried were apparently not sufficient to create the image he hankered after.

Approaching Fergie's close, I met up with the others who included Harry, nursing his head wound. The evening's entertainment was discussed until midnight, during which time I was roundly abused on two counts – for having taken a back-seat during the fight, and for walking a girl home. 'Yir lumber's a cow,' they informed me. My membership of the gang was at this time vague and undefined and it remained so. No initiation test or ceremony had been demanded of me. Yet I knew all too well how to win fuller acceptance. I had to take part in the action – in some role or other – and be seen to do so. How and to what extent I was able to comply with this requirement I am advised not to disclose. But I feel I must make it clear that at no time did I carry, still less use, a weapon. How I could refrain from violence and remain on friendly terms with Tim mystified Big Dave. Looking daggers at me, he mumbled that expressive approved school term: 'fuckin' bendin' edger.'

The boys were still talking about the fight with the Barnes Road, and encouraging a girl who was spraying 'Margrit' on a wall, when the police arrived from all directions in a number of Land Rovers, vans and cars. Tim had assured us earlier that the police were scared to come through Maryhill. 'Once in a blue moon,' he said, 'they fly past in a motor, but we rule here.'[10] At the approach of the police the gang scattered, running through closes to hide or throw away what weapons they were carrying. Whether through fear, lack of experience, or realization of the futility of flight, I remained rooted to the spot.

My lack of resistance did not prevent me, however, from being hit on the shoulder by a baton as I was bundled into a police van after being searched. Beano was dragged to the van, punching and kicking policemen and swearing at all and sundry. As he was pushed inside by two constables, a third standing by the door hit him on the side of the forehead with a rubber torch. 'That'll quieten ye,' the policeman said. Tim appeared at the van door struggling with two other policemen at whom he was shouting: 'You'll no rip me. Ah'm a gemmie.'

As the van drove off, the boys began taunting the police by banging the sides of the van with their hands and singing:

Up yir hole wi' a ten foot pole
An' doon yir arse wi' a scrubber ...

All noise stopped at a curt word of command from an officer who remarked that we would soon all be singing in the cells. This comment caused the boys to fall silent and, still in silence, we were brought into the police station and made to stand in a line facing a blank wall. I noticed as we entered that Beano's white shirt was now spotted with blood which was dripping from his right eyebrow. The eye itself had haemorrhaged and, as he walked, he left a trail of bloodstains on the ground.

Inside, one of the riot squad, as the boys called them, ordered Beano to take off his jacket. Beano did so and handed it over. The policeman rolled the jacket into a ball, mopped the bloodstains from the floor with it, and then handed it back to Beano who rushed at him, yelling: 'Ya black rat! Ya sick an' dyin' rat!' Beano lost control of himself and began thrashing about with his arms and legs, striking out in all directions; after a struggle, he was held firmly by two policemen.

The other boys took up Beano's cause and began to swear and abuse the police who reacted by splitting us up. I was taken into a side room, asked my name and address, and questioned about a money-lender who apparently employed chib-men to collect money from clients as they left the Ministry of Social Security. The police quickly realised that I had no information to give them, and so, finally, they told me to empty my pockets. The moment I put my hands into my trouser pockets to comply with the order, I was punched in the back by one policeman and kicked from behind by another as I fell. After a few more punches and kicks, the police withdrew and the door was locked. I lay oh the bed in the corner, on a blanket that smelled of urine and vomit, and wondered whether the police would break my pseudonym by phoning the approved school which I had given as my address. For reasons unknown to me, this did not happen. After four or five hours we were brought before a sergeant who warned us that he knew we had been involved in the gang fight at the dance hall, that he wasn't prepared to tolerate such behaviour, and that next time we would all be formally charged. At that we were led out onto the street and told to get lost. The other boys talked of having been punched and kicked and it was clear that they had expected nothing less. Beano, his face by now swollen and ugly-looking, was congratulated by Big Dave for the way he had tackled the police, 'Ye took the piss right oot o' them, so ye did.' It was now very early on Sunday morning and the boys decided to get some sleep.

I did not realise it at the time, but the fact that I had shared the experience of being picked up by the police with the inner core of the Young Team proved to be a turning-point in that I gained some minimal measure of acceptance. The agreement to remain silent which Tim and I had entered into for our mutual protection had now been fully tested and Tim's loyalty strengthened my determination to continue. Saturday nights, however, were proving dangerous from all quarters. A change of plan was needed.

6
On a Sunday afternoon

I HAD NOW met the gang on three occasions – all on Saturday evenings. It was time to observe them under different conditions, at different times of the week. The most obvious change to make was to tell Tim I had a previous engagement on the next Saturday of his leave and ask for a meeting on the following afternoon. Tim had to report at the approved school before 6.30 on the Sunday evening and so two o'clock in the afternoon was chosen. This switch in time was to increase the risk of being identified as I was now walking the streets in daylight, dressed in the dark blue suit with a light blue casual shirt substituted for collar and tie. And I came very close to being spotted. On the very afternoon I chose to meet Tim, the approved school bus out on its normal weekend run, happened to make its way through Maryhill. Luckily for me Tim recognised the bus as it approached and shouted out greetings to the occupants. I was given sufficient time to turn my back on the main road and walk down a side street.

The rendezvous Tim and I had agreed upon was the main corner in the Young Team's territory. Sometime previously they had been in the habit of meeting in a nearby café. But Tim had been banned from there over a year ago for calling one of the serving girls a cow and had smashed some large seven-pound jars of sweets as he left. Now he took up his stance at the street corner with those of the gang who had emerged from bed.

The previous evening had been a repetition of the Saturday nights I had witnessed. They had met in their own local pub, travelled down to the Fleet's pub near town, and at closing time walked to one of Glasgow's leading dance halls. Here, the management had (and still have) a policy of thoroughly searching all males entering the building and ejecting all those found in possession of weapons. That night Tim had been in the company of Joe Stevenson, a younger brother of Dick, who was also on his way to the same dance hall. One of the group was refused admittance and Tim and Joe, both being quite drunk, had immediately drawn their weapons and attacked the attendants. Dick, who had been watching the growing rumpus from across the street, noticed that his young brother was involved and, with a meat cleaver in his hand, had raced across the main road, jumped on the backs of the Young Team and plunged his chib into the forehead of one of the bouncers. I had read a report of this incident in the Sunday papers before coming out. The bouncer, after some time on the danger list, eventually recovered.

On a Sunday afternoon

According to Tim, Joe's girlfriend and her mate had 'jumped in, screamin' and greetin' and tore me an' Joe oot.' Joe had been butted in the face by one of the bouncers and the blood from his nose stained his shirt and suit. As the four of them withdrew, the other members of the Young Team and the Fleet had also taken to their heels. The two boys retreated to a public lavatory to clean up. There Tim saw that his own trousers were spotted with blood and remarked that he couldn't 'go oot tae a party like yon.' With Joe's face patched up, they had rejoined the two girls and had returned home to change their clothes before going to Fergie's party.

I now learned for certain what I had suspected, namely, that for the gang Saturday nights did not end at or around midnight. Fergie was accustomed to throw 'all nighters' on Friday and Saturday. The boy's father had deserted the home, leaving his mother and elder sisters in control. But in fact they were summarily ordered out of their own home every weekend and dispatched to an aunt's house. This left the flat unattended and suitable for parties. The latest of these had been, in the gang phrase, 'a right corker'. There had been 20 to 30 'blokes wi' their birds.' Tim blamed the subsequent condition of the guests on the wine, but Beano added that those 'on ra goofies goat intae some state.' At a similar party a month before, Dick Stevenson had appeared 'wi' eyes like tea-cups' having been 'oan the drugs fur two tae three weeks.' He had taken some more, staggered and collapsed. After much quarrelling over the chore, one of his mates had taken him to hospital where his stomach had been pumped.

Tim himself had 'been up at a lassie's hoose aw night' and took obvious pleasure in claiming to have 'beefed her'. He had woken up at 11 that morning, had returned home, eaten and gone to bed for a few hours. Now he was ready for the football match. The in-group among the Young Team had all assembled by the time I had arrived, together with others from the gang whom I had not seen before. Today we were to play football against 'the big boays', namely the Fleet. On previous Sundays, the Uncle gang from Possilpark had been played ('Uzz Young Team always tank them'). And on other occasions scratch games had been played amongst members of the Young Team itself. The normal venue for the match was Cadder football park, but this time we simply climbed over the railings of the nearest school and monopolised the playground. As the game progressed, more and more girls helped each other over the railings and watched the game from beneath a shed in a corner of the school yard.

Dick arrived with his boys. Big Bob Robertson or 'Robbie' was in attendance in the same respectful fashion as before. Mick, Tim's elder brother, was there, as were Bertie and Wattie Ferguson, Fergie's older brothers, Gallic

Gallacher, Big Hauf, Beano, Frank Murphy, Jack Stanton, Joe O'Neill and others. The competition for places in the football teams was fierce, the outcome being that Tim and Dick chose not only those with ability, but also those whose status and temper was such that they couldn't be omitted. I was picked by Tim but for what reason I am unsure. I was soon to regret my pleasure at being selected.

The game began with 22 players and 22 referees. I had played both with and against Tim at the approved school and so was familiar with his inability to accept decisions given against him or his team. He brooked no criticism of his play or of his general conduct. Time after time at school he had attempted to dominate the field by intimidating opponents with crushing tackles or murmured threats; and time after time he had been sent off for ungentlemanly conduct, i.e. swearing at the referee when being reprimanded. Tim as never the gracious loser. His immediate response, for example, to being beaten at table-tennis in the approved school was to hurl the bat through the air, with total disregard for the danger he thus placed his audience in. Now 21 boys began playing with an unbridled ferocity which I found infectious. Within a short time I found myself hacking and pushing and charging with the best of them.

The game was punctuated by stoppages for minor outbursts of fighting or quarrelling. The majority of boys had turned up to play wearing 'sannies' and old denims. But the rest, including myself, played in our suits. I at least divested myself of my jacket at the very beginning of the game; Tim, Beano and Dave Malloy were stripped to their vests by the end. But Dick Stevenson, Mick Malloy and Harry Johnstone completed the match still wearing their suits, which were by then badly dirtied, and in Dick's case, torn. Dan McDade informed me, with admiration on his face, that Dick would throw the suit away and change into another for the evening. The boys were unanimous in telling me that Dick always played while wearing a suit. In fact, once during the summer, he had 'done his goalie' wearing a stolen mustard-coloured suede coat, 'divin' intae the mud an' every-thin'.' Easy come, easy go.

As to the game itself, it was played at a raging pace with one side or the other controlling the play for long stretches. The Fleet, ably led by Eddie McIntyre, Jimmy Agnew and Bob Robertson, began piling on the goals to lead eight to one at half-time. Tim went berserk as their lead increased, swearing and punching his own players (including the much taller and older Dave Malloy) in an attempt to galvanise them into greater action. As we changed round at half-time to play downhill, Tim cried out for his elder brother John who was still in borstal and who had received offers to turn professional as a goalkeeper. (But even if he had been present, he would have played for the

Fleet.) Bob Robertson, whose skill and, more decisively, whose fitness were contributing so largely to the Fleet's success, played for a well-known junior football club. There were, however, weaknesses in the Fleet's team; it was obviously regular practice to take 'the piss oot o' Dick', as he was so badly co-ordinated and lacking in basic football skills. Running from man to man in a vain attempt to keep up with the ball, he soon became exhausted and left the field. He tried to laugh off his gaucherie and encouraged others to do likewise, but the loss of face was keenly felt by him. At the next stoppage (yet another disputed goal) I noticed that he had left the school yard altogether. Playing with the slope in our favour we won 21 to 16. It was that kind of game.

Yablonsky's account (1967, pp.70-1) of his first attempt to redirect a New York juvenile gang's activities from 'bopping' to baseball is relevant here. The baseball project shifted leadership positions within the gang in that two marginal members, Cisco and Rios, grew in prestige because of their skill at the game, while the two core leaders of the gang, Duke and Pedro, being poor players, lost prestige. 'Duke was an impossible first baseman. He dropped or missed almost every ball thrown to him.' The boys solved their problems by becoming more agressive, beating up other members of the gang – 'no doubt to let them know they were still boss.' Although not true of Tim, this was certainly true of Dick Stevenson, who was a figure of fun on a football park, and who made up for this further demonstration of his general inadequacy by resorting to even more violent acts.

One other matter, apart from bruised ankles, gave me cause for worry. Dave Malloy, the self-appointed protector of Tim, was becoming jealous of my (to him) inexplicable relationship with Tim. In the first half I had become in his eyes the sole reason for our defeat. This was a problem which was to develop.

After the game, the Fleet departed with most of the girls and Tim, Fergie, Dave Malloy, Beano and various others all trooped deep into Maryhill in search of refreshments. We entered a café and ordered glasses of hot orange. In all we numbered 12, or in Tim's account, which I was later to hear, 'twenty-handed we wir.' As we began to relax and discuss the game. Tim turned round and recognised a girl sitting in the corner with a friend. 'Look who it is, fur fuck sake. It's yon fuckin' pig wi' knickers Ah telt youse aboot.' At this, he and three or four others ran over and at Tim's instigation, they began spitting in the girl's face and hair. She began to scream and, with Tim man-handling her out of the door, as they all continued to spit at her, she became hysterical. Tim returned to roars of applause and laughter, shouting: 'Ah ran a pure savage wi' thae people, man.'

He recounted in anger the background to the incident. While in the approved school during the summer, he had been taken into town with another boy (both of them wearing short trousers and overalls), by a member of staff to collect pieces of furniture from a store-house. Despite the boys' protests about appearing in the centre of town dressed in this way, they were instructed to go. Entering the store, Tim had been recognised by a young shop-assistant from Maryhill. She had left her counter, as the boys struggled out with the furniture, and had started ridiculing their appearance. Tim had harboured this grudge for months and on spotting her in the café had taken the opportunity to both punch and kick her for her insolence.

A few weeks later, I had the odd experience of listening to Tim telling this story both to other boys and to another member of the staff during a school hike. Not once did he as much as drop a hint of my presence in the café although taken to task by the other staff member for his outrageous conduct. His description was substantially the one I have given, apart from his dwelling on the spittle running down the girl's face: 'Big greasers they wir.' His last comment on the subject was: 'A lovely wee thing she wis an' aw.'

The Italian café owner did not dare to remonstrate with us and I didn't blame him. Sensing his disapproval, however, we moved on, walking back towards the Young Team's corner. On the way we met Mick Malloy, who had been so drunk the night before that he had looked as though he was still 'steamin'' during the game. His passing remark was: 'Ah'm awae doon by – doon the Licey's.' He had to be reminded that this being Sunday, and he being in Scotland, all licensed grocers were closed. When the message penetrated, he was off to buy wine from the local punter at a pound a bottle.

Back at the corner, we passed the time by criticizing everybody and anybody who passed by. Typical of the comments was a remark shouted to young girls walking in the street: 'Hi! Sexy drawers! Ah want ma hole.' Or again, to girls and, surprisingly, to boys: 'Ah'll kick yir cunt in.' As darkness came down, their daring increased. The Young Trio broke into song, the melody being 'The Auld Orange Flute' with the words rewritten by themselves:

> I went to a party one Friday night,
> The Tongs were there and wanted to fight,
> I drew my blade out, quick as a flash,
> And shouted 'Young Team, Young Team, Ya Bass.'
> The first one that came was five foot four,
> I lifted my boot and he fell to the floor.
> The cunt was in agony,
> The cunt was in pain,
> So I lifted my boot and I fucked him again.

Another song in their repertoire, sung to the tune of 'Bless Them All', began: 'Stab them aw, stab them aw, the busies, the judges, an' aw!'

One couple walking down the road attracted particular attention. This was Big Sheila's sister and her boyfriend, a quiet young man, who was held close by his fiancée every time they encountered the Young Team.

'Are ye no goaney gee ra boay a free night?'

'He's no' goin' wi' youse hooligans,' came the girl's answer.

The very sight of a young couple who were going steady or on the point of marriage was sufficient to provoke a stream of obscene abuse from the gang: 'Yir ma's a pastime for a darkie, an' you're a fuckin' hing-oot.' Tim summed up the incident by concentrating on what had given the gang such pleasure, the boy's loss of face: 'Whit a showin' up in front o' aw the boays.'

It was time for Tim and me to return to the approved school. We moved off together, and, after a suitable distance, we parted and I headed for home.

7
The relevant murders

ONE TOPIC MORE than any other occupied the gang's mind that Sunday afternoon. It was the first anniversary of Henderson's murder. The boy had been stabbed to death at Charing Cross by a gang calling themselves the Wild Young Catholic Shamrock. Here were two Catholic gangs (both with Protestant members in their ranks) fighting because they came from different areas of Glasgow, or perhaps just fighting without any reason at all. On asking Tim how he felt when he realised one of his number had been murdered, he replied: 'Ah wis mad, aff ma heid. Ah ran a right psychey doon the toon. Ah ran amock wi' a big psychey blade. Didnae know whit Ah wis dain'.'

From the others I heard that Dick Stevenson had attended the trial of those accused of the murder. When one boy, McBride by name, was acquitted, Dick had punched him in the face on the steps of the Court and challenged him to a 'square-go' in Glasgow Green. They had set to, I was told, under the eyes of the 'busies' and, of course, Dick had 'murdered' him. Five other members of the Shamrock were sentenced to life imprisonment.

Some aspects of the trial still enraged them. One of the witnesses for the prosecution was a chip-shop owner from Castle Street. 'The Toon boays', i.e. the Shamrock from Townhead, 'wir laughin' aboot havin' bumped wan o' thae Fleet barn-pots' and the owner had overheard and reported the conversation to the police. Protection was given to the shop-owner for months before and after the trial, but members of the Young Team had heard that the Shamrock still stood outside his door and allowed only women to enter. While retelling this story, the boys made it clear to me that they hated the fish-andchip seller as much as the Shamrock did. They would have preferred to have settled the matter in their own way without the interference of the police or the courts.

The witness was praised by the judge, said Tim, mimicking: 'We need more of your kind, public spirited an' aw that.' Those members of the Young Team and of the Fleet present in the Public Gallery had burst out laughing. 'Imagine bein' called public spirited, man. Whit a showin'-up!' In the eyes of Tim and the others, justice had manifestly not been done: 'Wee McBride goat aff wi' the murder and started up the Shamrock again.' At the first opportunity, they took the law into their own hands. Months afterwards at a party in Cowcaddens, a district half-way between Maryhill and Townhead, one boy was heard to boast: 'Ma mate is dain' time fur Henderson.' 'Is that so?' Tim had said, picking up a glass flagon of cider and hitting him on the head with it. Two other Shamrock boys had jumped out of the window (luckily of a basement flat) and 'guyed the course'.

The Shamrock had replied to this move by attacking Tim himself. Shortly before his committal to the approved school, 20 members of the 'Toon' had arrived at a party at which Tim was present. With only two 'handers' he had prevented them from gaining entrance, but at the cost of being struck on the head with a bottle. 'Ah wis unconscious, man.' He had 12 stitches inserted in the wound. His greatest worry was that his hair would not grow back, or that he would be unable to flatten it down. He had been glad to spend most of this 'growing-in' time in the remand home. The approved school knew nothing of this wound.

The final comment on this murder case, as on every other incident, was: 'It wis aw in the papirs.' The papers were indeed scrutinised every morning for the slightest reference to gangs or gang warfare. Such an item was read first, out loud, and to an approving audience. The Pat Roller column in the *Daily Record* was the favourite spot for such stories. After a few lines about who had been stabbed where and by what gang, the Young Team would join in with the reader to form a chorus for the last sentence. 'As usual the thugs ran away at the approach of the police.' This was greeted with derision as though it were untrue.

I now had a method of verifying the gang's version of the murder. Armed with the actual date of the killing, it was an easy task to check out the story in the pages of the daily newspapers. A quick trip to the Mitchell Library enabled me to confirm what Tim and the others had told me. On the front page of one of the local newspapers for the morning in question I read:

MAN DIES AFTER STREET STABBING

Three young women knelt in rain-swept Sauchiehall Street late last night trying to comfort a dying man after he had been stabbed. The man died soon after in the Western Infirmary from multiple wounds.

The man, still unnamed early today, was found on the pavement. He is believed to have left a nearby dance hall.

Finding out the date of the court case allowed me to read the proceedings, which lasted four days. I shall quote at some length from these reports as they convey in their short staccato paragraphs something of the horror of the events.

Under a banner headline of GIRL TELLS OF DEATH FIGHT IN CITY STREET, an evening newspaper reported the first day of the trial as follows:

> The accused are Brian McNally, James Clifford, James Maxwell and two juveniles.
> Apart from the murder they are also charged with committing a breach of the peace in a restaurant in Castle Street, Townhead, and with having had razors, knives, bottles and a club – all offensive weapons – in their possession in Sauchiehall Street.

The 'attractive 19-year-old widow 'of the murdered man, Henderson then gave evidence.

> Mrs Henderson told the Court that her husband always carried a knife with him 'because of the gangs that run about the town.' She also said that she had a daughter nearly a year old and that her husband, a builder's labourer, was unemployed at the time of his death. She denied he had any connection with any gangs. Speaking softly, she said her husband had never been in trouble before and had not been a violent person.

A young nurse who had witnessed the murder and had comforted the dying Henderson was next to give evidence.

> The other boys advanced but the one I later learned was Henderson stood where he was, pulled a bottle out of his pocket, and broke it. He danced around with it and the other boys jumped on him. One of them pulled out a large wooden stick from his sleeve. Others had what looked like pieces of metal in their hands. The boy with the bottle was dragged from one side of the street to the other. They were all kicking and fighting.

The nurse was asked in cross-examination if she heard any shouts in Sauchiehall Street that night:

> She said, 'Yes.' When Henderson shouted 'Fleet' and 'Fleet Ya Bass', the others shouted 'Shamrock'.

She had been speaking to evangelists at the time and one of them had told her she shouldn't interfere. The judge then asked her if she was able to recognise in Court any of the 'six to eight boys' who had been attacking Henderson. The reply was 'No.'

On the second day of the trial two more girl witnesses were produced, one of whom identified McNally. James Maxwell, another of the accused, had handed her a knife and asked her to hold it for him. Shouts of 'Toon', 'Shamrock', and 'Fleet' had been heard by both girls. A fingerprint expert then reported that he had matched the prints on the knife with those of the accused.

McNally gave evidence in his own defence on the third day of the trial.

> I picked up a milk bottle which was lying on the pavement and ran back shouting 'Police' thinking they would run away. I thought it was my pal Maxwell who was on the ground and was being attacked. It was only after I hit the other man with the bottle that I saw it was not Maxwell who was being attacked.

With such a defence it was no surprise to read the front-page headlines at the end of the fourth day. FIVE GUILTY OF MURDER, proclaimed the evening paper. The oldest boy Clifford was jailed for life, while McNally, Maxwell (both 18) and two 15-year-old juveniles were ordered to be detained during Her Majesty's pleasure.

Just as Tim said, a photograph (or 'picter') of Henderson's young widow appeared alongside the story of the trial. No matter how close their connection with Henderson, no matter how embittered they were at his death, they could still say of his wife: 'She's a right beefer.' My eyebrows must have risen in curiosity, for the speaker explained for my benefit: 'Only good fur beefin'.'

Dwelling on Henderson's murder as they did that afternoon reminded them of their own successes in this field. Jimmy Barrow began recounting their exploits on the night they had visited the Bishopbriggs Bowling Centre – an evening which Baggy had touched on during my first outing. The Fleet and the Young Team had decided en masse to go bowling that Thursday evening. In Jimmy's reckoning over a hundred boys, some with girlfriends, had walked northwards from Maryhill through Milton and into the bowling alley. Situated on the outskirts of Bishopbriggs and facing the expansive Milton housing scheme, the Centre was a well-known playground and meeting place for the Milton Tongs.

Unaware that they were heavily outnumbered on their own 'pitch', the Tongs had shouted 'Milton Tongs! Tongs! Ya Bass!' at the Fleet and Young Team members they recognised. When they realised their true position, they made for the door. Tim took over the story at this point, recalling that he was sitting in the cafeteria when the fight broke out with a Fleet boy cracking an opponent on the head with a bowl. To prevent the Tongs escaping from the building, Tim claimed, without contradiction, to have dived through a glass panel six or seven feet high. Outside a chase began, with 30-odd girlfriends following as closely behind as they could. Across the scheme's circular road, up on to Liddesdale Road, and into the heart of Milton the pursuit continued. Boys were chased through closes and upstairs to their front doors. But one young boy of 14 turned and faced his hunters. On being knocked to the ground, he had rolled himself into a ball in an effort to protect himself. The Young Team who had cornered him proceeded to stab him in the back 'seventeen times' until he became unconscious. 'His back must hiv' been like a dart board,' was Tim's comment. And Fergie added that Big Sheila had strutted up to the inert body, dropped her handkerchief, and remarked: 'That'll help ye tae mop yir brow.' Having listened intently to this account of their exploits, the gang burst out laughing, as they had apparently done on the original occasion. 'Efter the chibbin' everyboady split up an' we aw went hame.' Squads of police cars were by that time touring the district.

This chapter ends with a record of my conversations with Tim about the murder his brother William had committed. Although these talks were spread out over several months, I have collated them, a technique that is employed increasingly in the remaining chapters. The date of the trial was still very much in Tim's mind: 'Ye don't forget a day like yon.' At the time, Tim was 14 years old, and claimed to have been expelled from his school for a year; John was 16, unemployed and on probation.

The reason for the murder, Tim told me, was a long-standing feud with the Black family. The vendetta went so far back in time that Tim had no inkling of the original cause. The seven Black brothers had always been warring with William, Peter and Michael Malloy and, finally, one of the Blacks had been killed. Now William was 'dain' life' in Perth Prison and Tim visited him when on leave. William's conversations always began and ended with this exhortation: 'Chib them. Every time ye see wan o' thae Blacks, chib them.' Before the trial had even started, one of the Malloy brothers (Tim didn't say which) had stabbed his own uncle for standing talking to one of the Black family in a bar.

On the night of William's arrest, the police had descended upon the Malloy home and had knocked the door down to find only Tim and John. They were taken to the station and questioned, Tim for two and a half hours and John for the same number of days. The elder brothers were hiding William in one of their married sisters' homes, the boys thinking that this simple subterfuge would save William from the police. The girl had recently returned from England and taken a flat with her husband. Here the door was knocked down as well, and William arrested as he slept in bed. The speed of the operation had been vital to its success, for Tim knew that his brothers had guns under their pillows. What surprised me when Tim was going over these events was that he didn't talk of the police in general, but of particular officers whom he knew well within what he called the 'Murder Squad'.[11]

Once, while discussing this major episode in his life, Tim looked me straight in the eyes and spoke softly: 'Ma ambition's tae murder some-wan. That wid be a laugh.' When I tried to deter him by dwelling on the sentence William was serving, his answer was, 'Ah'm no' worried. Ah'll take ma chances.' He then alluded to a Glasgow family of fighting brothers. The point of the reference was that all the older members of the family had been charged with murder and now the youngest had graduated in the best bloody tradition of his brothers.

Tim struck me as having a genuine attachment to William, but for Pete all he could say was: 'He's *really* aff his heid. He's a *real* mental case.' He had only been out of prison three weeks after serving a sentence of more than two years for serious assault, when he was again charged with assaulting a member of the Black family. Peter was due to be released the following April and the Blacks were ready for him. 'He's the wan they're really efter but they're scared fae him.'

The feud still continued. Mick, who himself had served one year for his part in this inter-family feud, had been sitting on the local Celtic supporters' bus, holding two bottles of whisky, when a member of the Black family had climbed aboard. After breaking both bottles over his head, Mick had been ejected from the bus together with his opponent, to fight in the street.

Having heard Tim fully on the subject, I turned once again to the newspaper files of the Mitchell Library to verify his statements. This was one of the very few occasions when I was able to test his creditability and it will be seen that his story varies considerably from that given in the press. The points of difference, however, are mainly of detail. Beneath a banner headline THE FATAL FEUD and beside photographs of the mudered man and of the Malloy parents reading a letter from William, the account reads:[12]

> The bad blood between two families led to the death of a young man at knife point ...
> And yesterday at Glasgow High Court a man was sentenced for his part in that night of violence.
> William Malloy (25) was jailed for life when he admitted murdering John Black (37) of Barrack Street, Maryhill, a father of three.

The judge, passing a life sentence on William Malloy, told him that he had set out on the particular evening armed with a knife to settle a grouse with the man he murdered.

'There is no question of accident or provocation in your case,' he told him.

Malloy had admitted stabbing Black repeatedly with a knife and kicking him repeatedly and did murder him. The charge said he had also previously shown malice and ill-will against him.

The Advocate Depute told the Court that the Malloy brothers of High Street, Maryhill, were members of a large family and so too was John Black. It appears there was bad blood between the families.

On the evening of the murder Peter Malloy went drinking in various public houses and was not in the company of his brothers.

He had a fair amount to drink and went to a club in Maryhill. Black had also gone there, and he had also been drinking. There was a row between Peter Malloy and Black, and, as Malloy was being put out, Black struck him.

Meanwhile, William Malloy was in a house in High Street, and he later met up with his brothers Peter and Michael.

Peter had an injury to his face, and he told his two brothers that Black was responsible. The Malloy brothers decided that William should settle the score with Black. William Malloy had a knife when he left to go to Black's house. When Black answered the door he set about him and left him dying. The Advocate Depute said that Black had a number of small wounds about his face, and two stab wounds on the left side of his chest, which were the fatal blows.

The reporters then turned to the 'human interest' aspect of the drama and, under a headline of HE WAS BAD, continued:

Last night the brothers' mother, greying Mrs Jean Malloy (56) sobbed: 'I know he was bad ... but he is still my son.'

Mrs Malloy, who gave up her boy to the police, was not in Court to hear her son sentenced.

She has not seen him since his arrest three months ago. 'It would have been too sad for me,' she said. 'After he was charged with murder I only wanted to die.'

'Each morning I've gone to church to pray. I keep asking myself where I went wrong.'

She said of the feud between her sons and the Blacks: 'We have not seen an end to it yet. There will be more blood spilled before it's over.'

More research among newspaper files disclosed some further information about the elder Malloy brothers. William, on his 20th birthday, had been put on probation for two years for assaulting a man by striking him with bottles, an ash tray and an advertising board. His counsel had stressed that William's victim had a whisky glass and a knife in his possession at the time of the assault. Moreover, he pleaded that William came from a good family but had got into bad company.

The day after being put on probation, William committed another assault in pursuance of the same quarrel, although on another man, and for this he was jailed for 60 days. This time his defence counsel informed the Court that William was the eldest of a family of nine, none of whom were working apart from himself. His father was a chronic invalid and was unable to bring any money into the house. The family depended on the money William could earn working on the roads. The second assault, explained counsel, was part of the same feud involving the same people, a feud which had for its basis religious bigotry. Prophetically, the judge cautioned the prisoner in the following words: 'The way you are going, you will spend the rest of your life in prison.'

One weekend when we were in the school and discussing the Black murder, Tim confided one interesting piece of information to me. At the time I realised that this was a test of my loyalty; for the information was such that it should have been passed on to the school authorities. 'There's a wee bird havin' a wean tae me,' he said, watching for my reaction. 'Do you mean Maureen?' was my reply. He did. Tim would be 16 in a few weeks and the girl was 17. Congratulations were hardly in order, so I questioned him about what he and the respective families were prepared to do in the circumstances. Tim was adamant that he was going to do nothing, certainly not marry the girl. Trying to make him feel consideration for the girl's plight, I suggested that the child would make it harder for her to find a husband. 'Naw, naw. They aw get married. They're aw cows hawkin' their mutton. The birds don't mind whit ye dae they don't mind havin' a wean.' He stressed that this was a normal situation for gang members to find themselves in, and he recited the names of other unmarried fathers, adding in a beautiful, if tragic, Irishism, 'Aw oor boays hiv' babies.'

Only days later he whispered to me that he was 'a Daddy', Maureen having given birth to 'a wee boay' in Oakbank Hospital. If Tim had been embarrassed embarking on this topic in the first place, any mention of the baby by me was certain to confound him. He pretended a total lack of interest in the future of his child, evincing no desire to go and see it. 'She's geein' it tae her Ma', was all Tim would say.

As to his own family's reaction, he remarked: 'Aw ma bruthers knew ma bird wis up the kite. Ma Ma knows, but Ah don't think ma Da knows. Whit's it ma'er oaneywae? Ah'm no carin'.' On the Saturday afternoon of his most recent leave, Tim had met Maureen's mother in the High Street on her way to see his parents. He had been able to head her off, at least temporarily: 'Ah only goat a big riddie when ma bruther started screamin' at me in front o' aw the boays.'

Maureen and he had been 'goin' thegither' for 15 months, Tim having gone out with other girlfriends before, during and after this period. Back at school after the Christmas holidays, Tim told me that he had 'seen the wean. Aye, it's aw right. But Ah don't like wee weans - they look like auld men.' Asked if he would work to help support it, he replied, 'Aye. If Ah wis merried tae its Ma.'

To this day the approved school is unaware that Tim became a father at the age of 15 - a startling illustration of how much in the dark one works in trying to help delinquents. Without any real knowledge of their families, their peer groups, or their activities, the well-meaning efforts of the staff are little removed from trial and error.

8
Saturday afternoon and Monday evening

I WAS KEEN to go out with the gang as often as possible before Christmas. This was only partly because I wanted a rest and time to rethink my position but mainly because a major gang fight with the Barnes Road was being scheduled for the holiday period. Challenges were soon to be issued for a full scale 'ba'le'. The vacation was chosen as both teams would then be at full strength, with approved schools and remand homes releasing large numbers of boys for the festive season.

On that first Saturday night at the pub I gathered that Tim was being given what amounted to a progress report. Since then I had discovered that he was being brought up to date with news of the Fleet rather than of his own gang. I was anxious to see if he held a similar briefing for the Young Team. This would mean meeting Tim early on the Saturday afternoon, shortly after his release from the school. The more Tim resisted the idea, the more I insisted.

At last we compromised. Tim would go home, sleep for a couple of hours, and then meet me at the same time as he regularly met the other boys. He had managed to talk the Headmaster into granting him an extra day's leave on the following Monday to visit William, who had been moved to Peterhead. Tim's plan was to travel to Aberdeen on the Sunday, thus leaving Monday free. Seeing the gang's activities on a week night was too good an opportunity for me to miss, so I made Tim agree to meet me on the Monday evening as well.

Fergie was the first boy on the scene that Saturday. He was still bubbling over with the happenings of the previous weekend. Tim arrived to hear Fergie describe a fight between the Fleet boys and the Young Team. It had started in the Fleet's pub on the outskirts of town. Bob Robertson of the Fleet had fallen out with Wee Midgie of the Young Team. No one knew, or, apparently, cared, what had caused the disagreement, but within minutes a brawl had started. Soon it developed into a massive free-for-all which spilled out of the pub and onto the pavement and roadway. The fight had been a clean one, no blades, just heads and boots, all 'square-goes'. What surprised me – and what ended the fight – was the arrival of Dick Stevenson, who had thrown in his lot with the Young Team out of a liking for Wee Midgie, who was being badly beaten up by the older boys. I was glad I had missed that night.

'Big Fry', to whom I was then introduced, and whose nickname was based on a chocolate advertisement, then reported the most recent break-ins. This was the first mention in my presence of any theft or shop-breaking in which the

Young Team had been involved, certainly Tim had said nothing. Now he stood, smiled nervously and blushed. From what I listened to, the gang seemed to concentrate on their own area. The local cash-and-carry store had been raided yet again. The normal method of kicking down the back door had failed-the owners had learned from past experiences. This time Dave Malloy had broken in by squeezing a car-jack between two iron bars guarding the windows, raising the jack, and bending the bars. Entry had thus been gained and the shop cleared of money and goods. The place was broken into again over the Christmas holidays, and the last time I heard it spoken of, an electronic eye had been installed opposite the doors and windows. Similarly, all the other shops in the gang's territory had been burgled, bar five or six which had been rendered impregnable by their owners. Fergie could even rattle off the names of whole streets which he claimed had been 'done' without exception.

'Big Dim', the acerbity of whose nickname was only tempered by its accuracy, had been caught housebreaking again. He had been so infuriated at breaking into a meter which contained filed-down halfpennies that he had attracted attention to his presence in the house. Perhaps he was complaining about the prevailing dishonesty. This type of crime, I had been told, was beneath the dignity of a gang member.

Big Dim was in a class of his own, Tim assured me. At one time, because of his size and weight, he had taken over the leadership of the Young Team during one of Tim's legally enforced absences. Tim, on his return, had simply met up with his closest mates and had accompanied them to their local pub for a drink. Big Dim had entered and challenged Tim to a 'square-go' outside. Knowing full well that he was no physical match for his opponent, Tim had felled him with a hammer which he just happened to have with him. Big Dim had been carried out and dumped in the street. No other challenge to Tim's authority had since been offered.

Beano then related the outcome of one of the skirmishes between the Fleet and the Young Team. The relationship between Dick Stevenson and the 'Mad Mexican', Pat McDonald, had been strained for some weeks, since Dick's release and resumption of complete command. The Mad Mexican – an awesome sight with his long black hair and sideburns, his scrawny, spindling physique, sunken eyes and hollow cheeks – had sulked at being relegated to the background. But the news that Dick had sided with the Young Team against his own boys was too much for Pat. On Saturday night, after hours of hard drinking, he had 'claimed' Dick. Beano, in a dramatic reconstruction of the scene, re-enacted how Dick ('the fittest boay Ah've ever saw – jist oot o' Polmont,[13] right enough') had crashed to the ground after receiving a kick in the stomach. Without using his hands to propel himself forward, Dick had jumped up and 'rattled Pat wi' his heid.' More butts with the head and 'boots in the chuckies' (alternatively described in rhyming slang as one's 'haw maws') were delivered before Dick knocked Pat out, leaving Dick undisputed master of the pitch. Tim's feelings were: 'It's gettin' ridiculous; too many square-goes an' no' enough chibbin'.'

Later, I found out that the Mad Mexican had 'given the boays up', taken a job as a conductor on the buses, and had 'settled doon'. (Towards the end of 1967, I read in the papers that he had been murdered by a very small gang in Maryhill who styled themselves the 365 after the wine of the same name. I shall return to the court case in Chapter 17.) Pat's reputation was redoubtable. In the Fleet's pub, he had asked a stranger for the penny-ha'penny he needed to pay for a round of drinks. 'Fuck off, beardie', had been the reply. 'Pat jist went mad and stuck it oan him'. One of the most far-fetched stories I heard concerned Pat. He was in the dock, charged with possessing an offensive weapon. Something the sheriff (i.e. the magistrate) said angered him, so he leaned forward, picked up exhibit A (or rather Production Number One in Scotland), his own hammer, and hit the offending magistrate on the head with it. Subsequent inquiry provided no basis in fact for this story.

As other boys joined us at the corner, more information about gang members 'bein' done fur gee-bee-aitch.' (grievous bodily harm),[14] or 'oh-el-pee' (opening lock-fast places) was produced. The conversation veered and turned and stopped. There was little to do except 'staun' aboot' until the pubs opened at five. Tim began walking, with the others trailing behind him. We had been walking for some time, 'jist dossin',' when Tim had an idea. 'Let's get right intae that lib'ry,' he said, pointing to one of Glasgow's public libraries.

Running into the building, we ignored the Lending Section because of its turnstile, and burst into the reading room. Dan McDade and Billy Morton began setting fire to the newspapers on display, as Tim and the others pushed books off tables and emptied shelves of encyclopedias and reference books. I 'kept the edge up' at the outer door and shouted 'Polis!' as soon as I dared. Dave Malloy was trying to set alight the newspapers being read by old-age pensioners or down-and-outs. One old man beside the door, wearing woollen gloves with the finger pieces cut out, was reading with his face screwed up against the print which he deciphered with the aid of a magnifying glass. Jimmy Barrow's last act was to knock this glass from his hand as he ran past. En route to the street, a male attendant in a green uniform was punched and kicked out of the way. Some, behind me, could hardly run for laughing.

Claiming that I was 'away up the road tae take a bird oot', I left Tim and Dave Malloy, reminding Tim I would see him on Monday. Dave Malloy was visibly relieved to see me depart.

The rain on Monday night was torrential. Not having an overcoat which 'wis in the style', my suit was soggy by the time I reached the corner. Tim had waited behind for me; the others had decided to go to the pictures and had gone ahead. On the way Tim told me that not only his own team but the Fleet and the Possil Uncle were all planning to go to the same cinema. Over the years Monday had become a ritual night for the pictures with the old Seamore in Maryhill Road the standard venue. And the standard procedure for entry was for a number of boys to pay themselves in, settle down, and then for one of them to sidle off and admit the other boys by opening the exit doors. Those who were caught were charged with fraud.

In the cinema, the fun had begun. Rows and rows of boys, some with girls, who were more like camp followers than real companions, sat heckling the film. The police had already been called and were stationed in the back row of the stalls. During the interval before the main film began, Big Sheila stood up from her seat near the front and turned to the boys behind her, yelling: 'Ah'll take any wan o' youse Fleet boays.' 'Come up here, ya big man ye,' was Dick's riposte. From the laughter I judged that she was held in some affection by the boys. As the lights dimmed, Tim observed: 'She's a big psychey case.' Times without number she had issued challenges like: 'Come oan then. I'll go right ahead wae any o' youse mugs.' The boys would humour her rather than fight with her; she countered by claiming that every such refusal was tantamount to a victory. 'I ran a right mock wi' his heid.' Her value to the gang lay in her willingness to secrete chibs in her handbag or even her underwear. 'Ye should hiv' seen her makin' up tae this young busy oot fur the first time in Possilland! Aw the big boays wir sayin', "Awae tae fuck", when he says, "Boys, come on, move along please." Big Sheila stepped oot an' in a dead sexy voice said tae him: "You've goat lovely come-tae-bed eyes." Brilliant it wis.' The girl herself was tall, solid-looking and built for comfort, with black hair and bad teeth; in sum, none too prepossessing.

We were watching Mutiny on the Bounty, and, looking along the rows, I was soon to see as many weapons being held openly as were visible on the screen. At one stage in the film, Marlon Brando made a comment to the effect that the fleet was approaching the harbour. As though in reply, boys rose to their feet screaming: 'The *real* Fleet's here.' This proved to be the last straw for a middle-aged man on my left. As the lights came on, he shouted across: 'Yir aw a bunch o' fuckin' hooligans.' Missiles were hurled in his direction, the police descended from the back row, and I made for the exit. Ten boys were arrested. Running away was keeping me fit.

We returned to our pub, a course of action which under the circumstances I thought, and said, though in different words, was foolhardy. The talk, once we had pints of beer in our hands, proved to be worth the risk for me – for by some means or other the subject of schools was introduced.

A few of the boys had attended Saint Monica's comprehensive school on the outskirts of Maryhill. This school, known quite unjustly to the local police as 'the concrete jungle', I myself had taught at for one year. Beano was withering in his scorn and hatred for the place. He had not been there; he had been a pupil at the same junior secondary school as Tim and the others. His young brothers had, however, all been sent to Saint Monica's. 'Ah punch thir wee heids in every time Ah see thaem wi' thir uniforms oan – thir daft school tie the thickness o' a scarf, an' thir big daft badges. Ye wouldnae get me intae a uniform.' This from a boy who was wearing the gang boy's uniform with as much attention to detail as any apple-polishing prefect in a school blazer.

Beano now began to wax eloquent on the subject. One of his younger brothers 'wee Frankie, pure mental he is, brass-necked it, walkin' up the road wi' his stupid, mid-grey flannels'; here he simulated the voice of a form teacher at a parents' meeting, 'his stupid big ugly shoes an' his wee handbag fur his books'; now the imitation performed was the mincing steps of the stereotyped homosexual. Beano reverted to this topic on another evening: 'Ah hated school 'cos Ah didnae hiv' the brains. Don't worry. Ma wee brother will learn sense; he'll take a tumble tae hissel' an' leave school. Ah'll guarantee it. Dae youse know whit he wants to be? An electrical engineer! Aw naw! Ah'm ashamed. Imagine earnin' a wage!' This provoked approving mirth even from boys like Fergie, the slater and plasterer, and Dave Malloy, who worked in a local paper mill. 'Podgie' reminded the group of the junior secondary teacher, Big Alec, whose opening words to the class every morning were: 'Right, those who want to work, put your hands up. Those who don't, go and sit at the back with your arms folded.' Predictably, charges of indecency and assault were levelled against all and sundry in authority. 'Heidmaisters' came in for heavy criticism. One, known to Baggy, was said to drop cigarettes down the dresses of the senior girls and then spend several minutes retrieving them. A member of the Cowcaddens Toi, who had attended the same junior secondary as the others, and was now attending a senior approved school, had drawn the figure of Leslie Charteris' Saint complete with halo on the bald head of a teacher who had collapsed in front of the class.

Tim himself had conducted a running battle with his science teacher. In reprisals for being belted, Tim had poured acid into the aquarium and, if that didn't kill the goldfish, he also roasted them with bunsen burners. As a climax to this feud, the teacher had dismissed the rest of the class early, ordered Tim to remain behind, locked the door, and announced that he was going to beat Tim up. As the teacher closed the distance between them, Tim had lifted a stool and split his head open with it. At the time, Tim was 14. He had been expelled by the headmaster, an action which he still resented almost two years later. Tim, however, had struck back; he waited for the man to leave the school one evening, and then, surrounded by his team, had followed him along the road, cursing and swearing at him.

'Aw Ah ever goat in that school wis techey drawin',' was Tim's considered opinion of his education. At the beginning of his secondary school career, Tim remembered being keen to work. He had started his homework one night amidst the mockery of his elder brothers. Finally, one of them had become so riled at his persistence that he had thrown Tim's school books into the fire. The following day Tim excused himself by asserting that he had lost the books. Never again did he attempt to do any homework.

Yet all the time he attended the approved school, he was fascinated by the books I was either carrying or reading. Without fail, he asked to look through them, returning most of them within seconds. His regular comment at this point was: 'Aw, Ah couldnae study. Ah'd crack up.'

9
'Jist dossin' aw day'

LIFE WITH THE gang was not all violence, sex and petty delinquency. Far from it. One of the foremost sensations that remains with me is the feeling of unending boredom, of crushing tedium, of listening hour after hour at street corners to desultory conversation and indiscriminate grumbling. Standing with one's back against a wall, with one's hands in one's pockets, in the late afternoon and in the early hours of the morning, was *the* gang activity. At times I longed to discard my passive role and suggest some constructive form of entertainment. Once, I remember, we were all slouching against the walls of 'wir coarner' when it began to drizzle. No one made any move to seek the protection of a close-mouth or a shop front and so, in my observer status, I had to stand there and let the rain trickle down my face.

Some boys whispered and at least some snatches of their conversation provided me with valuable information, which is presented later in this chapter. Others had no interest even in talking and were content to let their minds go blank. Smoking, chewing gum, recounting past exploits, deriding passers-by, and indulging in horseplay with each other and with girls, these were the only diversions from 'dossin'. Neither the young nor the old escaped their caustic and obscene abuse. Specifically delinquent activities occupied only a small fraction of their waking hours.

Late one evening, two old women, one with bloated legs, the other suffering from rickets, hobbled past us in sandshoes, sucking hot chips with toothless gums. With insults and curses, the gang pushed them off *their* pavement and into the gutter where, I was told, they belonged.

Every so often as we stood 'dossin', a thin jet of saliva would hit the pavement. The boys had their own 'gallous' way of spitting; they kept their lips and teeth motionless and squirted out the spittle with their tongues. The trick is a favourite with approved school boys.

On one occasion to break the monotony I took out cigarettes and asked a passer-by for a match. My action unleashed a torrent of criticism: 'Is that no' brass neckin' it, askin' fur a match? Aw naw! He'll think we cannae afford a boax. Ah'd rather dae wi' oot an' that's nae kiddin'.' Baggy signalled to me that he would help me out of my difficulties, so I asked him for a match. 'Don't kerry heavy timber,' he replied while producing a stolen lighter. His sally at my expense restored the gang's good humour.

'Wee Cock', who naturally preferred to be called 'Wee Eck', began recounting his experiences of the last few days. He had been arrested at two in the morning for breaking and entering, and had spent the first night in a police cell (or 'peter' as they call it). Unable to sleep, he had passed the time by whistling to himself to keep his spirits up. The cell, he claimed, was clearly marked as suitable for 18-year-olds and the injustice of a 14-year-old being locked up there rankled with him. In the morning a policeman had entered with an egg sandwich. ' "Take as many as you like," he says tae me an' laughs. Ah pit it doon the pan. It flushed fae the ootside. Scared ye strangl' yersel' wi' the chain.'

After an appearance in court he had been transferred to a remand home. 'Dubbed up aw day in ma peter Ah wis.' By dint of discreet questioning during the long hours we spent standing at the street corner, I was able to piece together the daily routine in the remand home. The boys were awakened at 5.30am and, after washing, they cleaned out their cells. Then came breakfast at seven, after which they were 'dubbed up' until lunchtime. Wee Cock was given a cowboy book to read; he skimmed through two pages and then threw it away. Shortly afterwards he picked it up and began reading again: 'Ah wis scared o' crackin' up.'

He had to eat his lunch by himself in his cell, a punishment for trying to escape. At five o'clock he joined the others for evening tea. From seven until nine television was watched but no talking or smoking was tolerated. If a comedian appeared, said Wee Cock, the prisoners were allowed to laugh, but not too much. He had envied the 'passmen', boys who in the afternoon were permitted to leave their cells to scrub floors and polish shoes. But only the 'edgers', the 'benders' were chosen for these tasks, I was informed. Wee Cock's hair had been shorn and he claimed to have had no more than one shower during his one week of imprisonment.

He had also been accused in Court of 'goin' on the demand', i.e. stealing clothes from younger boys at the point of a knife. Tim leapt to his defence: 'Its aw thae Tongs an' Shamrock that demand jaikets an' leathers. It wouldnae happen up here.' Yet Fergie remembered that he and Tim had 'taken liberties wi' boays.' They had forced one youngster into a lane and had made him remove even his shoes. Tim countered with, 'Ah widnae demand gear noo; Ah kin afford ma ain.'

Wee Cock had also met the 'Top Man' of the Tongs in the remand home. Asked why he had been arrested, the King had explained that he had inquired of one of his own gang: 'Are ye goin' doon tae the bookies?' 'Aye,' the boy had replied. 'Weil, Ah want tae pit this line oan.' At this he had cut the boy's jaw open. As the boy left the scene, the Top Man had added a final jest: 'Awae an' staun' in shite' (i.e. for good luck).

'Jist dossin' aw day'

There was a second charge for the leader of the Tongs to answer. Having been chibbed by a member of a rival gang, the 'King' had sent a letter to the perpetrator, threatening to kill him. (The boy's mother had delivered the letter into the hands of the police.) Not content with that, he had sent representatives from a firm of undertakers to the boy's home to measure him for a coffin. The boy had collapsed at the door. Admiration shone in the eyes of the gang.

Wee Cock had also learned (his phrase for this was 'Ah got tolt', i.e. I was told) the latest password among the Tongs, vital information for anyone who happened to be cornered by any of that gang. One replied to the opening remark, 'Ding, Dong! Ah'm a Tong!' with, 'Ha, ha! So am Ah!'

Apart from some rough and exploratory handling of the girls present, the gang's only other pastime was 'puttin' the mix in'. This was their expression for contriving a quarrel where none existed. Beano's attention, for example, was directed to a boy walking on the other side of the street. Though the boy could have given Beano a few inches in height and a stone or two in weight, the gang, at Tim's instigation, began to goad Beano into challenging him to fight.

'You could take him easy.'

'You're dead well built an' that.'

'Pit it this wae, you could go right tae town wi' him.'

At first Beano demurred. 'Naw, Ah'll see youse ra morra', he replied as he attempted to eschew the dare. But the pressure on him increased until he was shouting after the boy: 'Hauf-wit features! You're gettin' set aboot.' The boy took to his heels and fled. Beano returned in triumph. 'He's aw chuffed wi' hissel',' said Tim.

In the space of a few paragraphs I have summed up *all* the gang's conversation and activities over a number of hours. To relieve my ennui I studied the tattoos on the boys' hands and arms for I could not afford to ask too many questions. By far the most frequent tattoo was pricked into the skin of the four fingers of both hands between the knuckles and the first joint. It spelled out the message 'TRUE LOVE'. Another common one was a heart and a scroll which bore the one word 'Mother'. 'Mum and Dad' also made its appearance on the back of the hand and on the arm, together with girlfriends' names. In large letters, Tim had scratched on his arm the legend 'Born A Loser'. Mick, his elder brother, sported on his forearm a red dagger entering the top of a skull and reappearing through its mouth. It was considered to be the finest tattoo in the neighbourhood, surpassing Dick Stevenson's crucifixion scene where the traditional letters INRI had been replaced by the name of Dick's current girlfriend.

'Jist dossin' aw day' was the gang's ideal. School, employment, reading all took up valuable time which could be better spent in doing nothing. Many people in a word association test would answer to the stimulus 'Glasgow Gang' by some such word as 'violence'. The reply 'dossin' would be nearer the truth, and would sum up more of these boys' lives than any reference to isolated violent incidents.

The repetitive monotony of gang life has been remarked upon by many investigators, and perhaps Bloch and Niederhoffer's (1958, p.177ff.) account comes nearest to my own:

> Actually, the average gang existence follows a fairly monotonous routine. Its activities can be predicted in advance. Night after night, gangs can be found at the same street corner hang-out. Weekend nights may bring a slight variation. They may grace a dance or movie. This regular round of activities is broken by auto trips to pick up girls. This is life in the gang. The fighting, burglaries, delinquency, are a very small part of the total range.

In their description of the Pirate gang in New York, the authors suggest that such repetition is welcome to the boys because of their basic insecurities and inadequacies:

> Not versatility, but this regular patterned existence, the same hangout, the endless 'bull sessions', the familiar faces day in and day out, these are the very attractions that lure the gang boy. He desperately needs and clings to this security, this anchor, to keep him from drifting aimlessly in the Sargasso Sea of adolescence.

10
Uzz Gemmies

HOPING THAT I have conveyed something of the general atmosphere of the gang and its activities, I now propose to draw together conversations and items of behaviour which took place at different times throughout my 12 outings and which concern a single main theme. In this chapter I shall speak of the gang's concern with physical toughness, a concern which is made manifest by their respect for the 'gemmie', and of their relationships with other gangs in the city and in their own area.

I shall quote, to begin with, a composition written in my class by a 15-year-old boy deeply involved in his local gang. With the title 'Glasgow Gangs' as stimulus, he wrote in response:

> Most of the Gangs in Glasgow are Gemmies. I think that if you are in a Gang you just go for the fun of it. When you are in a Gang it is very easy to get birds whereas if you're not you don't get so many because most of the birds go for boys in Gangs because it makes them feel big. I go about with a Gang called the Possil Uncle; it used to be called the Fleet, then Border Troops, the Rebels and Possil Pigs. The Maryhill Fleet boys go about with us. Sometimes we go to the Granada dancing or go up to the Milton to fight the Tongs or the Thrush from Kirkintilloch. I get a lot of fun going about with a gang because we smash aw the bam-pots up that try to get fly when they get you yourself with their mates.

Tim's definition of a 'gemme boay' is now apposite: 'Uzz gemmies go *right* ahead wi' aw the mugs an' bent-shots o' the day. Ma motto is "Don't run fae anyboady, no ma'ter whit he's goat".' Big Fry once told us of a 'real gemme boay', his cousin, a Bowrie boy (a gang based in Yoker), who on being chased by the Partick Cross had turned round and faced his pursuers alone. 'Aw the others guyed, the crap-bags.' He was stabbed nine times in the back and legs and collected £300 from the Criminal Injuries Compensation Board for his pains.

Again, to illustrate the meaning of the expression, Tim had expressed a liking in the approved school for a very small, but highly aggressive boy from Rutherglen for the one and only reason that the youngster was prepared to tackle any boy with whom he disagreed, whatever his size. This is the mark of the 'gemme boay'; someone who is ready to fight, whatever the odds, even if defeat or physical punishment is inevitable. Consequently, the greatest insult one could aim at Tim was to contradict his oft-repeated claim to be a 'gemmie'. Part of the syndrome which Tim displayed was to make a point of smiling contemptuously at whoever chose to administer corporal punishment, a tactic which seldom failed to goad the staff member into giving more strokes than he at first intended. Provoking the teacher into losing his temper was deemed ample recompense for the additional pain.

The main outlet for the Young Team's aggression and hatred was its traditional enemy, the Calton Tongs;[15] by all accounts, the most hated gang in Glasgow. Early on in our relationship, Tim's attitude towards his main rivals was expressed as follows: 'If Ah saw wan o' thae Tongs lyin' in the gu'er bleedin' tae death, Ah'd stab him again. Ah'm swearin' it. Ah'd run a *right* psychey. Nae kiddin'! Ah wid.' Such phrases were uttered almost in a scream, with his teeth grinding together in tension. At the same time, all manner of actions were performed; the word 'stab', for example, was accompanied by a flashing stroke of his arm.

Towards the end of my involvement, the reputation of the Tongs deteriorated sadly in Tim's estimation: '*Thae Tongs* go on the creep nooadays, lyin' in wait fur ye in yir close fur hours an' jumpin' ye when ye come hame.' This accusation might equally have been made against Tim himself, as I explain later in this chapter. The Tongs were 'mugs, bam-pots, pure rides', and as a crowning insult, 'back-stabbers' – a charge made with all the venom and contempt at the speaker's command. Only 'mixers', boys who moved from gang to gang, were thought less of.

The leaders of the Tongs were spoken of with awe by Young Team boys. The King of the Calton, Jim Daly, was 'mad, mad, pure mental'. His reign had been bloody and brutal. One phrase came tripping off their lips every time Daly's name cropped up, in a manner reminiscent of a Homeric epithet: 'The stitches haud him thegither.' No less than 200 of them, I heard. He had been 'stabbed near tae death' by the Spur from Barrowfield who, catching sight of him without his usual bodyguard, had chased him up a close. In vain he had kicked at his mate's door but nobody answered. He had curled up into a protective ball and had been stabbed 'seventeen times'. Realizing they had caught no less a person than King Daly, the Spur gang had torn off his shirt and vest and traced a large 'S' on his back. With Jim Daly out of action for some months, Jim Nicholson had assumed command. Within a few weeks he was arrested for murder and sentenced to ten years' imprisonment. 'He broke doon an' started tae greet in the court – an' him meant tae be a gemme boay an' aw.'

With their leaders 'huckled' the Tongs had 'fallen away tae fuck'. So much so that Dan Donnelly, a boy who had been pointed out to me on the night of our trip to the cinema, had summoned up enough courage to drive his scooter right into Bellgrove, the heart of Tong-land, and to shout 'Real Young Uncle! Come oan youse Tongs!' As his opponents massed, he accelerated and drove through the centre of them. Circling a block of tenements, he repeated the performance, only this time as he turned the corner his scooter 'chucked it'. 'He'd tae pap it away an' guy up the road.'

Whenever the Tongs were mentioned, Beano needed no prompting. 'See wee Turner o' the Tongs. He's a nuthin', a bam-pot, an' he thinks he's a gemmie. See if Ah get him, he'll be the sorriest wee boay walkin' aboot oan two legs. He's nuthin' but a wee boay tryin' tae make a name fur hissel'.' Dave Malloy, although unable to see that every word of this applied equally to Beano, did make the point that Beano was only five foot tall. The answer was: 'Height goes fur nuthin'. A big blade doon yir throat brings ye doon tae size.'

Beano's remark reminds me of a comment made by Bloch and Niederhoffer (1958, p.168.), as they develop their theme that every part of the gang boy's life is coloured by a compulsion to become a man:

> The war against police and authority, against other gangs, requires the use of weapons. 'Men' no longer use sticks and stones but guns and knives. These are the legendary 'equalisers' which make the smallest adolescent the match for the biggest man.

Tim's knowledge of the Tongs, the biggest gang in Glasgow, was extensive. He could reel off the main charges against their more prominent members (of whom he knew about a dozen by name), their criminal records, their home addresses and places of work, if any. He told me that 'over a hundred boys' comprised the BCT (the Big Calton Team or the 'real' Tongs) which was 'led aff' by Daly and then Turner. Then came the YYT (the Young Young Tongs, equivalent to Tim's Young Team), admitting boys of up to 18 years of age and led by 'Chuckles'. The third section was the TT (or Tiny Tongs), none of whom were older than 15 and who were 'led aff' by Grant. Finally came the wee TT (or Toddler Tongs), boys of ten to 13 in a small gang led by McGregor, a 12-year-old. The monogram of the 'heavy team' had been carefully devised and it disfigured many a building; it stood for 'Real Calton Tongs'. The other gangs in Glasgow were not slow to follow their lead in drafting similar insignia.

Only one other gang, I was informed, could boast of an analogous hierarchy of Big, Young, Tiny and Toddler Teams – the Cumbie from the Gorbals. No such elaborate age divisions existed in Maryhill. The Fleet was the major gang, commanding the first loyalties of all gang members in the area. Boys to the age of 21 or 22 were involved, although the majority were 18 or 19. On being asked why so few boys over 20 remained in the Fleet, Tim replied: 'They used tae be in it but they've screwed the nut. Oaney wan o' them could take Dick but they're no bothered oaney mair.' The Young Team, coming from a distinct and identifiable part of Maryhill, formed a useful juvenile adjunct to the major gang. The relationship between the two was marked by a casualness and informality. John Malloy's position, for instance, struck me as anomalous. An older brother of the Young Team's 'leader-aff and a friend of King Stevenson, he fought on behalf of both gangs and wasn't clearly a fully committed member of either. Tim's answer to my question, as to what team John belonged to, the Fleet or the Young Team, was: 'They're baith the same, 'nt they?'

Tim's gang itself had no junior editions, the boys feeling that they were young enough. Beano, for example, was only 14. But some gangs were reputed to have groups of boys under ten, younger than the Toddlers, known as the Baby Cumbie, the Baby Govan and so on. The equivalent group among the Shamrock was called the Babysham. A sidelight, however, was thrown on the gang's influence over 11- and 12-year-olds by a scene I witnessed on one of my excursions. Dawdling at the 'coarner' with the other boys on a freezing night towards the end of January, I found my attention drawn to a thin little boy in a dark blue duffel coat, whose reactions to every situation were exaggerated. He acted in an over-excited manner, swearing and cursing, kicking the elder boys and being picked up and punched in a playful fashion by them. This was 'wee Georgie' McDade, Dan's youngest brother; 'He never stoaps', was the general account of his behaviour. 'He goes tae wan o' thae schools in the daft bus.' This meant he attended a special school for mentally handicapped children, an inference I had already made from his hyperkinetic behaviour. Judging from his stature, I took him to be about seven years old; in fact he was ten-and-a-half.

George's elder brother Tony came to collect him at half-past ten at night. Tony had just turned 12 and had started 'screwin''. Tim had this to say to him on the subject: 'Yir a brave wee boay that'll screw three shoaps in the wan night and knock leathers and jaikets.' This was tantamount to incitement to steal, and praise from a local 'leader-aff' was obviously music in the boy's ears. At the approved school, Tim admitted that 'patterin' up' of 11-, 12-, and 13-year-olds went on. Having been flattered and enticed to steal, these youngsters would then break into shops and come back with the stolen goods to prove they were capable of 'screwin'.' The Young Team would then step in, offering 'a dollar' (five shillings) for a hundred cigarettes, or ten shillings for a jersey and so on.

One gang, based in the centre of Maryhill, I have to date only mentioned in the list given earlier. Yet their differences from all the other gangs in the area lent them the fascination of the abnormal. The Blue Angels were a Rocker gang in the midst of Mods. Their café was situated right in the middle of Maryhill, which forced the Mod gangs to pass it frequently in the course of a weekend. I witnessed no friction between the groups but in the past the rivalry had been furious. At the height of the violence, the Blue Angels had roared down the streets on their motorbikes 'in wan big line, up oan the pavements an' everythin'.' Their main target had always been the Fleet's scooter squad, which they broke up by knocking the Mods off their scooters with chains. Once they had dared to attack the Young Team's café, one Rocker actually driving his cycle through the door and into the building itself.

The appearance and clothes of the Blue Angels were detailed for me. 'They're aw dead big boays. Big six-footers, man. This broad, they ur.' The boys insisted that all applicants had to be of outstanding size and build to stand a chance of being admitted. They wore leather jerkins, denim jackets, or suits with velvet collars and string ties. In music their idol was Elvis Presley, a star whom the Mods considered to be from a different decade. The Blue Angels copied their hair-style from Elvis, a cut called 'The Bop', where the hair is combed upwards from the sides towards the middle, which falls over the forehead like an overhanging cliff. To keep it in place, the hair was sleeked with vaseline. Even among the Young Team, shiny sleek locks greased with vaseline were fashionable.

According to McArthur and Long in *No Mean City* (1964, p.28) this preoccupation with hair and clothes was also a feature of the 1920s gangs in Glasgow. In a passage which describes their hero, Johnnie Stark, the authors comment: 'In the language of the Gorbals, he was "well put on" and proud of his "paraffin". There was actually a paraffin dressing on his sleek black hair, and, perhaps there may be some association of ideas between slumland's passion for smoothed and glistening crops and its general term for a smart appearance.' Another and more convincing explanation of the terminology, which has been suggested to me, is that again we are dealing with rhyming slang which has been abbreviated. The full phrase would be, 'he was proud of his paraffin 'ile' ' (the Glasgow pronunciation for 'oil'), which also rhymes with 'style'.

After the phase of conflict between Mods and Rockers, the Blue Angels had gone into decline. In 1966 they were 'tryin' tae bring thirsel' up again'. One last point of honour separated the two groups. The Blue Angels were said to take pride in the fact that nowhere did their name appear scrawled up on a wall. I challenged Tim on this since I had noticed the name once or twice near Bilsland Drive. As the letters appeared two to three feet from the ground, Tim excused this as the work of children.

In their list of enemies, the Young Team clearly placed the Tongs first, the Shamrock second, and the local gangs, the YRB and the Barnes Road, third. The Tongs were their most serious contestants for the hegemony of Glasgow, and therefore deadly rivals. Their hatred of the Shamrock, remembering Henderson's murder, was understandable. But for the life of me I couldn't discover the reasons for the conflict with the two local gangs. At one time, the YRB (roughly equivalent to the Young Team in age) had also 'handered' the Fleet; they had been considered 'gemme boays' for an exploit performed in the summer of 1965. Two of them, while riding past on a scooter, had thrown a petrol bomb into the police box in Bilsland Drive and had shattered it. Since then, something had happened to poison their relationship with Tim's gang. Now the YRB had thrown in their lot with the Barnes Road.

The history of the breakdown, as far as I can piece it together, was as follows. About Easter of 1965, Fergie and Tim resolved to withdraw from the Young Team and in fact did so. Apparently it was only a matter of telling the others they were opting out. 'We chucked the boays fur five month.' Both of them had started going to the pictures together, and had kept out of trouble. Returning one evening from the Vogue Cinema in Possilpark, they had been cornered by the Barnes Road who 'controlled' Bilsland Drive. Assertions that they were no longer members of the Young Team were of no avail. As they 'werenae kerryin'', all they could do was run; quitting the gang had not proved so easy after all. Tim made good his escape to the comparative security of Ruchill Street, but Fergie was caught by their most vigorous pursuer. Tim wheeled round and 'goat intae it'. The attack and chase were too great a blow to their pride to go unanswered. They had both re-entered the gang, although from now on Fergie's connection was to be tenuous; for during their period of withdrawal from the gang Fergie had met Frana.

More recently, the retaliation had been stepped up. One of the reports delivered to Tim on his release from the approved school concerned a confrontation between his brother Mick and Marty, the leader of the Barnes Road. Standing at the gang's corner, one of the Young Team had spotted Marty on a bus which was held up in rush-hour traffic one evening. Mick had boarded the bus and had 'dug him oot.' Leading Marty by the ear, he had returned to the gang, now eager for the fun. 'Come here, wee boay', Mick had said to the good-looking, nervous Marty. Mick, still twisting his ear, slapped the boy on the face until he cried. Then he had dismissed him, sending him 'hame tae his Maw.' 'Whit a riddie he hid', Baggy told us, 'whit a takin' doon – worse than gettin' chibbed.'

Of course, another reason for the mutual animosity between the Young Team and the Barnes Road was the 'chibbin'' of Frank Murphy, described earlier, and which I discovered had occurred in late autumn 1965. Tim's inability to place any of these events in chronological order made it impossible to unravel the original cause of the quarrel. In addition, Tim's tendency to exaggerate and distort may have made him unable, in the end, to distinguish fact from fancy.

Marty's revenge for his public humiliation provoked the all-out battle over Christmas. With Maureen unavailable because of the birth of the baby, Tim had 'picked up a wee bird fae Barrowfield at ra dancin'', Elizabeth Dawson by name. I was not so much surprised at the suddenness of her substitution as at the location of her home. She lived in Spur and Torch territory, the nearest gangs to the hated Tongs. My immediate inquiry was whether there was any danger for Tim when he walked her home. 'You kiddin'?' was the rejoinder. 'She goes hame hersel'. Ah take hir doon tae the sixty-wan stoap an' that's it.'

Tim's confinement within the approved school meant the girl received even less protection. The first time she was beaten up by the YRB, the kicks on her face left ugly bruises. Within a week, she was attacked again; this time she was stabbed twice in the shoulder and once in the breast, or 'chist', as Tim modestly called it. She had been on her way home from work on a Friday evening. Much later I heard that over the Christmas holidays Tim had repaid Marty and his side-kicks, Andy and Benny. For two nights he lay in wait for them at the foot of the stairs in Marty's close without success. On the third night, five hours after Tim had hidden himself, Marty returned with his two mates. In the darkness, Tim lunged forward and cracked Andy over the head with a lemonade bottle, leaving Jack Martin, a boy just outside the inner circle in the Young Team, to hit Marty a glancing blow on the side of the face with an axe. Benny ran for his life.

Both sides now wanted a showdown. Tim's 'goin' oan the creep' was considered by some of the more peripheral members of the Young Team as despicable as 'chibbin' lassies', but they were circumspect in not voicing their opinions too loudly. The only solution, Tim thought, was 'tae battle it oot.' During Christmas week, the gang talk became more frenzied. The pros and cons of various battlefields were discussed. It was up to the Barnes Road to make the first move. 'They says they're comin' up tae oor pitch, bi' they're aye sayin' it an' they never dae.' In this climate of mounting excitement every boy in the area within the aegis of the Fleet and all other associated gangs had been alerted and told to be armed. As one of their number, I was handed a hatchet.

My reluctance to carry weapons, noticed earlier, now aroused hostility. The situation had not been helped by my 'takin' a back seat durin' the action.' Dave Malloy was my principal accuser; whenever the conversation allowed it, he never failed to make a jeering remark at my expense. The sneering had turned to pushing and jostling and a 'square-go' between us was on the cards. Without Tim's constant interventions on my behalf I would have been unable to sustain my role. On one such occasion Fergie had stood up for me: 'Le'e him alane, Dave. He's a good wee cunt.'

11
A pause for reflection

I HAD REACHED a watershed. It was impossible for me to carry an offensive weapon. No one in authority knew that I was involved in this work and, even if anyone had known, no legal exemption for me would have been possible. Two or three outings in the new year to record the aftermath of the 'battle' I considered sufficient to complete the study. Active participation in the fighting was unthinkable.

Owing partly to 'observer fatigue', as Festinger (1956) calls it, and partly to what I can only call 'observer fright', no first-hand account of the 'battle' is available. However, the holiday period gave me time to ruminate on the evidence so far collected and various general points occurred to me.

From the very beginning the importance attached to territory had impressed itself on me. The gang knew its pitch and that of the other major gangs almost to the very last cul-de-sac. When crossing some other gang's territory, its members were only too aware of the fact. To violate the borders of another gang and daub your slogan or monogram on its walls was considered a major triumph.

A not uncommon gang name in Glasgow is 'The Border'. Such a gang would be situated between two major teams and would hope to do business with both sides. A small gang of this name was centred on the no-man's-land between the Possil Uncle, the Barnes Road, and the Milton Tongs. It contained no more than 12 members, some lukewarm in their support. Nevertheless, its narrow buffer area was emblazoned with the fantastic boast: 'UZZ BORDER KILL'. Another Border team was to be found near Parkhead between the Tollcross Wee Men and the Torch gang; others similarly named I heard of but cannot place precisely.

If a boy's family moved to another part of the city, he was expected to remain a member of his original gang; yet, as with every norm espoused by the gangs, exceptions abound. Earlier I stated that boys came from Drumchapel and Helensburgh to join the Fleet, such was its notoriety. Tim stubbornly contended that all Young Team members came from the one confined area even when I pointed out that Beano's home was in 'Toiland'. He seemed to think there was some advantage in having a gang from one district, unpolluted and unadulterated by strangers. In anger he protested at my enquiries: 'Naw, naw. They aw come fae Maryhill.'

When I asked him if he was prepared to hate and fight and stab another young boy simply because he came from another district, Tim agreed. 'See, if wan o' thae Tongs wis tae move tae the next close tae me, Ah'd chib him. Nae kiddin', man.' And he gave me a stiff warning not to interfere in a 'chibbin' case'. 'If we're gettin' intae a boay, don't dae *nuthin*' tae help him or you'll get it worser. Anyboady that stepped intae it wid get the same'.

A desire for status – status of any kind, won at any price – was also noticeable among the gang boys. 'Naeb'dy wants a bad name.' Tim once referred to a young boy who aspired to join the Young Team and whose name, which sounded Polish to me, he mispronounced and then derided. This xenophobia was taken up by the gang and one of their remarks about the boy lived in my memory: 'Aye. He *had* tae go screwin' tae live doon *yon* name.' This is an instance of the power of the subculture, the pressure of the group to force a young boy into delinquency.

One way of acquiring status or a separate identity was to sport a nickname or an unusual twist to a Christian or familial name. For example, a boy named Joseph, not satisfied with being called Joe, might alter his name slightly to Jody. Thomas, unhappy with Thos or Tommie, chose Tosh as his own highly personal first name. To frustrate attempts at tracing these names, I have selected examples from gang boys in the approved school in 1968, but the same principle operated in the Young Team. Fergie's girlfriend Frana had changed her name to avoid confusion with any other Frances. Standard diminutives of surnames, e.g. Fergie, Robbie and Mitch, were also used. But far and away the most envied name was the highly personal nickname. Apart from Beano, Big Dim, and Big Fry, others were: Podgie (because of puppy fat), Fingers (a reference to his skill at stealing), Blinky (the result of a movement of the eyelid which was so rapid that it was virtually disfiguring), Eldo (from a penchant for drinking Eldorado Wine), Peppy (whose love of pills was well known), Cocoa and Baba (for reasons unknown), Chancy Chalmers and Plum Duffy.

Bloch and Niederhoffer (1958, p.66) claim that the conferring of a name constitutes a symbolic landmark in the individual's quest for self-identity. They continue:

> Aside from the nickname cherished by a boy, we may observe the curious and meaningful artifices of young girls who go through a stage where they give their names a peculiarly elegant twist. This may be seen specifically in the affectation of an oddity in spelling and in the vehement insistence upon a desired pronunciation as well as in the caressing flourish with which a name may be written.

Equally indicative of their whole attitude to status was the exclusion of one boy from the Young Team. Davie Wilson had tried for some years to gain acceptance and had been rebuffed at each endeavour. The reason? 'He's a mental heid. A right heid-banger. Boy's daft – a lunatic.' (The last word was pronounced as though it rhymed with 'dramatic'.) 'See when it's a full moon, he runs amok.'[16] The rest of the gang agreed with Tim's assessment of this epileptic boy with the 'gammy' hand: 'He's mad. Tried tae set the polis station oan fire wi' petrol bombs. On a Sunday mornin', in his slippers, nae kiddin'.' The last sentence was delivered in a crescendo as though Tim was growing incredulous at his own words. Thrasher (1927, p.338) has an interesting comment on this subject:

> Every gang usually has its 'goat'. He is a boy who is considered uncommonly 'dumb'; he may be subnormal, as measured by psychological tests, and he can usually be depended upon to get caught if anybody does. Boys of this type are sometimes known as 'goofy guys', if they combine some special peculiarity with their dumbness.

The first time I encountered the gang's feelings about social class differences and status was when we were returning from town by way of Maryhill Road. As we passed Rolland Street, the home of the YRB, Harry Johnstone looked down and pointed: 'That's the senior sec'y doon there, where aw the snobs go.' The cry was taken up by Tim: 'Aye. That's Snobland. Ah *hate* them. Get *right* intae their nuts.' Big Fry's contribution to the conversation was: 'They're *snobs* aw right. They pit oot clean mulk boattles an' everythin'.'

On another night in January, walking along Woodlands Road, Tim demonstrated the very spot where Brian McBride (at that time in a senior approved school) had slashed a student from the university. 'Wee Brian *hates* thae students an' snobs an' aw that.' To placate what were (to Tim's mind) my offended feelings, he later added when we were alone: 'See thae students. They kin fight, man. See yon college up at Partick,' by which I understood him to mean Glasgow University, 'its crammed wi' thae snobs'. 'Aye it is', he tacked on at the end, both to convince himself and to deter me from contradicting. His conception of life at the university was rudimentary, summed up in a phrase tinged with jealousy: 'Aw thae birds an' aw that time.'

Perhaps the most illuminating story on this subject of status was the one I heard from Tim, when I bumped into him in the street six months after his release from the approved school. Dick Stevenson had married 'a college bird; she's at that college up the toon', he told me with pride. Still it was no barrier to being attacked. Although Dick had announced to all and sundry that he was 'screwin' the nut', getting married, and leaving the gang, he and his young wife were assaulted in the centre of the city by boys from a rival gang who were unaware of his sudden withdrawal from the gang scene.

Another symptom of the boys' desire to be noticed was, as I have mentioned already, their scrutinizing of the newspapers for any mention of their own gang or any other gang. No matter how offensive or disparaging the article, it was read avidly.[17] So I was delighted to learn from the local morning newspapers (1 March 1967) that the police had informed the press that publishing gang names only pandered to the 'mini-gangsters' craving for publicity. It has not always been apparent that the appeals were heeded. To give but one glaring example, the main Glasgow evening papers carried banner headlines and lead stories (10 October 1968) on the imprisonment of 'Two Tongs' for eight years each. A similar plea to the press not to publish names was made by the city magistrates in 1936. Faced with what they called 'the gang menace', the magistrates unanimously passed a resolution which contained the following sentence: 'that the attention of the press be directed to the undesirability of giving undue publicity to such cases ... '.[18]

The boys' disdain of smaller gangs or coloured people was part of the same syndrome. Someone, somewhere had to be lower down the social scale than they were. In full flight from the cinema that Monday night, a group of about 12 of us found ourselves running in the opposite direction from Maryhill. Within minutes we were in Springburn, waiting for a bus to return us to our own area. A group of boys approaching us stopped, looked long and hard at us, and then melted away.

'It's the Wild Peg, fur fuck's sake,' sneered Tim.

'Aye, aw four o' them', I added with equal disdain.

'Naw,' Beano rebuked me. 'Ye've goat tae gee them their due. There's at least five o' them.'

As the boys turned to go, Big Dave challenged: 'Are youse messin'? Dae youse want tae go right ahead?' Looking at their backs, he concluded sarcastically: 'There's *nae* messin' wi' *them*.' The last words went to Big Fry: 'Ah've threw better oot the wae tae get *intae* a fight.'

On our way back to Maryhill, one young boy was cornered in a closemouth by Big Dave. As Tim and I ran towards them I could hear Dave shouting: 'Who rules? Whit team are ye in?' The boy's reply was inaudible to me but Dave's counter wasn't. 'They're wankers, mad wankers. You're gettin' ripped. You're gettin' ma hoose o' Frazer [i.e. razor].' Dave turned to us hoping we would be able to supply the desired weapon. The boy broke from his grasp and ran through the close into the backcourt. His parting shot was: 'Whose goaney rip me? No' you, ya back-stabber ye.'

A pause for reflection

The gang were equally dismissive of the Cowcaddens Toi and the Port (Dundas) Toi, two smaller gangs on the periphery of Maryhill. 'Big JB', the 'leader-aff' of the Cowcaddens Toi, was 'a pure idiot, a pure mental case'. Proof of this statement was not long in coming. He had been serving a sentence of 28 days detention in the last week of which he had 'shot the craw' and 'jolted', i.e. absconded. He and his closest mate, Jack Clancy, were accused, each time their names cropped up, of 'runnin' a pure brothel' -a contradiction in terms, until I remembered they used the word 'pure' as an equivalent of 'nothing less than' or 'complete'.

Another major inference I drew at this time was the casual attitude towards gang membership. I had gained admission, if not acceptance, rather easily. No initiation ceremony or test was demanded of me, as I mentioned earlier. Tim and Fergie had the year before simply announced that they were leaving the gang and that had been accepted. Again, Tim and I were able to appear on a Saturday night, drink pints and eat fish suppers with the gang, and leave the next day to return to the approved school. I could turn up on the Saturday night and not on the Sunday; no questions were asked, as most others put in an appearance or failed to do so just as it pleased them. Consequently, the list of boys present on the occasions I met the gang was never the same. Apart from the in-group, as I have called them, who attended on a regular basis (Fergie is an exception even to this), the number of boys I met in the Young Team itself was 27. I could also, towards the end of January, recognise at least 14 members of the Fleet. These figures do not include boys about whom I learned a good deal but whom I never met because of their committal to borstals, approved schools, or remand homes. The total numerical strength of the Young Team was therefore subject to constant fluctuation. Here are Tim's answers to my questions on this matter:

'How many boys in the team do you know by name?'

'Aboot fifty.'

'And how many by sight?'

'Aye, aboot fifty. Know them tae talk tae.'

As with so much else, numbers were never given exactly. I estimated that the total strength of the Young Team, combining boys both central and peripheral to the gang and boys both 'inside' and out, was in the region of 35 to 40 at the most. Yet Tim and the others believed in the fantasy of their gang being a 'hunner handit'. Likewise, when a boy was stabbed several times, the preference of the story-teller was always for the number 'seventeen'. Dave Malloy was not alone amongst the gang members in his liking for the round number 'four hundred' which in his eyes was an accurate description of the size of the Tongs or of the Buck gang, or in fact of any opposing force.

As to the internal organisation of the gang and the relative status of the most prominent members, this is how Tim saw it:

'Who are your closest friends in the gang, Tim?'

'Jack Martin - he wis at school wi' me. Dave Malloy. Fergie, of course. Ma cousin, Beano - been ca'ed that fur years, don't know why. Eldo - he's jist oot the 'Grove.'[19]

The Young Trio were conspicuous in this list by their absence; and the more I saw of them, the more I realised how much of a group within a group they were. Jack Martin for some undiscovered reason I saw little of and Eldo I met once in January and so was unable to appreciate the strength of their relationships with Tim.

'How do you control them all?', I asked next.

'Seven or eight o' uzz go' roun' thegither. If there's a battle oan, Ah send them up tae the hooses, tae the Youth Centre, roun' the pubs. Ah kin get o'er a hunner boays in fifteen minutes.'

'Why do they follow you? Why are you "leader-aff"?'

'They've goat tae follow some-wan, hiven't they? An' it's me. They aw know better than tae chib me. Mick and John both hiv' sawn-aff shotguns. Big double-barclled things they ur, man.'

Unquestionably the infamy of his elder brothers, added to the fact that he himself had all the qualities of a 'gemmie', had allowed Tim to assert himself as 'leader-aff'. He was the real initiator of events, charging into action and drawing the less enthusiastic with him. Over the last few years, Fergie had been his closest friend, but they had moved apart because of Fergie's growing relationship with Frana. Becoming more settled and secure in his own masculinity, Fergie had less need of a gang.

With the waning of Tim's friendship with Fergie, Dave Malloy's star had waxed. On almost every occasion that I 'jumped aboot wi' the boays', he was present. He was an 18- or 19-year-old boy with a good job in a nearby paper mill, whom I suspected of some latent homosexual affection for Tim. On all accounts he should have become a member of the Fleet by now, following the same trail as Tim's elder brothers, Mick and John. Instead he stayed in the junior gang, contentedly playing second fiddle to Tim. From time to time they diverted themselves with a game of identification with heroes. Meeting them both one night, I overheard them calling each other 'AT and 'Frank'. It did not take me long to complete the names with Capone and Nitti. *The Untouchables* was one of their favourite television programmes, a predilection they shared with many Glasgow viewers. Dave assumed command in Tim's absences and reported to him on his return. My arrival and connection with Tim annoyed him from the beginning. On our first meeting he was silent, menacingly so. Just as he was developing a closer relationship with Tim, I had introduced myself as a mate of Tim's from the approved school. I could appreciate the pained expression he wore each time I showed up. To avoid a fight, or rather what he proudly called his 'right sleekit heid', I soon realised that my association with the gang would have to be a temporary one. It wasn't temporary enough for my face. For he turned on me one evening without any immediately justification, grabbed the lapels of my suit and butted me in the face with his head, all the time screaming: 'Ah'm intae you, Ah'm intae you.' As the ensuing scene won me some reputation as a fighter, my standing with the other members of the gang was immediately enhanced. Dave's solution to his loss of face I relate in Chapter 16.

Next in the line of affection to Tim, though not in the hierarchy, stood Beano who owed his rank to the blood relationship with the Malloys. He was too young, too small, and too ineffectual to hold higher office.

After him in the pecking order came the Young Trio, Harry Johnstone, Dan McDade and Jimmy Barrow, who remained something of an enigma to the end. As they floated in and out of the inner circle of the gang, I never fully understood their position. When they were present, they were a force to be reckoned with. Their deeply disturbed personalities, the highly aggressive Harry and Dan, and the more withdrawn but no less violent Jimmy, made the whole gang wary of their every move. Even Tim admitted to an uneasiness in their presence. Tim, I think, feared their intense loyalty to one another, but no threat to his leadership was ever offered; the prestige and fighting-power of Tim's elder brothers scared off contenders.

The majority of the boys in the gang had no close relationship with Tim. They lived in the area, knew Tim and were recognised by him; some of them were only vaguely connected with the Young Team and so liable to be enlisted. Really there were two amorphous groups among the 'hundred' boys which Tim invited me to believe were at his command. Some of the more active boys sprayed, daubed and chalked their names wherever possible; they roamed streets aimlessly in search of diversion, lounged against hoardings in sheer boredom, and listened to pop music in states approaching coma. But in the main, the boys of the district were on the fringe of the gang or quite definitely outside its influence. Most of the fringe members, it appeared to me, could have done without the gang and its leaders. The gang leaders, on the other hand, needed the status which the gang conferred upon them. And it was they who determined how active the gang would be. The Fleet collapsed each time Dick Stevenson 'wis huckled'. The Tongs similarly fell into disarray at the loss of their leaders. Nevertheless, even with Dick at the helm, the Fleet and the Young Team had been in decline with numbers falling away rapidly when

Henderson was killed. This gave them a new pretext for aggressive activity. Both gangs suddenly became bigger and more active than ever. The Glasgow juvenile gang, then, in my opinion, has little internal cohesion of its own; it exists to oppose others and to provide coveted status for its members and especially its leaders.

Another conclusion I came to at the time was that it wasn't the strongest or the fittest, the tallest or the brightest boys who became leader or lieutenants in gangs, but the most psychologically disturbed, those with lowest impulse control. A further illustration of this was provided by Dave Malloy, who once recounted in my hearing how as a young boy he used to live in Dennistoun. There his chief source of pleasure was to be admitted by the older boys in the area to the Meat Market where, he claimed, he was allowed to lacerate carcasses. The look on his face as he remembered this pastime betokened the disturbance of his mind.

Shortly after I ceased my connection with the gang, I made the following comments: in the Young Team's favour, above everything else, stands their loyalty. I found little of the 'no honour among thieves' mentality, at least in relation to 'squealing'. They kicked and butted each other in the face; at times they even threatened each other with blades and on an odd occasion one gang member would stab another or leave a sick or injured boy unattended. On the other hand nobody, but nobody, informed the police of his assailants. A common hatred of authority banded them together. Tim, as so often, put their case succinctly: 'Naeb'dy grasses. Some o' oor boays hiv' been malkied and never wance hiv' they went tae the polis. If they did, Ah'd stab them ma'sel'.'

Rereading that passage after some time has elapsed, I am struck by the strong identification it reveals with the boys. Maybe at the time I needed to believe that this gang norm was faithfully upheld, at the very least, to act as a cover for my minor delinquencies. But since I left the gang, evidence has been presented to me that the 'no grassing' rule is more often violated than vindicated. One prominent member of the gang was arrested and within 24 hours all other members had been questioned by the police. The inference was obvious to everyone except the gang. Yet their misplaced belief in gang loyalty was not discarded or even diminished, but became all the more extreme and passionate. (A similar response to disconfirmation was documented by some American psychologists (Festinger et al., 1956) who joined a group which was making specific prophecies of imminent cataclysmic floods. When the deluge failed to appear, the group's proselytizing activities far from diminishing, increased enormously.)

My experience in the approved school also makes me question the boys' claim that they never grassed. For there, gang leaders were prepared to inform on their friends, relatives, and fellow gang members to escape punishment themselves.

Conversations with Tim invariably led away from the original point. After such a remark as, 'Ah'd stab them ma'sel', I would ask Tim if he ever felt remorse or anxiety after attacking someone.

'Ye never think aboot it efterwards', came the reply.

'But suppose you were to kill someone.'

'Aw, Ah'd be worried then. Ah mean, if the polis wis tae catch ye fur that, ye'd get done ... '

'Have you ever felt sorry for anyone you have chibbed?'

'Aye, when it wis wan o' ma ain boays. Ah felt sorry fur Big Dim. "Mon," he says tae me, "you an' me's hivin' a square-go". He goat seventeen stitches in his heid.'

Tim also talked about what he would do after leaving the approved school. 'Ah'm no workin'. Ma bruthers hiv' never worked. Never man. No' since they left the school.' This statement was totally untrue. 'How are they able to afford money for drink and clothes?'

'Oaneytime they want suits an' 'at, they go doon the toon an' take them.'

'But what of your own future?'

'Ye only think aboot the noo, the present. Aw Ah want is birds, drink, fights, an' parties.'[20]

'What do you think will happen to you when you leave here, Tim?'

'Get ma borstal', he replied resignedly. 'Whit can Ah dae? Cannae leave Maryhill, are ye kiddin'? Whit boays wid Ah go aboot wi'? Naw, Ah'll never leave Maryhill.'[21]

12
Birds, birds, birds ...

TIM HIMSELF WAS unsure and uncommunicative on the topic of the role of girls in gangs. (My earlier warning about obscenity applies particularly to this subject.) His opinion differed as often as I questioned him on this. At first he defended them: 'Birds are aye stoapin' fights.' Later, this changed to: 'They try to stoap fights.' And finally came: 'Right enough. A loat o' battles are aboot birds.' I acquired more information on this topic from Moira McManus than I did from Tim. One story she told me will introduce the main points to be made.

Some months before meeting me, Moira 'had been goin' wi' a boay fae the Govan Team.' They were 'led aff' by a character calling himself 'Rebel.' 'He's only five fit somethin' but he's the gemmiest – aw these great big blokes wir' aw around him.' While they sat talking in their café at Govan Cross one evening, a girl entered and delivered a message to the effect that 'So-an'-so fae the Bowry can gee it tae youse half-wits.' She had been promptly set upon by the Govan girls, one of whom took a hatpin from her handbag and lunged at the intruder with it. The pin entered the girl's chin. Rebel at this point stepped forward, and, according to Moira, 'wi' a wave o' his haun'' he brought the fighting, if not the screaming, to a halt.

Though Tim was reticent about girls, his preoccupation with their opinion of him broke through now and then. In the approved school one evening, I found him in a bitter mood. 'See if Shewie [i.e. Hugh] Cairns comes here, Ah'll kill him.' Tim went on to explain: 'In the 'Grove he wis annoyin' me so Ah kicked his heid in. His nose wis aw smashed an' 'at. An' he's jist efter telt the birds ootside that he took a len' o' me. Aw the birds wis askin' me if it wis true – fur aw the birds like the gemme boays. Ah'll kill him, Ah swear it.'

The theme of 'birds like the gemme boays' struck me as central to the life of the gang. It was a theme to which Tim often returned: 'They like them that go *right* ahead. A leader-aff can get a haud o' any bird he wants.' In spite of his contempt for birds, he was prepared to take into consideration their occasional usefulness. They came into their own when the police arrived in the midst of a battle and started 'cairtin' boays'. The girls' duty was to offer their arms and, if they failed to do so, boys had been known to grab the arm of the nearest girl and intimidate her into assuring the police that they were 'oot thegither'. Boys were normally only stopped or searched when they were on their own.

An indication of a deeper level of commitment to the gang than this mere masquerade of courtship was evident in the case of a number of girls who were prepared to conceal weapons for the boys in their handbags and in their underwear. This subterfuge gave the gang access to 'blades' in dance halls and in the streets, as both bouncers and policemen hesitated to search young girls.

The relevant literature indicates that this practice is by no means confined to the gangs of the 60s. Sillitoe (1955, p.128), when discussing two of the most notorious gangs of the 30s, namely the Norman Conks and the Billy Boys, comments: 'Both gangs used hatchets, swords and sharpened bicycle chains habitually and these were conveyed to the scenes of their battles by their "queens". This was because they knew that the police dare not interfere with or search a girl, who would at once protest that the officers were improperly assaulting her.' John Mack (1958, p.645) similarly depicts the girls of the same era as a 'travelling armoury', who occasionally took part themselves 'in the heat and fury of the battle'.

Spergel (1964, pp.88-9), in his exploratory study of delinquent subcultures in 'a very large eastern city' of the United States, observed that one of the roles 'the girlfriend played in relation to the fighting gang was that of weapon-bearer. The weapon was usually concealed under the girl's blouse or skirt.' The girlfriend in 'Slumtown', like her counterpart in Glasgow, contributes highly to the maintenance of the gang-fighting system. 'She was the carrier of tales – the magnifier, distorter, and fabricator of derogatory remarks which served to instigate conflict among the various clubs. On occasion, an insult to a girlfriend was cause for the boyfriend to avenge not so much her, but his own honour.' Tim and the other members of the Young Team were caught up in the same ritualistic pattern of behaviour.

Tim's girlfriends I have mentioned already. He had two, or at least two I found out about, in the short time I knew him well. Maureen, the girl he had made pregnant, I never met. Big Fry, however, told a story concerning her one night. Tim and Maureen had been walking along together when Maureen had suddenly slipped her arm round his waist. Almost in the same movement she had withdrawn her hand, asking, 'Whit's this'? Pulling open his jacket, she had revealed a hatchet stuck in his belt. 'Oh!' Tim had countered, 'Where did that come fae?' Everyone had laughed. The truth was, Tim now told Big Fry, that he was carrying the hatchet to hand in at the cloakroom of the dance hall so as to be left with his open razor. 'Like Dick Stevenson', Beano commented; for Dick had taught his young brothers to carry a second weapon, hidden in their suits or in their socks. Maureen had been delighted at the deception.

One more item of information I learned about Maureen. She was two years older than Tim. This age difference she had in common with Lizzie Dawson, her successor, who came from Barrowfield, and who was 18. Tim volunteered this information one day as he was describing his activities on one of the Saturday evenings I had decided not to meet him. He had met Lizzie, taken her 'up tae the hoose', and, when his parents had conveniently retired to bed, they had sat down to watch television. When both of them became bored with the programmes, Lizzie had suggested an alternative ploy. 'Why don't ye go away oot fightin' ?' she had inquired solicitously. 'Ah like older birds', Tim concluded.

Towards the end of January I met Lizzie at the party described at the end of this chapter. Her pretty face was marred for me by jaws which constantly chewed gum. She was dressed in a purple fur coat, which was the style at the time, purple plastic shoes, and carried a matching plastic handbag. She was slightly taller than Tim. When I first met them, they were quarrelling. The previous evening, Lizzie had called on Tim to stop fighting outside a major dance hall in the centre of Glasgow. Her request had been an attempt to prevent him from being arrested. For her pains, she had heard in reply, 'Aw, shut yir fuckin' mooth.'

Dismissive as he was of girls, Tim could not tolerate the situation in reverse. The Saturday afternoon we invaded the library, Tim spotted Henderson's sister in the street. As we passed her, Tim showed that he recognised her by greeting her in friendly fashion. The girl walked on without looking to right or left. The affront to Tim's dignity proved intolerable to him. Running after her, he booted her in the behind. The girl, distressed and in tears, fled before his wrath. Returning to us, he kept muttering how much he loathed being 'cut deid'.

His attitude to girls in general was epitomised by the gang aphorism: 'Shag 'em and sling 'em.' I suspect Tim realised that I would oppose such a crude sentiment. Anyway, he gave me some heart-thumping minutes by addressing himself directly to me and continuing: 'That's aw birds are fur. Whit's it fur, then ? Ye jist get it and sling 'em away.'

The older boys in the Fleet gang had their own version of the maxim. Their favourite sport was to steal a car, drive to Saracen Cross in Possilpark, pick up a girl, and travel deep into the country. There, the car would be stopped and the girl presented with this Hobson's choice: 'Cock it or walk it.'

Thrasher (1927, p.238) has a strikingly similar passage in his chapter on 'Sex in the Gang':

> There is a common practice among young men in Chicago, and this is by no means confined to boys of the gangs or the underprivileged

classes, of picking up girls, utter strangers, on the street and taking them for – a ride in an automobile. During the course of this ride it is customary to indulge in passionate petting, and often the affair culminates in the sex act. If the girl refuses, it is commonly supposed that she is put out of the car some place in the country and asked to walk back.

A lack of finesse and an absence of deep emotional commitment characterised most of the gang's dealings with girls. Their regular remark made to girls passing in the street was: 'Up ye!' In general' the recipients of this pleasantry were well chosen and well able to reply in kind. The girls' counter was a vigorous 'vicky' or 'V sign, normally accompanied by some choice 'swearie words'. The majority of the girls who were associated with the Young Team were in the 14 to 16 age range. Groups of them huddled together at our own corner or at Saracen Cross, smoking, gossiping, and 'eyeing up the talent'. Apart from the bolder ones, the groups kept separate, with the odd boy or girl crossing over to convey a message, a dare, or an invitation.

The general coarseness of behaviour towards girls can be seen again in the way the gang dealt with Harry Johnstone's sex problems. He was one of the most violent and callous members in the gang, and yet he was too shy to talk 'tae the bird he fancied'. The others teased him mercilessly about her. Typical of their ridicule was: 'Everyboady's rattled her. Aw the Young Team hiv' had her. She couldnae walk up the road, hir legs wir that bloated.' And the final crudity was spoken with their arms pumping out that obscene gesture: 'She's a punch-up.' They continued until Harry was virtually beside himself with rage: 'Ah'll wrap a blade roun' yir fuckin' throats, ya rides ye.'

Apart from their own girlfriends, three other types of girl featured in the life of the Young Team: firstly, the 'gang shags' as they are called in Thrasher's work (1927, p.237), or the 'gang bangs' as Yablonsky (1967, pp.219-21) termed them; secondly, local girls who wished to have nothing to do with boys involved with gangs; and lastly, common prostitutes.

Of the three 'cows' associated with Tim's gang, I met only one. Sandra Lawrence's reputation preceded her with all the stealth of a sonic boom. To the Young Team she was 'a pure pump, a pure bun, a fuckin' cow'. Big Fry remarked that she would agree to intercourse at the drop of a hat. She performed numerous times on Friday and Saturday nights to deal with 'the big line-up' that followed her about the streets. The expression 'a line-up' is also a favourite among American gangs.

Baggy described one incident involving Sandra. Big Dave, Dan McDade, Jimmy Barrow and others had pursued her to her close in Lambhill. Bob

Robertson induced her to go with him into the back court where her mother observed her in flagrante delicto. Her father rushed downstairs, but seeing what manner of boys danced attendance on his daughter, he refrained from physical violence and pleaded: 'I'm sorry she's like that. I'll hiv' tae take her up tae the hoose.' Bob, not so self-controlled, punched him and his daughter and then left.

Sandra was pointed out to me on the solitary occasion when I joined the gang on a Sunday evening. Her appearance was drab in comparison with her reputation. She stood, not five feet tall, on stumpy legs which were covered with torn stockings. Her squat little body was encased in a lime-green coat, the hem of which was visible at the back. Her face was so 'pot ugly' that entertaining a 'line-up' was the 'only wae she kin get boays'. In all she was a pathetic little girl in need of care and protection. She was one of the crowd standing at the corner who were trying to out-stare the police diagonally opposite. With the advent of darkness and the departure of the 'busies', Joe Stevenson approached her and commanded: 'Get roun' the back, Sanny.' This latter word, a diminutive also of 'sand-shoe', had become the unfortunate girl's nickname. It encouraged such jests from Joe as, 'Aye, an' hir breath's like a smelly sanny an' aw.' Whatever the girl whispered in reply, she moved towards the nearest close with the words of Big Sid in her ears, 'I'm comin' in efter, Sanny.'

At the conclusion of a composition written for me in the approved school, a gang member from the Gorbals wrote:

> Nowadays the gangs only fight for kicks and mostly show off to daft girls who like a lot of attention and that's where the rape comes in. They take a girl round the back close, kiss her a few times, and then expect her to drop her knickers. If she doesn't she gets raped and there's nothing the poor cow can do about it because there's nearly always boys and only one girl, so you see.

Rape I did not witness; Sandra was too compliant for that charge to stick. But I did see boy after boy trooping through the close to the backyard. Only two or three had intercourse with her, the others were spectators. Fully clad as they were, they returned within minutes from what must have been a joyless experience. Tim found the proceedings, with me present, intensely embarrassing particularly when I asked him if he was going to join the 'line-up'. 'Hiv' ma ain bird,' he stammered self-consciously.

Two other girls, who rejoiced in the nicknames of 'Hotpoint' and 'Skidmarks', were reputed to be in the same class as Sanny Lawrence. All three were in their third year at a local comprehensive school and on the point of leaving. Dave Malloy told me that Hotpoint had been taken into a condemned tenement building by her boyfriend. 'She gave it tae him an' then his two mates slipped roun' an' she took the three o' them. Then three other boays said tae her: "Take us an' aw or we'll kick yir fuckin' heid in".' All six boys, who were well known to her, were 'taken', Dave told me.

Skidmarks had come by her name through the boys' practice of kicking her naked behind after they had 'pumped' her. These three girls were conforming to a pattern of female juvenile delinquency well known in this country and in America. As Howard Jones (1967, p.137) puts it:

> Several boys queue up to have sexual intercourse with a local girl of a notoriously experimental disposition. Only when she baulks at going round a second time, and avoids compulsion by running to the police, does the incident come to light.

A good example of the boys' attitude to girls in the second category, local girls antagonistic to gang life, is provided by their treatment of one very good-looking girl from the district who was engaged to one of the boys on the very fringe of the gang, The same highly repetitive charges were made against her: 'We've aw been up her. Some rid neck Benny must hiv'.' On his own or in the company of his girlfriend, Benny was a target for their vilest abuse: 'Yir maw does press-ups oan a carrot-field.' 'Aye, yir ain maw,' responded Benny. 'Aye, yir maw an' yir two da's,' chorused the boys. Such treatment was meted out to the young couple every time they encountered the gang, and the closer they came to the date of their wedding, the more obscene became the abuse. I felt that their vilification of the girl was directed not so much at her morals, as at her engagement and impending marriage to one of 'their boays'. The proximity of a conventional, warm relationship enraged Tim and the others.

When in town, the boys were fascinated by the Glasgow prostitutes. The first time we wandered up to Blythswood Square and down St Vincent Street, Tim was at pains to convince me that 'gemmies' had no need of 'birds on the game', because all the best-looking girls flocked round gang leaders. At 'five poun' fur a strip an' a short time', I felt the reasons were more probably economic. Tim, 1 think, was right in saying that his boys never picked up a prostitute but they burned with curiosity about the profession. All bragged of their extensive knowledge of 'kip shops' (brothels), but no one was privy to the exact locality of one, though many girls were known to ply their trade in Maryhill. (I must confess that the first time the gang said they were heading for a kip shop, I thought we were on our way to buy fish suppers in a chip shop.)

The coffee stall at Charing Cross attracted the boys on a Friday and Saturday night after the pubs closed. There, while washing down fish and chips with cups of coffee, we could 'chat up brass nails'.[22] The ladies of the town had the situation sized up; the boys provided no custom but they did provide company and sometimes amusement until the main trade of the night began. Within minutes I was 'chattin' up the big woman beside me, great style.' She belonged to Newcastle, had been married and divorced in London, and was now in hiding from her husband in Glasgow. In a plaintive voice she moaned: 'I was told the business was good up here but it's not.' With Tim listening in, I heard myself defending Glasgow's ability to provide her with clients as if the lack of business she talked of constituted a typical 'Geordie' smear on my native city. One remark of hers was recounted by Tim over and over again. That evening she had been visiting 'one of the girls who's pregnant to the darkie, him that keeps her.' She had taken the girl the small sum her colleagues had collected to help tide her over the period of temporary unemployment.

It was the following day before I fully realised that I had conducted most of this conversation. The others had stood around the coffee stall, sniggering and elbowing each other. I had been accused earlier in the evening of being a 'back-seater' and subconsciously must have leaped at this opportunity to show some courage when little was at stake. One exchange between the 'big brass nail' and myself I cherish still. Endeavouring to keep the conversation alive, I asked her what was her busiest night. To my surprise she replied: 'Mondays is our best night – for they've been wi' their wives an' girlfriends all weekend an' they're lookin' for a bit o' fun.'

Finally, the one and only party I attended in the company of the gang deserves an abridged description. After the fierce fighting season of Christmas, I decided to return to the gang partly to hear what had taken place in the interval during my absence and partly to attend a Saturday night party, an event which, as Tim had by now admitted, took place regularly.

I fully expected that Fergie would be throwing the party, for such was the information I had gathered. However, as we made our way to the house after closing time, carrying our 'screw taps', fish suppers, and bottles of wine, I was told that it was no longer possible to hold parties in Fergie's house. At a marathon function in his home at the very beginning of the Christmas holidays, Tim and Dave Malloy had chibbed Fergie's uncle and cousin for trying to stop the guests from becoming riotous. They had since regretted their actions but had not seen Fergie to apologise to him. As things had got progressively out of hand, Fergie had burst into tears. He had been sitting beside Frana, being comforted by her, when he suddenly leaped to his feet and started 'crackin' his heid aff the wa'.' In an attempt to explain this odd behaviour, Jimmy Barrow added: 'His Da left him when he wis wee.'

So instead of Fergie's house, we arrived at Rose Brennan's. Climbing the stairs, I noticed that the fiat at the opposite end of the landing was protected by a large padlock driven into the door and into the lintel. Inside the front room, the talk was all of Mick Malloy. At the 'advanced' age of 21 he had just become engaged. Tim caused me much amusement by his description of his elder brother's courtship. 'They've been goin' thegither fur four year and he's been gettin' nuthin', not even the coat open. His bird used tae say tae him: "Pit a ring oan ma finger an' ye can hiv' it".'

Couples were dancing in the front room to music from a record player. Throughout the evening and into the early hours of Sunday morning, one song by The Kinks, Dead End Street, was played more than any other, and was adopted by the gang as their song. Without over-emphasising its significance (the music, too, was catchy and it rose high in the national charts), I want to quote it.

> There's a crack up in the ceiling,
> And the kitchen sink is leaking,
> Out of work and got no money,
> A Sunday joint of bread and honey.
>
> What are we living for?
> Two-roomed apartment on the second floor.
> No money coming in,
> The rent collectors knocking, trying to get in,
>
> We are strictly second class
> We don't understand,
> Why we should be on dead end street.
> People are living on dead end street,
> Gonna die on dead end street,
> Dead end street, dead end street,
> Dead end street, dead end street.
>
> On a cold and frosty morning,
> Wipe my eyes and stop me yawning.
> And my feet are nearly frozen,
> Pour the tea and put some toast on.

What are we living for?
Two-roomed apartment on the second floor,
No chance to emigrate,
I'm deep in debt and now it's much too late,

We both want to work so hard,
We can't get a chance.
People live on dead end street
People are dying on dead end street
Gonna die on dead end street
Dead end street, dead end street,
Dead end street, dead end street.

The chorus is then repeated and the song ends with the line:

Dead end street, how's it feel?

When this record came off the turntable for perhaps the 20th time, Big Fry, now deep in drink, rose up and tauntingly called out: 'We're the slummies!' Normally the music at parties was provided by Jimmy Barrow and Dan McDade playing their guitars, with Fergie accompanying them an odd time on his mouth organ. The arrest of Dan McDade – for reasons I never discovered – and the disappearance of Fergie, had put paid to that.

The only home-made entertainment that evening was a song started by Tim amidst giggles and guffaws. As others joined in, the volume of noise increased until the boys repeated the Glasgow primary school chant with full-throated voices:

Ah want ma hole,
Ah want ma hole,
Ah want ma hole-idays.
Tae see the cunt,
Tae see the cunt,

Tae see the cunt-ery.
Fu' cu-,
Fu' cu-,
Fu' curiosity.

To provide drink for the party, a local public house had been raided and the stolen bottles of whisky, wine, gin and vodka were poured into the kitchen sink and stirred. Guests were handed cups to sample the brew. I decided to stick to the cans of beer I had brought. One of the boys picked up a bottle of advocaat, which he had mistaken for whisky in the darkness, to add it to the 'punch'. 'Christ!' he remarked, 'puddin' in a boa'le!' (i.e. bottle).

Harry Johnstone, who without contrivance could look dirty and untidy even in his best 'tin-flute', performed his party piece over and over again for the assembled company. Whenever a girl or boy wanted a light for their cigarette, the match was handed to Harry who struck it on the zip of his fly.

The bedroom door had been purposely left open to allow fellow guests to watch the performance of the occupants. At one point in the course of the night, there were three couples on the one double bed, but they were 'winchin' (or 'petting') rather than having sexual intercourse. On a trip to the toilet I met Tim who was heading in the same direction. Of Lizzie and his chances of gettin' it' he had this to say: 'Ye cannae dae nuthin' – no' in front o' aw her mates. That wid take her right doon.'

The combination of alcohol and drugs began to have its effect; one guest in particular, a petite girl in black, was 'stoatin' aw ower the place – pure puggled she wis'. Noticing Tim spill wine on the floor, she staggered in front of him and ordered: 'Right, you get oot get oot the hoose.' Tim was in no mood to be mocked by a 'daft wee lassie'; there were too many onlookers for that. He pounced on her, and manhandled her out the room, tearing her dress in the process. The company filed out of the door to see the outcome. The girl, now in tears and on the point of vomiting as a result of punches to the stomach, was being hurled downstairs. Tim rushed past us into the house to snatch the girl's coat from Rose's arms. Ripping the patch pockets from the garment, he threw it after the girl. The party spirit was beginning to disintegrate. It was six o'clock on Sunday morning; Rose thought it time to encourage her visitors to leave. She had no success. Later on, as I walked Moira home, she told me that Rose had, in desperation, 'cracked the wean oan the heid'; it certainly wailed and bawled as if it had been struck. The baby, who 'belangs tae Rose's mither', did the trick. The boys took the hostess's gentle hint, the Glasgow barman's standard cry: 'Hiv' youse nae hames tae go tae?' Some had to be awakened from their beery sleep and pointed in the general direction of home. Baggy was half-way through the door when Big Sheila shouted after him: 'Ah took it oot an' measured it when ye wir drunk, ya mad wanker, ye.' Not to be outdone, Baggy retorted: 'Y'd need a helluva big measurin' tape.'

As a parting shot to repay Rose for her hospitality, the boys slipped some of her long-playing records into their coats and made for the door, which was slammed behind them. This final act of provocation could not be allowed to pass unanswered. A game of 'knifey' began with Rose's front door as target. Bayonets and commando knives streaked across the landing and sank into the woodwork. Whoever hurled his 'blade' deepest into the wood won the contest. Harry's weapon, 'a big psychey machete', clattered onto the stone-work after every throw. And so we took our leave.

13

Gallous gear, brilliant patter and the writing on the wall

LOQUACITY DOES NOT come easily or naturally to these boys. One of the few subjects where their interest and knowledge adds fluency to their speech is clothes and they held detailed discussions on, for example, ticket-pockets, flaps and vents. The importance they attached to 'gear' and to 'bein' in style' I had long been aware of. A major part of my preparations for entree into the gang was discovering precisely what cut of suit would be acceptable at that time. Fashions changed within a matter of weeks or months rather than years.

As I have already described in Chapter 1, the 'gallous gear' then was: a dark suit with a middle vent of 12 to 14 inches in the jacket (two vents were 'played oot'); two- to three-inch flaps over the pockets (a ticket-pocket was *de rigueur*); tight trousers with one-inch turn-ups (the season for two inches was to come before my four months were over and the fashion of no turn-ups at all was already passed); ties had to be spotted with a matching handkerchief 'fur the toap poakit' (by January the white polka dot was out, and 'college ties', bought or preferably stolen from Forsyth's, Rowan's, or Carswell's, were all the rage); shoes, otherwise known as 'yir manoeuvres', were ridiculed unless they were London toes (this later changed to brogues, which like the 'college ties' are more middle-class items of dress). Tim advised me when ordering a suit to ask for 'a finger-tip jaiket', i.e. one which stretches to the end of the boy's middle finger when his arm is at his side. Alternatives were reefer or denim jackets and suits ('Eddie's goat a right cracker'), patch pockets, pleats for vents, hipsters (really 'on thir way oot', but still acceptable if cherry-red and split over the bridge of the foot), and, for those with more exotic tastes, leather and suede and mohair coats and suits. The whole effect was summed up in the phrase, 'aw geared up'.

By general agreement one married boy in the Fleet was accorded the title of the 'best wee dresser in Maryhill'. By all accounts, he changed his suits as regularly as the Duke of Windsor. His camel-hair coat, mohair suit, silk shirts and painted ties were the talk and pride of the district. For an unemployed labourer 'on the buroo' he set a high standard in dress. The explanation given me was that with so many children (i.e. family allowances) he could not fail to be 'in the money'. Within the Young Team itself, big Dave Malloy was acknowledged as the sharpest dresser: 'He's goat the maist gear'. One evening he was holding the floor with his description of the latest suit: 'It's soart o' a bluey-green cloath wi' a chalk stripe, peaked lapels, finger-tip length, wan inch turn-ups, two inch poakit flaps – aye, an' caught in at the waist.' The gang phrase for a boy with such a collection of, and interest in, clothes was 'over-gallous, an over-gallous boay's oor Dave.'

Tim claimed, as I mentioned earlier, that his brothers acquired new clothes by 'goin' doon the toon an' takin' them'. John had been arrested for just such a raid on one of the city's newest clothes shops and sentenced to borstal. In the company of Dick Stevenson, he had entered the shop and seized ten pairs of trousers and eight 'casuals'. Dick had drawn a 'malkie' to dissuade the assistants from impeding their escape. Nevertheless, as they ran for the door, the employees chased them. A passer-by in the street, who inadvertently blocked their way, was pushed through a plate-glass window by Dick and John. 'Aboot twelve people in the street clawed John but Dick guyed.'

Prestige and status could be won with clothes. And those without 'gear' were labelled 'tramps, pure tramps'. The gang in Possilpark, called the Border, laboured under a more accurate title given them by their rivals, namely, 'the Clatty Dozen', who 'hadnae a stitch o' gear'. A further charge levelled against them was that they 'couldnae rise tae a pair o' Levi's'.

Tim's reference group for clothes was the teenage record scene. One half hour in the week, 7.30 to 8pm on a Thursday evening, was sacred in his eyes. The groups, the comperes, and the dancers appearing in Top of the Pops were the final arbiters of taste and the supreme creators of fashion. Often the music was secondary to earnest discussions on the latest 'gear' of the leading performers. Howard Jones (1967, p.143) emphasises the importance of clothes to these adolescent boys:

> Their solidarity is important to them, and a uniform both strengthens that solidarity and gives them continuous and reassuring proof of its existence. But their interest in their appearance goes much further than this. Boys, who seem otherwise to lay great emphasis upon their masculinity and toughness, will give as much thought to the cloth and cut of their suits as any woman. They will also spend hours and a good deal of money at the hairdresser's and a good deal of time in front of the mirror – before going out to join their friends at the café, or out in the street. Not only does this show how skin-deep their male confidence really is, but it seems to hint at an enforced withdrawal on their part, back to infantile narcissism. Lacking love from other people, they must compensate by cherishing themselves.

Another focal concern of the Glasgow boys was the capacity to deliver 'brilliant patter' (this pronounced 'pa'er'). They shared this concern with the adult community of Maryhill, where I noticed, for example, an advertisement chalked up in the window of a local greengrocer. 'Fresh Grapefruit', it proclaimed, 'Stolen only last night.'

At first, I found their jokes amusing. But as I came to know the boys better, I realised their witticisms were even more repetitive than those of most other people. For example, there was one remark which was reserved for a scrawny female of the Twiggy type: 'I've seen mair fat oan a cold chip.' Every time a girl of slender proportions passed, this phrase was trotted out. Other clichés in conversation were: the vulgar simile, 'she's goat a face like a badger's arse.' Tim's standard reply to enquiries as to his intentions on release from the approved school, 'Ah'm goin' straight – straight tae a screwin' joab'; and the regular metaphor for a 'boay oan the goofies', was 'a fart in a trance'.

I would not claim that my highly subjective selection of their banter is recorded correctly. The constant repetition was of considerable help, but their general inarticulateness hampered me considerably. Although on each occasion, I committed to paper my recollections shortly after leaving the gang, mistakes are inevitable. Big Dave Malloy expressed some of his aggressive feelings towards me verbally. Towards Christmas when my reputation was at its lowest, Dave remarked amid laughter: 'If ye wur dyin' fae lack o' breath, Ah wouldnae fart in yir face.' A variation of his on the same theme was: 'Woudnae' gee ye a pat oan the back if he hid convulsions.'

The gang wit was unquestionably Big Fry, 'the boay wi' aw the answers'. His verbal felicities won him the title of 'pa'er merchant' and, after one of his conversational flourishes, he was invariably asked: 'Whaur dae ye get yir pa'er fae?' One of his interventions I hope will do him justice. Beano, as we sat in a pub one evening, was describing an incident in his class the day before. The teacher, talking to school-leavers on the glories of medieval Florentine sculpture, had mentioned a word which Beano pronounced as 'ali-baster', and the class had dissolved in laughter, as our group now did. Harry Johnstone, thinking that the joke was over, screamed in disbelief: 'Aw, naw. Beat it! There's nae such word.' Beano assured him of its existence, and, as though to rout Harry completely, he asked him what it meant. The ensuing silence was broken by Big Fry who volunteered the definition: 'A darkie wi'oot a Da.'

Their idea of crisp, trenchant 'pa'er' was to say to young boys or girls, 'Take a fast cab!' or 'Blow a fuse!' when their company was not desired. To older 'hangers-on' like the epileptic Davie Wilson the phrase was 'Get snazzled' (i.e. castrated). Younger children were silenced with the admonition: 'Buy stickin' plaster fur yir mouth.' The version used to adolescents was: 'Button it, queer arse.' A more military-sounding expression was also fashionable: 'Awa' an' take a regimental fuck tae yirsel'.'

I return for a final time to rhyming slang, which is certainly not exclusive either to gangs or to Glasgow. Their own idiomatic expressions, however, have a fascination of their own. Scars were 'Mars Bars' and Mods were 'Sods'. One phrase baffled me completely and I had to prise the explanation from Tim at the cost of intense embarrassment to him. 'Geein' oot hammies in the remand' involved the standard difficulties caused by an abbreviation which I explained with the phrase 'jist yir Donald'. Here 'hammies' turned out to be a shortened form of 'ham-shanks' which rhymes with 'wanks'. But my own favourite among these examples of rhyming slang is typical of Glasgow humour in that it is a neat combination of obscenity and religious bigotry. The gang thought that, because of her promiscuity, Sanny Lawrence would one day end up in Black Street (which formerly housed Glasgow's VD clinic), since they suspected her of carrying 'a dose of the John Knox'.

In one particular set of circumstances their words became almost ritualistic. This happened when other boys started 'actin' fly' or 'comin' wide' and challenges had to be issued. Even within the approved school the fear of being tricked or made to look foolish made the saying, 'Don't come fly, pal', the most frequent sentence in their vocabulary. The use of the word 'pal' was intriguing; I heard it tacked on to such unlikely openings as 'goaney shatter ye, pal', or 'goaney bust ye, pal'. But faced with an enemy, the phraseology changed to: 'Dae ye want yir go? Jist you an' me. Anytime. Ah'm goaney go *right* tae toon wi' yir nut.' If squaring up to a rival team, the boys shouted almost hysterically: 'Dae youse want tae mess? Dae youse want tae go *right* ahead? Youse are goaney cop yir whack. Goaney cut yir heid *right* aff yir boad-ey.' Tim's own war-cry was: 'Young Team! Young Team! Forty rapid in the stomik!' All this was shouted when the fighting was about to break out.

If insults were being hurled in a slanging match like the one I witnessed in a dance hall between the Young Team and the Barnes Road, then their respective mothers were introduced as a matter of course. One such exchange went as follows:

'Aye, yir maw.'

'Aye, yir maw's in the 'Grove waitin' oan a psychey report.'

A very similar pattern of behaviour is reported by many American observers. One of them (WB Miller, 1958) defines 'ranking' or 'doin' the dozens' as involving 'two antagonists who vie with each other in the exchange of increasingly inflammatory insults, with incestuous and perverted sexual relations with the mother a dominant theme'. Harrison Salisbury (1959, p.52) refers to the practice as 'mother swearing', and Yablonsky (1967, pp.229-30) writes of one type of New York gang boy who 'will approach a stranger with the taunt, "What did you say about my mother?" An assault is then delivered upon the victim before he can respond to the question ... '. Hans Toch (1969, p.192ff.), commenting upon the stereotyped behaviour of 'playing the dozens', sees a striking parallel in the duelling among German university students, and jousting among medieval knights who uttered a 'prescribed sequence of insults' before each encounter.

Ritualised actions were also very much part of any challenge. One gesture in particular, made from the top of buses and from the other side of streets, will be difficult to capture in words. I would call it the 'Come oan, then' gesticulation. To the accompaniment of these words, the hands were outstretched, palm upwards, and the fingers moved up and down as if beckoning the opposition to approach. The final stage of the hand movement came when the boy drew his two index fingers across his cheeks in imitation of slashing razors. Two 'Mars Bars' were being wished on the adversary's face.

Some of the expressions used by the gang boys have lasted 40 years since the time of the Razor Kings described in *No Mean City*. Phrases like 'Ah'm gled', 'Ah'm no' carin'' remain the same; Glasgow words like 'kip shop', 'the busies', 'bein' carted', 'two thousand-handed', 'the slummies', 'flymen', and 'winchin'' have also remained unchanged. But in the 1920s in Glasgow, 'leaders off' meant something quite different from gang leader. In those days the local dancing champions at the minor dance halls 'led off' at the beginning of each number. This may be the origin of the modern gang king's title 'leader aff'.

The third and last topic for this chapter I have entitled 'The Writing on the Wall'. This is the one feature of gang life which all Glaswegians have taken cognisance of, mainly because it is virtually impossible to walk the streets even of the centre of the city without one's eyes being accosted by such slogans as 'Tongs, ya Bass', 'Wild Young Derry, 1690', 'Toon Boys', and 'Randy Andy fae the Pak'.

Some of the graffiti are truly memorable. On a tenement wall in Maryhill Road I read the proud boast, 'WE ARE THE PEPOLE'. In Possilpark, deep in the housing scheme, amid homes that look more like slovenly-kept barracks, a call for unity and loyalty was emblazoned at a close-mouth:

One Team
One Scheam
One Uncle

Another slogan, popular with the gangs, which I have deciphered at locations as far apart as Parkhead Cross and Bilsland Drive, reads: 'Born to raise hell'. The ultimate in self-advertisement came with the proclamation: 'Me. OK'

To turn to the slogans and emblems of particular gangs, the largest and more disfiguring one among many contenders was the sentence painted up in letters a foot high on a street corner in Bridgeton.

> SPUR OK
> THE PHANTOM PAINTER
> STRIKES AGAIN. THE
> POLICE'S WORK HAS BEEN
> <u>IN VAIN</u>

The walls of Maryhill and Possilpark were and are marked in similar fashion. There, the Protestant element had replied to 'Wild Young Catholic Team' with a three-letter word of intense topical importance, namely 'KAI'. In blue paint with letters four feet high, garage doors and pub walls carried this word – the Christian name of a Danish footballer who had scored the winning goal for Rangers in a cup-final reply with Celtic. The Young Team waited until the 11th of July to strike back. That night, armed with green, white and golden paint, they sallied forth to brighten up the local Masonic Halls. Both Dave Malloy and Big Fry, the two 'Prodisants' in a 'Karflick' gang, joined in the fun. In addition to redecorating the building, the gang tore down the wire guards protecting the windows and smashed the glass. All this must have put the marchers in fine fettle on the glorious twelfth, particularly when they saw the main doors of their headquarters daubed with the saying 'Catholic Young Team Rules'. The usual, abbreviated form 'CYT' had been expanded in full to cause the maximum damage.

In the Young Team's pitch the commonest slogan was:

> FUCK
> ALL
> CALTON
> BASTARDS

Second in frequency came 'YMF' or 'MYT', the full versions of which read 'Young Mental Fleet' and 'Mental Young Team'. On some walls the word 'Mental' had not even been abbreviated. The phrase 'Young Trio' was seldom seen without being preceded by the word 'Mental' as well. And one of Harry Johnstone's phrases, 'Ah'm goin' radio', was explained to me by Tim as an abbreviation of 'Radio Rental', chosen to rhyme with 'mental'. That the boys *themselves* should choose the words 'mental', 'crackpot', and 'psychey' to describe their gang is indeed surprising.

Gallous gear, brilliant patter and the writing on the wall

The names of nearly every gang member appeared in various colours on the buildings, lampposts, bridges, bus shelters, telephone boxes, Post Office pillars and hoardings in the district. 'Dougie', a boy close to the in-group, had decorated the area liberally with his name the night before appearing on a charge which he knew would sent him to borstal. But some names (Tim's in particular, and the Malloys' in general), were not to be seen on display anywhere in the district. Tim was firm on the point that neither he nor any of his brothers had ever written their names on walls. This was stated as though it was a point of honour with him. In fact, he continued by referring to the Blue Angels, the Rocker gang in Maryhill, and to a gang in Bridgeton called The Nunny, part of whose mystique was that 'nane o' their boays write oan wa's.' Not once did I spot Tim's name publicly displayed but one curious fact I did notice. Tim was inordinately proud of his good looks. He told me frequently of his close resemblance to the pop star Steve Marriot of The Small Faces and that numerous girls had commented upon this likeness. A number of entrances to closes in Maryhill were disfigured by the name of this young singer. Of course, literally anyone could have been responsible, but I have often wondered.

With chalk, magic markers, but most often with stolen tins of aerosol spray paint, the pitch was marked out with slogans for all to read. Knives and tools of all sorts were used for engraving the name of the ruling team on any surface capable of taking the inscription. Even the gents at the Close Theatre bears witness to the efforts of Glasgow's literati to learn to live with – and make light of – the gang problem, in the form of a scribbled slogan: 'Ibsen, ya Bass!'

14
Malkies, goofies and the busies

HERE AGAIN I draw together three disparate subjects, their only connection being that by their very nature (weapons, drugs and the police) this chapter is necessarily selective. The more spectacular the subject, the more dramatic the occasion, the less am I able to record.

The variety of weapons I saw was manifold, the types I heard of legendary. Hatchets, hammers, knives, meat cleavers, meat hooks, bayonets, machetes, open razors, sharpened tail-combs, all these were the regular chibs. Bottles of all sorts and tumblers and bricks and sticks were employed in emergencies. Berettas, double-barrelled shotguns, swords, scimitars, and hand-grenades were lovingly described, but mercifully never appeared in my presence.

The sources for these arms were also various. The home provided such items as the bread knife, the coal hammer and the poker. Antique shops were 'screwed' and their armouries raided. A military store was reputed to have been emptied by Dick Stevenson. But apart from the home, the place of employment seemed to be the main supply depot. One job above all others was coveted in this respect. The butcher's boy had access to the most terrifying of weapons both for his own use and for sale to his mates. The approved schools continue unwittingly to place boys, known to be gang members, in the meat trade.

To be more particular, Dougie, the borstal boy I never met, had always been attached to hatchets. Convicted of carrying an offensive weapon, and having served his term of detention, he bought a new hatchet on his release and went out at night 'tae break it in'. He walked into the centre of the city, claiming a total of 33 windows on his way, and was finally arrested 'fur a daft wan doon the toon'.

'Big M', whom I found myself calling 'wan o' oor big boays', dreamed up the following ruse to trick the police. His weapon was a claw-hammer, carefully wrapped in brown paper and string, so that, if stopped, he could pretend to have just bought the tool for his work. I do not know what ironmonger's he could have cited as being open at three o'clock on a Sunday morning.

The Malloy brothers had earned the revered title of 'chib-men'. This was no honorary title, but one accorded few members of any gang. Not everyone 'kerried' by any means, and even amongst those who did, some used their weapons mainly on property, while others carried them only intermittently. Those who carried chibs or malkies (i.e. any kind of weapon) more often than not, and who had used them 'successfully' on people, were 'chib-men'. The Malloys boasted of being able to outwit any policeman who searched them; Tim, for instance, claimed to have been 'raked' one night while 'kerryin'' and to have escaped arrest for possessing an offensive weapon. The trick he had picked up from his elder brothers, none of whom had ever been caught in possession. Before leaving the house, John used to tie a short blade to his wrist with a piece of string; he then concealed it by rolling down his shirt sleeve over the knife which rested alongside his forearm. Tim adopted the same technique, but in addition, was fond of carrying his favourite weapon – an open, lock-back razor. Harry Johnstone thought this 'sleekit'. At nights when they met, Harry would ask Tim, 'Are ye kerryin'?' 'Me kerryin'? Are ye kiddin'?' Yet in a fight, I was told, 'a wee blade comes oot oan the sleekit – a wee loak-back or somethin'.'

I asked Tim how he kept his parents from knowing about his weapons. Mick and he shared a room, the door of which was always locked – 'ma Maw wouldnae dare go in.' The guns and knives were hidden in the dresser in this bedroom. Bill, the oldest son, had been in the habit of leaving his favourite malky, a coal hammer, in the fireplace and had thus been hoist with his own petard. For, climbing in the window one Saturday night, 'steamin' he wis', he had been hit on the leg by his own weapon. His future brother-in-law had been sitting in the front room, 'winchin'' in the dark with one of the Malloy girls. Thinking someone was breaking into the house, he had hurled the hammer at the intruder and broken Bill's leg.

If the reports can be believed, the parents of some of these boys also recognised the less conventional uses of the domestic coal hammer. At the start of the 'battle' with the Barnes Road, Joe Stevenson was sitting at home with his mother, watching television. The father of the family ('auld man's mental', was Tim's comment) burst into the house from his pub and announced: 'Thir's a ba'le doon the road.' Handing Joe the hammer, Mr Stevenson exhorted his son: 'Get doon that road an' soart oot thae Barnes Road.' The Young Team spoke of the father of the Stevenson family as having been a Razor King and a gang leader in the 30s. With his eldest son Dick now a King in his own right, talk of a hereditary monarchy in Glasgow is not too fanciful.

One Wednesday evening some members of the gang had gone out drinking. As the pub closed, a 'kerry-oot' was bought, but the screw-tops and cans of beer were not so much for drinking as for use as missiles. The group had charged up Maryhill Road, knocking pedestrians out of their way ('makes ye feel great, man'), and hurling the beer through shop windows. Men's and ladies' outfitters were prized as targets. For here, not only were the windows smashed and the displays wrecked, but blades were produced and the tailor's dummies were beheaded.

Moving in a group with the gang was always a nerve-racking experience. One boy or other would run forward and dance provocatively in front of a girl on her own and pull her hair or head-scarf, murmuring: 'Dae ye hiv' plenty o' love juice?' Anyone walking up the middle of the pavement was jostled on to the road or into a shop front. The slightest turning-up of the nose by the offended party could spark off violence. Thus did the Young Team rule their pitch. Within the team itself all differences were supposed to be settled by 'square-goes', weapons being reserved for all out-groups. Tim's treatment of Big Dim (mentioned in Chapter 8) is just one of a long list of exceptions to the rule. A 'square-go', although the phrase itself is not used, is neatly described in McArthur and Long's *No Mean City* (1964, p.121):

> It is to be noted that a 'fair fight' between gang champions is one in which nobody interferes, at least as long as both men are on their feet. But it is fighting, not boxing. There are no rules and no rounds and no weapons except fists and feet. It is sheer primitive battle that ends-and can only end-when one man is battered into senselessness.

The term amongst the New York gangs is apparently 'a fair one' defined as a 'fight between one or more members of a gang in which weapons are not involved' (New York City Youth Board, 1960, p.295).

There is not much to be said about my second topic for this chapter, namely 'Goofies'. I neither came into contact with, nor heard of any gang organised round the use or peddling of drugs. Tim's silence on this subject was almost total. Only after I had been involved with the gang for three months was Tim prepared to talk to me about drugs; and it took him another month to admit to having taken them in the past. In fact, he was bringing them into the approved school when he returned from leave and taking them in small doses – to counteract boredom, he told me. Appearing to condone this practice was part of the price I had to pay for Tim's silence about my own activities; for, although making clear my reasons for condemning such a habit, my hands were tied as far as informing the authorities was concerned. I also believed that Tim's confession should be accorded the confidentiality normally extended to privileged information. Tim himself was worried about the effects drugs could have on him. For days after he returned from leave, his eyes were puffy and swollen. Every morning he could be seen rubbing them with cold water in an effort to reduce the swelling. 'Eyes like tea-cups' was the gang expression.

I did not learn the source of their drug supply from Tim, but from the general conversation of the gang. A member of the Cowcaddens Toi, 'Fingers' by name, worked in a chemist's shop and stole pills of all sorts to sell to the gangs. The lounge bar of a specific pub was the meeting place, or alternatively, the Granada dance hall. The names they had for the drugs were: French Blues, Black and Whites, Black Bombers (the most common name, irrespective of colour). Big Fry tried to impress us with his chemical knowledge: 'Black Bombers – Perpexedrine or Dexedrine's the legit' name.' The normal price was two shillings or two-and-sixpence each. Fergie remembered the days when they were a shilling. When Fingers first raised his prices, Fergie had remonstrated with him. By way of explanation the boy replied: 'Ye know there's inflation in the country an' aw that'.

The habit of drug-taking seemed to be widespread among the leaders of the gang. All feared 'the horrors' which followed days of drug-taking, and the common practice was to save one pill for the 'come-doon'. Four to six pellets would be taken together and washed down with cheap wine or beer. Beano once insisted to me that he had just swallowed as many as eight – this after a night's drinking. His subsequent behaviour gave me no cause to disbelieve him. With no control over his limbs, he staggered and stumbled, mouthing inarticulate nonsense. No one, apart from myself, thought of taking him to hospital.

At the party in January, Tim was presented with 20-odd pills and took four right away. A few of these half-red, half-black pellets were pressed upon me and I was invited to sample these 'Black Bombers'. Putting two in my mouth I stuck them to the inside of my cheek and drank deeply from a can of lager. Only one of the pills stayed in place and I spat it out at the first available opportunity. But by then only the capsule was left and the white powder covered my tongue.

This experience provided me with the opening I needed and for once Tim spoke at length on the subject. After 'bein' in the clouds', he dreaded 'the horrors' the following morning. 'Ye imagine everythin' yir afrighted fur. Chibbin' some-wan tae death in the street wi' everyboady at the windaes watchin' whose dain' it – and the polis chasm' ye, and you runnin' fur miles an' miles.'

Hard line drugs, such as heroin, however, lay outside the gang's experience; nor did they know anything of cannabis and they had only read about LSD. But at the party both boys and girls took pills of all shapes and colours like Smarties, in sheer ignorance of their ingredients or of their effects. Harry Johnstone, with his antipathy to all things medical, refused to take drugs and was unique in this respect. To the others this reluctance was considered to be a further example of Harry 'shitin' hissel.' As with so many other activities, Dick Stevenson was the acknowledged champion drug-taker, ready to boast at a moment's notice of the number of occasions on which he had had his stomach pumped; drug-taking was yet another way of proving his masculinity.

The local 'busies', with whom the boys had most contact, had all been given nicknames. The districts of Maryhill and Possilpark produced such characters as 'Cross Swords' and 'Big Johnny Last Chance', so called because their opening gambits were invariably, 'Hiv' Ah no cross swords wi' youse afore?' and, 'Right, yir oan yir last chance.' These two were as well liked by the boys as it is possible for a Glasgow policeman to be. Others like 'Flappy', because of his protruding ears, 'Black Arse', and 'Big Gonk' (a word normally reserved for the inmates of the Lennox Castle Institution for the mentally handicapped), were involved in a love-hate relationship with the gang in that they tried to make friendly contact with the boys who for their part detested and despised them. But the very fact that the local constables were given nicknames at all suggests, I think, that they were not totally abhorrent to the boys, in whose eyes the real villains of the piece were what they called the riot squad police who were total strangers to them. At the time of this study, such police arrived *en masse* in Land Rovers from headquarters; later, the police employed mini-vans and 'personnel carriers' to rush numbers of men to 'group disorders'.

A phrase of their most 'brillian' pa'er' was used almost exclusively to the police and never failed to achieve the desired objective – a loss of temper on the part of the 'busy'. It was an intensified version of the pejorative dismissal of young boys and girls, 'Away an' pap peas at the moon!' The police were treated to the more full-blooded, 'Away an' pap shite at the moon!', or more common still, 'Pap shite at yersel'.' Their demeanour in dealing with the police was always uncooperative, hostile, and abusive, and it is exactly this fractious behaviour which Piliavin and Briar (1964) have shown (in a Californian study of police encounters with juveniles) is the major criterion for determining what action a policeman will take.

The sergeant, Jimmy Grey, 'knows uzz aw – knows everyboady's name', and his favourite charge was said to be for loitering. 'A big squad o' boays' would stand at the corner, staring across at the policemen on the other side of the road. On one such afternoon, we were eyeing up two sergeants, one of whom was Jimmy Grey. The process continued for full ten minutes, at the end of which the sergeants were joined by Big Johnny Last Chance and the 'polis' crossed over. On being moved off the corner, Tim curled his lip in disdain. 'Watch the material, Mac', he threatened. This proved too much for one of the sergeants. Grabbing Tim by the front of his casual, he strained in an effort to lift him off the ground with one hand. The chain round Tim's neck broke and a tiny golden cross fell onto the pavement. Big Johnny, later identified as 'a Tim' (i.e. a Roman Catholic), intervened, saying, 'Aye, well, we'll ha'e less o' that.' The situation was thus saved from deteriorating.

With all members of the police force, life for the gang was a constant struggle to better them in argument. A typical exchange was reported by Big Fry. Arriving in an ugly mood one evening, he launched into his grievance:

'Ah wis pulled up doon at the Croas'.

'Whit are ye dain' oot?', he says.

'Ah'm workin', labourin',' Ah says.

'That's a joab fur a man, no' a wean.'

'Aye, an' that's how you'll no' get a joab at it yirsel'.'

'Get up that fuckin' road an' keep aff ma pitch,' he says.'

A different type of approach to the police was taken by Joe Stevenson. Ordered to move on or be arrested, he put his left hand on his waist, stuck out his elbow, and began mincing up the pavement. In his best 'toaffie' voice he would squeak: 'Ah wis jist goin' up tae ma boyfriend's.' Big Sheila indulged in the same sort of 'mickeytaking'.

Charges against the police were legion: everything from common or garden assault and battery to homosexual interference. Being struck in the face with a baton, being made to sleep in soiled blankets, being robbed of one's possessions – all these accusations and countless more I listened to. The staffs of remand homes, approved schools and borstals were also alleged to have perpetrated the vilest of crimes. Every so often, however, a story was told which had the ring of truth about it – a very subjective judgement, I agree. One such involved Beano. Separated from the others during a skirmish with the YRB, he had been stopped by two young constables, 'two fuckin' tea-boays, they wir'. As they jostled him into a close, Beano called out to two passing women, one of whom recognised him. To stop the kicking which was aimed at his groin and belly, Beano pleaded that he had ulcers and called upon Mrs Thomson, a neighbour of his, to verify the story. When the woman did as she was asked, the police officers desisted. They claimed (and rightly) that Beano had been part of a disorderly crowd and they were taking the opportunity to sort him out.

The boys sought to convince each other with endless stories of the brutality, duplicity and corruption of the police. My concern in describing and discussing the events of the night the inner core of the Young Team were taken to the police station is neither to accuse nor to pillory the police but to render with fidelity the phenomenon under consideration. The police violence I witnessed that night could not be called sadistic cruelty nor was it an isolated case of the police being too handy with their fists. Rather, I formed the impression that such police action was a calculated and standard method of control. The whole operation was conducted in an efficient and workmanlike manner, and, on the authority of the boys, was repeated at irregular intervals. I feel inclined to believe this claim because their matter-offact acceptance of the visit to the police station struck a truer chord than their wilder flights of fancy about police practice. Furthermore, I judged that the attempts of the police to combat the growing incidence of adolescent gangs carrying, brandishing, and occasionally using offensive weapons in the streets was more than a spontaneous exercise in law-keeping; it was a reaction to the strident pressures of both press and public. The mood of the majority of Glasgow's citizens was so inflamed at the time that, even if they had been acquainted with the treatment given to gang boys, they would have regretted only that the police acted with such restraint. Their tactics were to make periodic raids on these gangs, hold them for questioning, and demonstrate in a very primitive way who was really in command of the neighbourhood. The defect of such a policy of containment was, of course, that it was counterproductive, for it increased the boys' personal sense of outrage, it embittered their feeling towards the police even more, and it stiffened their resolve to strike back. I let the boys speak for themselves:

'The polis is aye tryin' tae come wide wi' me. No' supposed tae hit boays under age wi' their batons but they dae. Wan o' oor boays goat his heid split wi' a baton an' wis goaney charge the busy but the polis drapped his charges against the boay, the fat rat.'

On another occasion I heard the following: 'If you've no' goat a blade oan ye, they throw a chib at ye an' when ye catch it, they say tae ye: "Right, yir dabs [i.e. fingerprints] are oan it, we're chargin' ye".'

Or again: 'They slipped a loak-back [i.e. open razor] intae ma brither's toap poakit. An' they tried tae stoap him bendin' ower tae get rid o' the blade wi'oot touchin' it wi' his haun's.'

There were also innuendoes about a 'crooked cop'. 'Big Ken' McDonald was taxed with 'raking' boys on their arrest and pocketing whatever he found. His forte was surprising them during their housebreaking. The gang alleged that he then chose what he wanted from the stolen goods or from the household generally; and only when his greed was sated, had the boys hopes of being turned loose. These stories should be treated with caution. I have recorded them from the conviction that they have a value in that they were taken seriously by the boys themselves, who attempted to justify their own behaviour by quoting them.

Tim's views on the police were unvarnished: 'Hate them, wi' thir riot stick' an' thir dug vans.' The latter were vehicles used by the riot squad, some of whom were accompanied by alsatians on leashes. What infuriated the Young Team so much was the open contempt the riot squad had for gang members. The boys were convinced that even the local police singled them out for questioning whenever the slightest breach of the law had been committed. Their sense of justice was offended by the police constantly 'digging them up', forcing them to move on, and accusing them of all manner of crimes. They even objected to being sworn at by the police, their attitude being that, although swearing was standard practice for gang boys, it ill became policemen. They were only beginning to appreciate that their 'uniform', their hair style, their previous convictions, the area they lived in, the criminal families they came from and the fact that they were known by name to the police, all made them obvious targets for investigation. Werthman and Piliavan (1967, p.81) have emphasised the depth of feeling among Negro gang boys in San Francisco about this issue: ' ... gang boys thus tend to regard their more or less permanent place in the situation of suspicion with considerable resentment that quite often spills over into outrage.' The two groups appeared to me to be locked in eternal combat, the police treating the boys like dirt and the boys goading and taunting their opponents at every opportunity.

Tim's attitude about 'grassing' to the police was exemplified in his conversation with Sergeant Grey late in January. 'Big Jimmy' was quick to see the bruises on Tim's face and enquired:

'Whit happened tae you?'

'Ah wis roon' the back wi' this bird an' Ah tried tae molest her, but she goat intae me wi' her haun'-bag.' The policeman laughed in scepticism, so Tim continued:

'Naw. I goat set aboot by a gang o' daft boays.'

'Dae ye want tae make a statement?'

'Naw, its jist yir Donald.'

'Weil, fuck aff then', said the sergeant in exasperation, 'don't come tae us if ye get really chibbed.'

Tim and I, the only witnesses to this scene, walked on in silence. Tim turned to me and protested: 'If ye dish it oot, ye've goat tae take it.'

To the gang, then, the police and all others whose task it is to enforce the norms of society, are brutal, corrupt and stupid. To Matza and Sykes (1957, p.668) this condemnation of the condemners, this rejection of the rejectors is one of the ways delinquents seek to justify their deviant behaviour; it is one of the 'techniques of neutralization'. The authors explain:

The delinquent shifts the focus of attention from his own deviant acts to the motives and behavior of those who disapprove of his violations. His condemners, he may claim, are hypocrites, deviants in disguise, or impelled by personal spite.

A final word on this theme. The boys were aware that the police in the area were adopting disguises in order to learn more about the delinquent sub-culture. Two police officers were spotted at a distance even by the most naive, because beneath their denim jackets and football scarves the boys could see their black ties and light blue shirts. But their fondest memories were of an old sergeant who toiled under the affectionate nickname of 'Bull-nose'. ('Bull' here rhymes with 'Mull'). Bull-nose had donned the costume of a street-sweeper in an attempt to eavesdrop on the conversation of the gang at the corner. Recognising their adversary 'dain' his midge-man', they had pelted him with offal.

15
Tim

THE CENTRAL CHARACTER in this work is unquestionably Tim. I want now to draw together some disparate strands in his make-up, to record the little I found out about his parents, his family and the picture he had of himself.

We fell to talking one day about his parents, who have lived in Maryhill 'aw their days'. Both had been born there and Tim had been brought into the world in their present house in the High Street. Neither his 'Ma or Da' were working; his immediate and totally false explanation was that 'they've goat money', and so did not need to work. Tim came closer to the truth when he later remarked: 'See ma Da – he's a cripple. Weil, no' a cripple esactly but he cannae walk.' According to Beano, the father had been employed in a rubber factory and had there contracted some disease which had left him crippled. I witnessed this disability myself as well as the quality of the relationship between father and son. Arriving with me at the door of his home one evening, Tim hammered on the woodwork. Recounting the incident later, Tim felt he had been 'waitin' fur 'oors fur somewan tae open the door'. It was opened well within five minutes by an old man in a torn grey jersey and slippers who hobbled forward to greet us. Brushing him aside, Tim complained about his tardiness: 'Whit fuckin' kept ye?'

There was no love lost between them. 'See when ma auld man's bevied, he's a pure needle. Tae Mick he says, "Aw, here's the fuckin' borstal boay." Ah says tae Mick, "Yir no' goaney let him aff wi' that? Hit him!" Then the ba'le starts. Every Setirday night it's the same.' The only favourable comment he had to make about his father was: 'He still shouts the odds fae the windae when there's a ba'le oan. "Get right *intae* it, Tim", he says.'

His mother comes from a family of 12 and had herself produced nine children. Tim was called 'the baby' by his mother and he reacted violently to this: 'Wid that no gee ye a rid neck?' This privileged position in his mother's eyes had compensations; she had often seen him drinking in pubs and turned a blind eye. She had heard that he had fathered an illegitimate baby and had said nothing. 'Whit's yir Maw fur?' he questioned me rhetorically. 'Maws are fur tappin', man. That's aw aboot it. Fur buyin' ye claes an' geein' ye money.'

On the only occasion I was in Tim's home, I met Mrs Malloy. Excusing Tim's treatment of her husband, she commented, 'he's a right rage, aw right', by which I took her to mean that he was quick-tempered and liable to flare up within seconds. 'It's aw the wae ye talk tae him', she continued, 'taken the right wae, ye can get the Kingdom o' Heaven oot o' him.' A social welfare officer from the approved school reported that, in answer to his questions about Tim's violent behaviour, Mrs Malloy remarked: I see nuthin', an' I hear nuthin'. As long as it doesnae come tae ma door, I'm no carin'.' As recorded earlier, Tim absconded from the approved school a week after being admitted to it in December 1965. The headmaster informed his mother in a letter, the relevant sentence of which runs, 'It appears that Tim was a little disgruntled at not receiving a visit.' The boy had been away from home since the middle of October. The school files have it that the only visit Tim received during his 18 months in the school was a short one from his mother in April 1966.

Yet the day he was committed to an approved school, his mother had been in court. She had offered to buy him a new suit before he was dispatched to the school from the remand home. 'Ah refused', Tim told me, 'Ah says tae her, "Ah'll take command o' wan masel'." That's how I annoy ma Ma ... refusin' her when she wants tae gee me things.'

He gloried in the infamy of his brothers of whom he was also wary. Mick, while drunk, had beaten him up on several occasions and Tim's politic behaviour in his presence made me doubly cautious and circumspect. The relationship with John, who was closer in age to Tim, I judged to be altogether more easy-going and intimate. Mick was phlegmatic, morose, withdrawn; John, never to be called 'Johnnie' or 'Jack', was bright, boisterous and explosive. 'John kin take a joke but no' Mick.' Beano remembered how he and John had stood trial on the same day. John had been dealt with first and as he was being returned to his cell, Beano had called to him, 'Whit did ye get?' 'Ma borstal,' John replied. 'Laughin' he wis, laughin' an' laughin',' continued Beano. He himself was sentenced to 28 days: 'Ma Maw wis cryin' an' aw. Ah wisnae. Ah jist went back doon tae ma cell an' slept. Ah wisnae botherin' ma arse.' To Tim's mind, John and Mick shared one saving grace: a propensity to go berserk if he, Tim, was involved in a fight. I suspect – without any real evidence – that Tim played on this to implicate his brothers and their mates in his private quarrels. It was no excess of brotherly love which brought Mick and John to Tim's aid. Rather they construed any attack upon their younger brother as an attack upon *their* status.

As he grew up, Tim had been in the regular habit of attending the youth club run by the local Protestant school, there being no Catholic equivalent. For three years he had been a regular member until the opening at the end of 1965 of the non-denominational Kelvin Youth Centre. There were ping-pong tables and a five-aside indoor football pitch. Membership cost two shillings for the year and the youth club leader was energetic and popular. Once, twice and sometimes three times a week the gang invaded the place, but only to participate in the games or maybe paint a slogan or two on the outer walls. Monday or Thursday were the regular nights, with Friday and Saturday reserved for going 'doon the toon fightin'.' On the Sunday afternoon that I met the gang, they were planning to go along to the club after Tim and I had departed. But even this well-equipped centre failed to provide sufficient outlet for the aggressive drives of the gang's hard core members, though it catered well for the nominal, peripheral member of the gang. But, to Tim's mind, the centre closed too early, leaving him and his mates on the streets. It was then that suggestions like, "Mon doon the Barnes Road', cropped up.

Albert Cohen (1955, p.184) sees no magical therapeutic virtue in the provision of facilities for 'wholesome recreation'. And long before Cohen, Truxal (1929) had found in Manhattan that the provision of recreational facilities had little effect on delinquency rates. Robison (1964, p.685), commenting on this and similar studies, makes the point that in certain neighbourhoods delinquency *is* recreation for so many boys. The argument is continued by Henry D McKay (1959, p.183) who writes: 'organized recreation and delinquency are not mutually exclusive activities.' McKay, in this article, quotes Ethel Shanas who concluded, after an investigation into recreation and delinquency in five areas of Chicago, that delinquent boys spend more time in recreational activities than non-delinquent boys. Another reason why 'recreation programmes' will not of themselves prevent delinquency is that 'participation in organised recreation represents such a small proportion of the total life experience of the child'. Translating McKay's own conclusion into British terms, to suggest that a boy will not be delinquent because he plays football is no more valid than to say that he will not play football because he is delinquent. He may do either, neither, or both. And in my experience the Glasgow gang boy does both.

Tim himself certainly saw no prospect of change in the gang culture of Glasgow nor in his own life. Being presented in class with the question, 'If you could start your life all over again, what changes would you make in it? What would you keep the same?' as the title of a composition, Tim wrote the following:

> If I were to start my life over again I would stop stealing and drinking and I would go to Mass every week. I would not go about with gangs. I would help the police in every way I could. I would do everything my mummy told me to, and I would not go about with girls. If somebody in my class did something wrong I would tell the teacher right away, and if I saw somebody breaking into a shop I would go to

the police and at Xmas I would get Mummy and Daddy and my brothers and sisters a present. Well that is how I would lead my life. O.K.

He was beside himself with delight as he saw me read this sustained caricature of the strongest-held values in our society. Tim's essay gives evidence of what Cohen (1955, pp.129-30) calls 'the hallmark of the delinquent subculture', namely, 'the explicit and wholesale repudiation of middle-class standards and the adoption of their very antithesis ... The member of the delinquent subculture plays truant because "good" middle-class (and working-class) children do not play truant.'

Tim's view of himself was already hardened and immutable: 'Ah'm illiterate' was what this boy with an IQ of 105 (and that no doubt depressed) kept insisting time without number. The last class of which he had been a member at school had the title of 'III DF', which he explained was 'the daft class'. He felt that school had rejected him and he in turn rejected school. As I listened to Tim, a remark of Basil Bernstein's came to mind: 'The more rigorously we select, the more we increase the sense of social failure among those whom we do not select.' Presented with class-work which was at all difficult, but within his capacity, Tim gave up in despair: 'Ah'm an eejit, a hauf-wit, Ah cannae dae it. Ah'm stupit – tell me Ah'm stupit, wull ye?' Someone had been doing just that for years.

One of the conclusions which I reached and shall discuss in detail in Chapter 20, was that the core members of the Young Team showed symptoms of what I would call severe maladjustment or personality disorder rather than psychopathology. Yet I find difficulty in answering the question: does this conclusion apply to Tim? I have no hesitation in saying that Dick Stevenson was in need of psychiatric care, but critics could rightly point out that I only managed to strike up an acquaintance with Dick whereas I came to know Tim rather well. A remark of Matza's (1969, p.25), ' ... intimate knowledge of deviant worlds tends to subvert the correctional conception of pathology', has made me wonder whether it is only lack of empathy or knowledge which allows me to label Dick as severely maladjusted.

Though I have reservations about being so dogmatic in Tim's case, he was by no means a placid, stable and well-adjusted boy, as the reader will have gathered already. His response to frustration of any kind was always primitive and physical; he was deeply insecure, fatalistic, and domineering, violent, callous and fearful. On a number of occasions, when I was on night duty at the approved school, the night supervisor and I came upon him shouting and screaming in his sleep. Tim later pretended that these outbursts were deliberate practical jokes meant to provoke members of the staff, but such explanations only revealed his concern not to lose face in front of the other boys in the dormitory and convinced nobody. The state of terror in which we found him was all too real for that.

16
Exit

I AM UNABLE at this point in time to give a full account of my outings in January or to mention all the circumstances which forced me to quit. The following is as full as I can make it. Chapter 10 narrates the events before Christmas, when I was handed a hatchet. I disposed of it at the first opportunity which presented itself, withdrew from the gang over the Christmas period, and then renewed my connection with it on the first suitable Saturday evening in the New Year.

To my great relief the boy who had pressed the weapon upon me, Dave Malloy, was not present. Serving 28 days detention for his part in the battle with the Barnes Road, he was due to be released in two weeks and had sworn vengeance on me for my nonappearance. 'He's gettin' his jaw ripped', had been his constant threat. My days in the gang were numbered.

My reception was cold. Tim, of course, I had already met in the school, but he had been evasive and uncommunicative beyond the simple statement that they had 'shattered thae mugs.' I needed the gang and particularly Beano and Baggy to enlarge on the subject. Walking into the pub, I was confronted with the core members of the gang minus Dave Malloy but including Big Fry, Baggy, and Podgie. Offering to buy pints, I sensed the hostility with which Harry Johnstone, and the newly released Dan McDade, refused my offer. As soon as I could, I expressed regret at missing the battle, explaining how I had been taken hiking and camping with the approved school over the holidays as I had 'nae hame tae go tae'. This was the story I had asked Tim to sow in their minds if asked about my absence. Podgie took up the reference to 'the big fight' and soon the conversation became animated.

When Jack Martin chibbed Marty, the leader of the Barnes Road, during the Christmas holidays, the Young Team had known that this meant open war. But, as the Barnes Road were inferior in numbers and had never ventured much beyond their boundaries before, Tim had felt the initiative lay with him. So he had been surprised to hear one night that the Barnes Road were on the move and heading along Maryhill Road. The pub in which the Young Team were sitting had cleared in a frenetic rush, as boys ran to collect their chibs and rouse the neighbourhood. I am not sure whether the Barnes Road and the Young Rolland Boys advanced deep into Young Team territory by chance or lack of foresight, or whether they were allowed to do so by design; in any case, within 15 minutes of their vanguard being spotted, the Wild

Young Team, numbering 'over a hundred', were on the streets, armed and 'ready to go *right* ahead'. The Barnes Road and their allies were attacked from all sides; bottles and bricks were showered upon them; and Tim, Dave Malloy and others of the in-group led the charge which scattered and routed the opposition. 'The streets wir black wi' boays, runnin' aw ower the place. It wis a laugh,' commented Tim. 'Ye go mad. Ye slash aboot at oaneywan. And that's aw aboot it'.

Big Fry, the boy 'wi' aw the answers', who was easily the most fluent and effusive member of the gang, described the sensation as follows: 'See the feelin' in yir belly goin' intae battle, it's like the feelin' ye have when Rangers are attackin' the Celtic goal. Yir heart's racin', ye feel sick; it's better'n sex.' The others agreed that gang fighting was what really mattered to them; sex came a poor second in their list of priorities.

Considering the number of boys reputed to have been involved, the list of causalties was infinitesimal. WB Miller (1966, p.110) notes the same situation among the gangs he studied in the United States: 'A major objective of gang members was to put themselves in the posture of fighting without actually having to fight.'

Benny of the Barnes Road 'goat twelve boatles ower his nut', and two or three others were said to have been slashed, before Marty yelled to his team: 'Git oan yir sannies' (i.e. 'Get off your marks'). The order was unnecessary, as the invaders were already pouring from the field, diving through closes, and dodging through traffic. The most frightening aspect of the whole affair had been the arrival of the team, moving across the city like a storm cloud, terrifying pedestrians with their weapons and chants, and totally out of the control of the constables on the beat. When the police reinforcements arrived in the shape of the riot squads, the Young Team had also dispersed, with the exception of Dave Malloy, who was 'huckled' while still screaming full-throated challenges in the middle of the street to the 'fuckin' shit-bags' to stand and fight. He had tackled the first few policemen as if they were members of an opposing gang; perhaps his irrational behaviour is explicable in terms of a desperate effort to recover status and position within the gang. Harry Johnstone ended the discussion with a remark, loaded with meaning for me: 'There hid been too many square-goes. *We aw* goat right intae it. An' if ye shit yirsel' in a ba'le, the boays get intae yir heid – wi' weapons.' Honour demanded that the Barnes Road should be invaded for reprisals. I began to prepare Tim for my imminent departure. I had had enough.

In between warlike encounters with other teams, habitual acts of petty delinquency had continued. Dick Stevenson and Mick Malloy had entered a licensed grocer's before Hogmanay and, with pound notes in their hands, had ordered bottles of vodka, whisky, and beer. Although he didn't smoke, Dick asked for 20 cigarettes, as though it were an afterthought. The woman behind the counter turned round to fetch them. Dick, with the bottles already in carrier bags, walked through the door which was held open by expectant members of the Young Team. As the woman screamed for help, Mick leaned across and punched her on the face. To acquire their own stock of drink to welcome in the New Year, the Young Team had concentrated on 'raking' old men leaving pubs with their 'kerryoot'. Following them up side-streets and closes, they had robbed them of their Ne'erday bottle.

The first Saturday night out in January ended with the party referred to in Chapter 12. The following Friday evening, I was informed that Dick Stevenson had fled to London in the company of the faithful Bob Robertson and a few others. He was wanted on three stabbing charges, the assaults having been carried out over the Christmas and New Year period. With the last knifing he had gone too far. In the Young Team's pub where he was well known, he had stabbed a barman who refused to serve him the free drink to which he, as the local King, thought he was entitled. The management had banned both Tim's gang and the Fleet from the premises. Unaware of the ban I sauntered into the place only to be run out by a couple of new waiters who would have struck terror into the heart of Jack Dempsey. I found the gang in the Fleet's pub.

That night I was given yet another good reason for withdrawing from the gang without further delay. John was being released the following weekend, and the family were throwing a 'comin'-oot' party on the Saturday night. While I was always afraid of Tim's brother Mick, who was liable to explode at any time, he was quite decidedly a member of the Fleet and only nodded to members of the Young Team. John, on the other hand, mingled with both gangs indiscriminately. He was over-protective where Tim was concerned, and was bound to inquire about me more closely.

Tim himself provided me with the best get-out line. He had been selected by the headmaster to work outside the school for a few months prior to his release. As I had claimed on my first night out, and in the presence of the gang, to have entered the approved school on the same day as Tim, it was reasonable that I should be starting work too – only my job was going to be in England.

That Friday I inserted this piece of information amidst excited chatter about the arrests of Mick and Big M. Tim was listening stoically to this recital of his brother's misfortunes. The two boys had been 'dain' their salesmen in soaft felt hats an' raidin' oaffice holy ash boaxes.' Tim had heard it all at home before joining us in the pub: 'They're goin' up afore a sheriff an' jury.'

Tim then informed the gang that he was starting work the following Thursday and left us in no two minds as to his intentions. He was prepared to take a job in order to hasten the date of his release. Once he was out, he would continue working for a month or so to placate the school and to save enough money to buy 'gear'. Then he was going to 'chuck it – fur good. That's the *right* gemme.' He was found employment as a store boy in a paint shop which was situated in the territory of a rival gang; and so going to and from work soon became dangerous. Tim was not only a 'chib-man' but a 'leader-aff'. Many a boy had a score to settle with him. One in particular was the Mad Mexican, Pat McDonald, who had retired from the Fleet after the fight with Dick Stevenson, and had become a bus conductor. But on hearing that his young brother, who had since joined the Barnes Road, had been slashed in the battle with the Young Team, he arrived at Tim's place of work to challenge him to a fight – with blades.

It was now Tuesday, Tim's fourth day at work. He fled from the store at 11 in the morning, terrified to leave at the end of a day's work in case he was set upon on his way back to the school. Having crossed the city, he went home to tell Mick, who became so enraged that he rose from his bed and took out his shotgun. At least, so ran Tim's account of events. They searched for the Mad Mexican all afternoon but, finding no one, Tim returned to the school at half-past-six to say he had been sacked. 'Mick'll go right up tae his door the night an' kill him, Ah swear it.' He didn't. Another year was to pass before the Mad Mexican was murdered.

Now that Tim was a 'working-out' boy at the approved school, he was entitled to far more privileges, the chief of which was being allowed out on leave every weekend instead of once or twice a month. Despite his 'sacking' the previous Tuesday, he was allowed home on the day before John's release from borstal. That Friday night he met me for the last time in the presence of the gang. He told us that the Barnes Road and the Young Rolland Boys had all learned of the whereabouts of his place of employment. On two consecutive evenings they had chased him through the streets. The first time, Tim had just met Lizzie as she came from her work. They were going to spend half an hour together before Tim was due back at the school. Something about Marty, Benny and Andy from the Barnes Road and two others from the YRB attracted Lizzie's attention, and she had time to warn Tim to run for his life. Moreover, a phone call had been received at the school from someone purporting to be Tim's cousin from London. When this pretence did not bring Tim to the phone, all simulation was dropped and the voice asked for a message to be delivered to Tim. The message was that he was 'goaney be chibbed'.

In the pub that Friday night, Tim was adamant that the Barnes Road and the YRB had to be 'soarted oot' – and quickly. I advised Tim to wait for the arrival of John and Dave the following day, but he would not hear of any postponements. In the company of the Young Trio, Beano and Big Fry, Tim and I set out to hunt the enemy down in their 'locals'. We went the round of all their usual pubs, but drew a blank. Long before ten o'clock Tim suggested 'goin'' on the creep'; he wanted us in position in the close to await the homecoming of the Barnes Road boys. Dan McDade was the only one 'kerryin'' and the weapon was a bayonet. A quick return to Maryhill was suggested to collect weapons. We decided to meet back at 'oor coarner' and then walk up Bilsland Drive to Barnes Road. After the group split up, I was able to tell Tim I couldn't go through with this, and that I was leaving. For the last two weeks I had prepared him for this moment. As an excuse to the others, I told him to say that I had gone to say good-bye to Moira before leaving for England in the morning. Using the same story, I said farewell to the girl.

17
Epilogue

THE FIRST EXPERIMENT of sending Tim out to work having proved such a disaster, the headmaster confined him to the school again, and so it was May before Tim was found a second job. During this interval of three months, of course, I often met Tim within the school, but as he was only permitted leave on three occasions, he had little to report. John's 'coming-out' party had been a great success. Tim had returned to his home at 11 o'clock on Sunday morning from another party to find the 'hoose still crammed wi' people'.

Mick was tried towards the end of March for assault and robbery. 'He goat aff but Big M pleaded guilty an' goat eighteen month.' Within the space of three weeks John was questioned about two separate attempted murders but was charged with neither offence. Tim told me this with all the delight and respect one reserves for an old master who has not lost his touch. Over the Easter holidays, when he was granted minimal leave, Tim claimed to have been taken into custody three times in connection with breaches of the peace, but was not charged. Beano, Podgie, and the Young Trio had not been so fortunate. Twelve in all had been 'huckled' but only five charged. Tim volunteered no further details and I, reacting against all I had been through, did not pursue the matter. The role confusion in which I had been involved had taken its toll of me. But while escorting a group of boys to a Wednesday evening football match in mid-April, I had an opportunity to talk to Tim in private. The latest news was that Lizzie had been stabbed again and was in hospital. Although he had no idea how serious her condition was or (more important to Tim) who had committed this latest attack, he still preferred to attend the match than to visit his girlfriend.

In May, he began work as a shot firer in a factory close to the approved school and far from the territorial claims of Glasgow's gangs. After a month's hard work without incident of any kind, he was finally released. The night he left I was on my way home and so I gave him a lift to the borders of Maryhill; he knew I would never be returning to the corner. My last question to him was whether he considered his release a turning-point in his life. As he did not fully comprehend, I asked him if I could expect a change in his behaviour for the better. For answer I received his oft-repeated phrase, 'Are ye kiddin'?'

Tim's subsequent progress was recorded by the external welfare officer in charge of after-care who submitted reports to the school. These reports (from which I shall quote) reveal that within a month Tim was off work, claiming to have been injured in the factory, and yet he was playing football when the after-care officer called. Six weeks later he had lost the job through absence, and was in custody on a charge of breach of the peace:

> The boy stated that he was walking down Maryhill Road on his own when he was arrested, and that he was not causing any disturbance. He pleaded guilty, thinking that he would be fined and that that would be the end of it, as 'there is no good arguing against the police'.

Sentence was deferred for a month but before he reappeared in court, Tim found himself back in custody on another breach of the peace charge. He was granted bail of five pounds but ten days later he was still in the remand home as his family had been unable to find the money. From this point onwards further charges and court appearances became the order of the day. In January 1968 he was tried, found guilty of breach of the peace and fined £20, payable at one pound a week. He was still unemployed in March when he and another boy were charged with theft by housebreaking. The police evidence, to the effect that they had seen the two boys run off, was dismissed by the sheriff as the constables admitted to being over 200 yards from the culprits at the vital time. This charge against Tim was found not proven, but he had three other charges to answer in April, when he was finally committed to borstal nine months after his release from the approved school. One could hardly have expected a change in his behaviour after a year and a half in the approved school, when one remembers that he had continued to commit violent and property offences throughout his period of treatment. Tim's remark, 'Ah'll get ma borstal', had proved to be a self-fulfilling prophecy.

It is a predictable yet still a pathetic record. In his last months at the school an intensive effort was made by the headmaster, the whole staff including myself, and the visiting psychologist to change Tim's basic attitudes. Apparently to little avail. My connection with him, perhaps to my discredit, is now non-existent. Though horrified by his brutalities, I became quite fond of him, and I presumed the feeling was reciprocated. Nevertheless, since he left the school he has never telephoned, visited, or written to me, although I not only invited but encouraged him to do so – whether he was in trouble or not. My first reaction was that Tim must have looked upon our relationship as ephemeral, tenuous and without significance; but this may be a misinterpretation.

For my part, the break with the gang had to be incisive and permanent. To prevent myself becoming 'seduced by the group' I kept re-reading a passage of DJ West's (1967, p.249):

As the Roman Catholics found with their worker priests, social participation carries with it special dangers. Sometimes it becomes doubtful which side is doing the converting. If the 'detached worker', as he is called, becomes too much identified with the gang and its problems, he may take their side against authority.

With regard to other members of the gang since my departure from the scene at the end of January 1967, three incidents involving them have been reported in the local press. The first, which I have already referred to, concerns the murder of the Mad Mexican; the second, the conviction of Beano; and the third, the murder of a boy whom I remember as a young aspirant to the gang.

Pat McDonald, the Mad Mexican, was murdered on a Friday night in the summer of 1967. He was stabbed in the heart, the knife penetrating to a depth of five inches. Pat's brother admitted that the boy had been a member of a gang before he was sent to borstal, in fact, 'he was the leader of the Fleet.' Another relative added: 'Since Pat came out of borstal recently he seemed to be a changed boy.' Jimmy Barrow, called as a witness against the member of the 365 gang charged with the murder, said that he had been hit on the head with what he thought was a bottle and had fallen dazed to the ground. He had not seen his attackers.

Tim stated in court that he, Jimmy Barrow and Pat McDonald had been attacked by about six to eight youths. He had not seen what had happened to the murdered boy. When the fighting broke up, Pat had collapsed and it was then that Tim had realised that he had been stabbed. Tim could not recognise any of his attackers. Little wonder that the judge's address to the jury included the following sentence: 'You may perhaps have thought it surprising that a good many witnesses, who seemed to be in a reasonably good position to remember what had happened, seemed to have seen or remembered very little, if anything at all.'

The press reports ended with the information that hours after Pat was stabbed to death, his friends began a collection for his mother. In all more than £30 was handed to the woman who remarked: 'This was a wonderful gesture by the young ones to collect money after Pat's death. It shows you what they must have thought of him.'

The second incident I noticed in the press early in 1969. Beano was sent to a young offenders' institute for five years for 'an unprovoked razor assault on a fifty-seven-year-old man'. Beano admitted severely injuring and permanently disfiguring the man by striking him on the arm with a razor. The man, a motor mechanic, had been out with friends on the night of the assault, and was walking with them in a main street near the city centre when Beano approached. 'The youth was brandishing a razor and slashed the victim's left forearm.' The man 'was in a state of collapse when taken to the Western Infirmary and required blood transfusions'. He has been unable to use his left arm since the slashing, because nerves and an artery had been severed. Counsel for Beano said the assault was entirely without motive and occurred because the accused had been 'inflamed with drink'.

Thirdly, in May 1972, I read that a boy, whom I had last seen at the age of 13 in 1966, had been murdered by two 18-year-olds, one of whom had held the victim, while the other had stabbed him five or six times in the stomach with a knife. The two accused, who were sentenced to life imprisonment, pleaded in their defence that they had been provoked by the boy shouting 'Young Team!'. The violence continues unabated, and the traditions of the subculture still retain their hold upon the area.

On finishing the fieldwork for this study, I reached two immediate conclusions. The first, and one of crucial importance for approved schools, was that Tim, a gang leader, conformed as best he could within the system and used his leave at weekends to act out his aggression. The school never really witnessed what he was capable of; the staff suspected and guessed the truth of the matter, although they had only occasional outbursts of temper to work on. But of Tim's external conduct, his parental status, and of his own notoriety within the subculture of Glasgow's street gangs, they knew next to nothing.

This brings me to my second conclusion, also of relevance to approved schools. Educational sociologists normally encourage teachers to study the subcultures from which their pupils come. I tacitly agreed with the idea but did not fully comprehend it, until I realised that an approved school through lack of knowledge could endanger a boy's life by sending him to work in the territory of a rival gang. A pupil could be knifed or even killed – and this is not being melodramatic but all too realistic – through the ignorance of those whose professional duty it is to protect him as would 'a good and wise parent'.

An immediate result of my work with the Young Team was that the approved school where I was employed reviewed the leave granted to boys known to be gang members. At that time they were being released every so often on Fridays, Saturdays and Sundays – far and away the most likely times for gang activity. Seasonal holiday periods such as Christmas and Easter and all public holidays are also critical points, during which the whereabouts of gang leaders should be carefully noted and their movements supervised. However, approved schools generally continue to release boys at what appear to me the worst possible moments, even though Mays (1955, p.153) had already warned of these 'periods of exceptional danger'.

One final matter. Although I emerged from the gang physically

Epilogue

unmarked, there was one possibility which, if it had materialised, would have made my position as an approved school teacher untenable, i.e. the arrival in my own school of another member of the gang. In Scotland at that time, there was little classification of juvenile delinquents beyond that of age, sex and religion; but this alone could have brought some members of the Young Team sentenced to approved school training within my province. Fortunately not one of the boys I associated with appeared at the school. Nevertheless, one committal order gave me momentary cause for worry – the advent of a younger brother of one of the boys described in the previous pages. But the boy was a stranger to me and I to him. I have since left the approved school service.

18
Housing and gangs in Glasgow

GLASGOW HAS AN international reputation for slums and violence. But to her credit, the evils of organised crime, of vice rackets and of serious drug-taking, which plague other major cities in Great Britain, are virtually unknown. To deal first with her reputation for slums, housing conditions in my native city have not always been appalling. In 1723 Daniel Defoe rated Glasgow in *A Journey through Scotland* as 'the beautifullest little city I have seen in Britain.' Two hundred years later, after the Industrial Revolution had taken its toll, William Bolitho thought fit to call Glasgow the 'Cancer of the Empire.'

To this day, despite massive redevelopment and overspill schemes, Glasgow's housing problem remains unique in Britain and is of monumental proportions compared even with London, Birmingham or Liverpool. I shall attempt to outline this problem in two ways. Firstly, I shall give a brief, impressionistic description of Glasgow in the middle and late 1960s. And secondly, I shall quote a few statistics to substantiate the claim made in the first sentence of this paragraph, to indicate the dimensions of the task the city is faced with.

Glasgow today is not to be pictured as a collection of multi-storeyed blocks, although, unfortunately, we have our share of these egg crates.[23] In fact, those on the Balornock Red Road Development Scheme with 31 storeys bid fair to be the tallest blocks of flats in Europe. It is the tenement type of building, rare in England, which remains typical of Glasgow, accounting as it does for 85% of all dwellings (Cullingworth, 1968). The four-storey tenement blocks with their common staircase, off which passages run to the front doors of the flats, stand, in Chaim Bermant's phrase, like 'rows and rows of bad teeth'. Originally of good red sandstone, they are now begrimed with soot and dirt; the stonework itself is crumbling. Many a close-mouth is awash with stagnant and foul-smelling water through which children paddle and float sticks. Litter and refuse of all kinds are strewn about back courts; dustbins are either overflowing or lying empty on their sides with their contents spilled on the ground. What I remember above all is the stench of dampness and decay, an odour which, when I first encountered it, had me grinding my teeth together to prevent myself from retching. The total effect is not helped by the gang slogans daubed on walls, lampposts, hoardings and shop fronts.

Not even the four extensive modern housing schemes of Pollok, Castlemilk, Drumchapel and Easterhouse escape this outward manifestation of gang activity. Started in the early 1950s, these dormitory estates, situated in the south, west and east of the city, were built well in advance of any supporting services. For years they consisted of nothing but houses, shopping facilities were minimal, and there was a total absence of commercial entertainment. A Town Council resolution of 1890, which was not rescinded until 1964, forbade the provision of licensed premises on municipal housing estates.

As there was no money for basic amenities, it is not surprising that homes were constructed without character or elegance or imagination. So in the understandable haste to provide decent living conditions for vast numbers of people, cultural, social and psychological deserts were produced. Street after street of these houses look today for all the world like army barracks.

It was one of these housing areas, Easterhouse, which hit the national headlines in 1968 with regard to juvenile gang violence. I have calculated[24] that the population of Easterhouse in 1967 was more than 45,000, a concentration of people greater than that of the city of Perth, or Scarborough or Folkestone. Yet Easterhouse had no swimming pool, no dance hall, no cinema, no café, no library, no township centre. And nowadays when so many young people rebel against organised recreation, the provision of facilities for 'scratch' games of football, for meeting informally in coffee bars, is all important. No such facilities existed in Easterhouse in 1967. As the *Report on Community Problems*[25] in Glasgow concluded: 'The area remains a collection of houses and not a community in which its members find a meaningful place.'

Grieve and Robertson (1964) are right, however, in arguing that too much attention has been paid to the black side of Glasgow life:

> This negative attitude may be characterised by the popular renown of the Gorbals as an area of evil social conditions. Story, play and even ballet as well as countless newspaper articles alike testify to this as a place of ultimate despair. Yet in truth much imaginative planning has gone into the redevelopment of the Gorbals where a new and challenging environment is now being created – the first large-scale example of an ambitious series of redevelopments now in process of planning and implementation.

Glaswegians have other legitimate reasons for taking pride in their city: the Gothic Cathedral, the two universities, the art galleries, Charles Rennie Mackintosh's School of Art, the 60 public parks, the Victorian architecture of the city centre, Pollok House and so on. Today Glasgow remains a major commercial and manufacturing centre (despite the decline in world importance of her shipbuilding yards), and is engaged in building an ambitious new internal motorway system which will enable the city to continue as the industrial heart of west central Scotland.

But if Glasgow has given birth to Scottish Opera and the Citizens Theatre as well as to Rangers and Celtic, there is a stark side to life in the city as well. The drabness, the ugliness, the dirt are there for all to see. Only statistics, however, can tell us the extent of the housing problem and how Glasgow compares with other cities in the United Kingdom.

To begin with, 25 of Britain's 40 most overcrowded districts are to be found in Glasgow.[26] The percentage of the population in Greater London living in overcrowded[27] conditions was 4% in 1966, in the West Midlands and Merseyside the figure was 4.5%, but in Central Clydeside it was 15.5%. In actual numbers this meant more than 260,000 people living in overcrowded buildings.

For a more detailed picture, one must turn to the report, 'Scotland's Older Houses'.[28] There one reads:

> In May 1966, the Corporation [of Glasgow] assessed that of the total housing stock within the city of 326,000 there were 10,000 houses which were classified after individual inspections as unfit; 75,000 as sub-standard and not improvable at reasonable cost; and 49,000 as sub-standard but susceptible to improvement at reasonable cost. In other words over 41% of the city's stock of housing was estimated to be below standard. All these houses are in worse condition than a great many houses which are being demolished as unfit by many other local authorities in Scotland. And this we suspect is not the full extent of the problem even *as it exists today*. At the current rate of clearance it will take at least 25 years to deal with the backlog. Yet this is only a snap-shot picture of a situation which is constantly changing. It does not fully take account of houses which are deteriorating into slums or of houses which though not slums are inadequate for relatively modest contemporary standards of living. [Italics as in original.]

This report contains many an apposite passage, but I shall restrict myself to one further quotation:

> Glasgow has a reputation for bad housing conditions and, despite great efforts by the Corporation, we have found that this reputation

is unfortunately justified. The statistics alone cannot adequately describe the problem: indeed, they misleadingly suggest that the problem is not as great as it is. We have seen conditions in Glasgow that can be described as only appalling. Families are condemned to live in atrocious conditions which should shock the national conscience and, we, believe, would do so if they were better known. But even the Glaswegian who sees only the often imposing (yet, on closer inspection, often crumbling) front exterior seldom appreciates how revolting and inhumane are the conditions inside the closes, on the common staircases, and in the back courts. And even if he does occasionally glimpse the physical squalor which is out of sight to the passer-by, he can have no conception of the extent of the problem.

The Corporation has struggled to combat such conditions in two main ways: redevelopment areas like the Gorbals and Hutchesontown are being gutted and rebuilt, while numerous other citizens are being rehoused in the overspill plan in the new towns of East Kilbride, Cumbernauld and even as far afield as Inverness and Arbroath. But the uniqueness of the situation lies in the fact that: 'Glasgow with twice the population of Sheffield or Edinburgh is no larger in area than either of these cities.' (Oakley, 1967, p.9)

Apart from this acute shortage of space, the congestion and overcrowding is also to be explained by the spectacular rise in the population during the 19th century. The growth of the new heavy industries brought an influx of hundreds of thousands of people to the city. A population of 77,000 in the year 1801 had increased to 762,000 by 1901. (Robertson, 1958, p.58)

What has been Glasgow's answer to such fundamental problems? Since 1919 more than 150,000 municipal houses have been erected, of which total more than 80,000 have been completed in the period 1945-68. And in the ten years from 1958, more than 17,000 families have been rehoused outside the city, while in the 27 redevelopment schemes within the city, more than 36,500 families have been given new homes.[29] And yet one house in three in the mid-60s was sub-standard, and a crisis situation with regard to housing still exists in the city. Instead of the main political parties indulging in hollow arguments about their respective building records, it would be more realistic for them to concentrate on the number of houses which are still urgently needed. For the problem to be solved in the next few years, I sincerely believe that certain districts of Glasgow would have to be designated disaster areas and treated accordingly, with aid of all kinds flooding in from all over the country to the stricken zones.

What has to be remembered is that if every third house in Glasgow in

1966 was sub-standard, there was a time in the 1930s when one-third of the adult working population was unemployed. Both poverty and violence have a long history in Glasgow; and it is to this second theme, that of violence, to which I now turn.

Gangs in Glasgow are no new phenomenon; they were such a social menace in the 1930s that Sir Percy Sillitoe was brought from Sheffield, where he had 'smashed' the local gangs, to Glasgow as Chief Constable to perform a similar job. His autobiography[30] gives some illuminating insights into the situation then prevailing. According to Sillitoe:

> The Glasgow gangs were born soon after the First World War, and it was about 1919 or 1920 that the Redskin and Black Hand gangs became notorious ... Most of the gangs simply grew up around their own districts or just around one particular street corner ... They certainly were never, in any sense, organised teams of experienced criminals who grouped themselves round a 'master mind'. (1955, pp.123-4)

John Mack (1957, pp.11-14; 1958, p.644) agrees with Sillitoe that the Glasgow gangs were almost entirely a phenomenon of the interwar years. I respectfully suggest that this is not so. There is ample evidence in newspaper files that Glasgow gangs were in existence not only during the First World War, but as far back as the early 1880s.

Two articles in *The Times* (19 January 1920; 23 September 1936) carry reports of a gang called the Penny Mob which operated in Townhead and the East End of Glasgow almost a hundred years ago. 'This gang had a common fund to which all contributed, and when members were fined at the police courts, the money was always forthcoming – hence the name "Penny Mob".' Their picturesque name should not disguise the fact that they were 'a gang of hooligans, who for long were a source of serious annoyance to the community.'

The second article, based on personal reminiscences of one who had close contact with the ringleader of the Penny Mob, makes it clear that there were other participants in the street fights of that day, namely, the boys of the Wee Do'e Hill and the Big Do'e Hill. About the same time, there was also a gang styling itself the Drygate Youths, who on one occasion, 'while holding high revel, fell foul of the police and a battle-royal ensued.' The battle ended with the arrest of the 'chairman' of the gang.

The Times continues by referring to two rival gangs in the Central district at the beginning of the century. These were the San Toy Boys and the Tim Malloys, the slogan of the former being given as: 'We are the young San Toys, and we can fight the Tim Malloys.' After they had been suppressed, the trouble switched to the South Side, where the Mealy Boys, the McGlynn Push, the Village Boys, and, at a slightly later date, the Gold Dust Gang established a reign of terror in the district by committing unprovoked assaults upon citizens.

The phrase 'a reign of terror' was to be used again by the *Bulletin* (16 May 1916) and the *Sunday Chronicle* (21 May 1916) about another serious outbreak of gang violence in 1916, when the Redskins who are described as having 'their happy hunting ground in the East End', began to assert themselves. Again, though the Redskins were the most notorious gang, they were by no means the only one. A study of the press of that time produces such gang names as the Bloodhound Flying Corps, the Hi-Hi's, the Hazel Bells from Mile-End and Bridgeton, the Kelly Boys from Govan, and the Baltic Fleet from Baltic Street.

A fascinating article in the *People's Journal* (18 November 1916) includes a list 'by no means complete' of other Glasgow gangs of the same period, 'whose principal delight is to shout their own particular slogans and war cries, and set about each other.' The article, entitled 'Glasgow Apaches on War-Path', lists in addition to the Redskins and the Kelly Boys, the Brig Ahoy, the Silver Bell, the Death Valley Boys, the Beehive Boys, the Waverley Boys, the Cowboys, the Ging-Gong, and the Bell On Boys.

It was on 23 March 1916 that the *Bulletin* first announced the 'regrettable revival of the hooligan menace'. Unlike the earlier gangs, the Redskins were an organised body whose numbers were put as close on a thousand. The report goes on to mention two features of this 'nefarious organization'; firstly, they all had a peculiar whistle whereby one member of the gang could rally a crowd to his support; and secondly, they carried and used 'lethal weapons'.

Throughout the summer months of 1916 news items on the gangs continued to appear in the local press. Shopkeepers found their premises wrecked and ransacked, 'to prevent which they were forced to pay protection money'; pedestrians were kicked unconscious and stripped of everything of value in the open street. As the number of cases of assaults on the police began to rise, one of the leaders of the Redskins was arrested for attacking a man with a knife in one hand and a bottle in the other. Amongst the sinister weapons found on gang members were heavily leaded batons of wood and rubber, a revolver (unloaded), an iron bludgeon, and a steel club which 'would easily have brained a bull, let alone a man'.

There was much public concern expressed at the time about the number of girls who ran with the gangs. The *People's Journal* claimed that besides having 'kings' these gangs also had 'queens'; and in some of the gangs there were reputed to be more females than males. These 'pretty girl hooligans' were mainly aged 14 to 18. And so were their male counterparts: a fact at variance with the commonly held view that the gangs of the past were composed of adults occupying their time during long periods of unemployment. The press reports are quite clear on this point. The *Glasgow Herald* (29 June 1916), for example, records the case of a crowd numbering 30 to 40 youths, which 'shouted and yelled as they passed along several of the leading thoroughfares to Bridgeton Cross. Crying "We are the — Redskins", they jostled and otherwise interfered with a number of people ... '. Three of the 'rowdies' were arrested on a charge of breach of the peace; their ages are given as 17, 18 and 21.

The same point is made by two court cases reported in the *Southern Press* (27 May 1916). In the first incident a crowd of juveniles, while returning home from a party at five o'clock on a Sunday morning, had broken over 20 panes of glass in houses, shop windows, and public lamps. Three people, two girls and a boy, all of them 16, were arrested for the offence, the superintendent of police complaining in court that the law of the land unfortunately did not permit girls to be whipped. The second case concerned a group of over a dozen boys and girls, from 15 to 17 years of age, who were all charged with creating a breach of the peace in the Tradeston district by shouting 'and making an unseemly noise ... at a late hour at night'.

Similarly, in the 20s and 30s most of the gangs had junior sections according to John Mack (1957, p.13), who gives an account of the battle on the Albert Bridge in 1928 between the South Side Stickers and the Calton Entry, two junior gangs in the 15 to 17 age range, the latter gang being led by a 16-year-old. During the battle, one member of the Calton Entry was murdered by being stabbed in the back with a sword.

Gangs, therefore, are deep-rooted in Glasgow's history and gang lore and customs would appear to have been handed down from the 1880s to the turn of the century, to 1916 and to the gangs of Sillitoe, to whose work I now return.

One of his characters, the leader of The Parlour Boys, James Dalziel, 'or "Razzle Dazzle" as he was known, scorned so profoundly the delicacies of life that he would dance only with other burly members of his gang, considering it effeminate to dance with girls.' The favourite weapon of Dalziel's gang was the pickshaft, 'weighing nearly three pounds and measuring forty-two inches in length.' One police sergeant, endeavouring to interfere with this gang, 'was struck full in the face by one of these murderous missiles.'

When Sillitoe arrived in Glasgow, 'two of the most notorious gangs were the "Norman Conquerors" (known more familiarly as the "Norman Conks"), who came from Norman Street and were Roman Catholics, and the "Billy Boys", who were William of Orange Protestants ... '.

Sillitoe also records that every Sunday morning, the Billy Boys deliberately went out of their way to march through their enemies' territory on their way to church: 'Bottles, bricks and pickshafts would fly like hail from the windows of Norman Street as the "pilgrims" passed on their provocative way. The Billy Boys did not enter the church itself. They felt, apparently, that their job was concluded when they had created the Sunday morning riot.'

In 1935 the Billy Boys organised a drum and flute band, and on all Catholic Saints and Holy Days the entire gang marched through Norman Street playing inflammatory party tunes:

> As soon as the distant strains of the offensive music were heard by the Conks, they manned all upper windows, and even the roofs in their street, and when the Billy Boys' band tried to march past, it was met by a downpour of bricks, missiles, buckets of filth and broken glass. If the Norman Conks could have made boiling lead, I am sure that they would not have hesitated to use that too. It was certainly all that would have been needed to complete the picture of a medieval siege.

The police decided that the citizens of Glasgow had suffered long enough, but it took a charge of mounted police to scatter the parade:

> It was the beginning of the end for the Billy Boys, whose final chapter soon followed this wholesale defeat. Only one of their men, incidentally, escaped injury. He was Elijah Cooper, the big drum player. When the police charged, Elijah dived into his drum and used it as a shelter until he could surrender peacefully.

A series of articles in the Glasgow *Evening Citizen* (17 January 1955) include a number of facts about the history of gangs not to be found anywhere else. Billy Fullerton, the leader of the Billy Boys, recounts how each of the 800 members of his gang carried membership cards on which a weekly payment of 2d was marked up. 'At one time we had over £1,200 in a Bridgeton bank, lodged under three names.' The money was used to pay the fines of gang members after street battles and to maintain the dependants of married men who were sentenced to gaol. Sillitoe claims that fines were paid at once by levies upon the shopkeepers in that district. Eventually, it was decided to spend £600 on the formation of a flute band (obviously the one referred to by Sillitoe) on instruments, uniforms and transportation to Belfast for the Orange Walk of 12 July 1936.

Ten years earlier Fullerton had witnessed the wedding of one of his Billy Boys. 'The bridegroom stood before the minister with a sword concealed in his morning dress. The best man had a gun in his pocket ... I'll never forget the scene as they left the Church. The gang waiting outside threw bottles instead of confetti.' These are the traditions of violence and bigotry which were handed down to succeeding generations.

Bill McGhee's novel of the Glasgow street gangs *Cut and Run* (1963), makes the point that gang activity continued to be rife in the 1940s both during and after the war. And Brennan (1959, p.138ff.), while studying Govan, a redevelopment area in Glasgow, discovered in the mid-50s the presence of 'a loosely organised gang of boys who refer to themselves as the Bingo Boys'. Fighting rather than thieving had always been the Govan speciality according to Brennan, and this gang of younger boys, 'ranging from 13 years of age to 18 or 19', upheld the long traditions of the neighbourhood. So the resurgence of the gangs in the late 50s and early 60s should have surprised no one, as the continuity of gang warfare within the city seems unbroken even by two World Wars. Gangs in Glasgow have become institutionalised over the years, forming a violent or conflict subculture within the city.

For a hundred years, then, Glasgow has suffered from appalling housing conditions. For the same length of time gangs have been known in the city. The inhabitants, I fear, have become inured to both evils, to cramped, verminous houses and to brutal, barbarous violence. Middle-class citizens react to the situation by retreating into repugnance and repression or into indifference and inhumanity. 'Cordon off the areas and let them battle it out', is one typical comment. 'Hammer them – it's the only language they understand', is another. The very same aggression condemned in the behaviour of the gang boys is here verbalised and legitimised. This, briefly, is part of the background against which Glasgow's juvenile gang problem has to be understood.

19
British research into gangs

THIS CHAPTER CONTAINS no new theory, no integrating thesis, no synoptic overview of juvenile or gang delinquency. The task I have set myself is far simpler: to place my findings within the context of research into gangs. No more should be expected of a study which was purely exploratory, which was an attempt to acquire some hard inside information on Glasgow gangs.

Merton (1957, p.93) has called this type of empirical research 'post factum sociological interpretation', where analysis and explanation take place after the observations have been made and where there is no testing of a pre-designated hypothesis. According to him, such interpretations 'remain at the level *of plausibility* (low evidential value) rather than leading to "compelling evidence" (a high degree of confirmation).' But where we are faced, as in Glasgow, with a major social problem about which we have such little reliable information, I would have thought like Liebow (1967, p.12) that 'merely plausible' explanations are better than none.

And certainly, a reading of the literature on gang delinquency makes clear just how far theory has outstripped research. The theoretical writings, particularly of Cohen (1955) and of Cloward and Ohlin (1960), are unsatisfactory mainly because the reader is so rarely given the feeling of what it is like to be a delinquent gang member. The flavour of the delinquent act is missing because their work is based on second-hand evidence. The social distance between the investigator and the gang member is often so wide that behaviour is seriously misinterpreted. The free-ranging delinquent, observed in his natural habitat, is a very different character from the timeserving, compliant boy in the artificial setting of an approved school or borstal. Investigations which employ questionnaires, standardised or tape-recorded interviews, as the main method of collecting data, are almost bound to miss the complexity and the confusion of the delinquent process. We are in the absurd position of having very few first-hand studies of, but numerous theoretical speculations about, juvenile gangs.

No one theory of the causes of delinquent behaviour adequately explains all the data I collected on the Young Team; and yet, as Hardman (1967, p.25) found in his study of four small-town gangs in the United States, neither was there any accepted theory which did not contribute something to his understanding of the gang behaviour observed. The approach, then, in the following pages will be unashamedly eclectic, though in general my interpretation is closer to that of Yablonsky in *The Violent Gang* (1967) than to any other theoretical formulation.

But before I turn to the literature relevant to adolescent gangs in this country since the war, two problems must be aired: namely, the applicability of my findings and the validity of cross-cultural comparisons. Is my description of the Young Team typical of other Glasgow gangs, of gangs in other cities and societies? I have presented a sample from Glasgow gang culture and the possibility exists that it may be grossly unrepresentative, particularly as the gang I joined was not selected for me by random sampling. It is possible but not probable; in my view, Tim's gang is typical of the large number of juvenile gangs to be found in Glasgow's slum districts, and the further one travels from these districts to the new housing estates on the outskirts of the city, the paler become the imitations. I would predict that any findings from a study of other Glasgow slum gangs which at all conflict with my own, would be variations on a basic theme; but this is a matter for future research.

The argument is further complicated by temporal and geographical differences, which continue to be glossed over in studies of adolescent gangs. Mays (1968, p.249) poses the relevant question: 'What right have we to assume that what was apparently found to be true of Chicago in the nineteen-twenties is true of Baltimore in the nineteen-forties, or of Liverpool in the nineteen-fifties?' In many books which attempt to achieve theoretical parsimony, serious injustice has been done to the empirical data. For instance, there has not been sufficient recognition of the fact that there are important qualitative differences between the gangs which have been investigated in the U.S.A: Yabonsky's Balkans and Miller's Junior Outlaws, Kobrin's Eagles and Jansyn's Dons, Bloch and Niederhoffer's Pirates and Keiser's Vice Lords do not form a homogeneous group. To give one example, WB Miller (1966, p.111) concludes that violence was not a dominant activity of the gangs he studied in 'Midcity', nor a central reason for their existence. Whereas for Yablonsky's (1967, p.242) Balkans in New York 'free-floating violence, pure and unencumbered by social restrictions, conscience, or regret, is the goal'. In other words, the gangs of New York appear to differ in kind from those of Boston, Chicago and Los Angeles, and nothing would be gained by incorporating them all in one theory which ignores their essential differences. I believe the same to be true of this country in that the Glasgow gang finds no parallel in Liverpool or London. So theories which were evolved to explain highly specific conditions in England may have precious little relevance to the situation in Glasgow (cf. Klein, 1967, p.v). I am not suggesting that we abandon the attempt to produce a comprehensive theory of gang delinquency: all I am saying is that theories which ignore essential differences are bad theories.

English Research into Gangs since 1945

At the very time that David Downes (1966, pp.116-23; 1968, pp.61-72) was writing and broadcasting to the effect that 'research into gang delinquency in this country is in my view a fair reflection of its absence', the citizens of Glasgow were awakening to the fact that juvenile gangs had returned in force to the city. However, if Downes's remarks about the 'gang myth' and the 'non-existent gang' are restricted to England, then on the whole they would appear to hold good, as the following chronological review shows.

BM Spinley (1953) in her participant observation study of a London slum touches on the important part played by the adolescent gang in the social life of the area. According to this source, gangs in the early 1950s ranged in size from cliques of three to large groups of 20 'with perhaps ten supporters on the fringe'. The boys carried weapons, mostly knives or sharpened nail-files, but they seldom used them. In-group feeling was thought to be so strong that it prevented in-group fighting and no matter how unpleasant, conceited or mean the individual member, he was apparently tolerated and supported against outsiders. The boys displayed 'certain textbook signs of maladjustment', in particular a generalised aggression which spilled over into violence which was approved of by the gang.

Turner and Spencer (1955) did not find it so easy to locate and make contact with juvenile gangs in the Hoxton district of London. The research was entering its 11th month, and only the most superficial relationships had been established with the Junior Hoxton Boys, when the leader, interestingly called the King, made his first appearance. 'As a King, he was not impressive. He was the "average" boy, who was neither taller, nor heavier, nor stouter than one would expect of a sixteen-year-old. It was equally certain that he was not tough. He was talkative and boastful. But he was not unlikeable ... '. The boy was involved 'in cases of assault, with the accompanying "beatings" and "kickings" 'and his boast was: 'Nobody grasses up and gets away with it.' Unfortunately, the King and his mates 'disappeared' shortly after this breakthrough and the work came to an abrupt end.

Spencer (1950) and Turner (1953) have also written accounts of the Barge Boys' Club, 'showing the value of building a club around a small gang already in existence, and of utilizing a sailing barge in the fulfilment of the adolescent's sense of excitement and adventure.' These boys were undoubtedly rough, aggressive, and reacting against a neighbourhood which had singularly little to offer them; but they neither carried nor used weapons, they did not explode into violence nor did they belong to a gang culture.

A more systematic investigation is presented by Peter Scott (1956) who, calling upon ten years experience as a clinical psychologist working with delinquents in a number of settings, divides the London groups he studied into three categories:

1. Adolescent street groups, the majority of which were 'quite innocuous and, indeed, perhaps necessary and useful.' The boys indulged in group rowdyism rather than planned crime, and the weapons, which they carried for their symbolic and prestige value, were rarely used. Leaders of the 'mob 'or 'click' (the terms used by the boys) were nominal and Scott concluded that such groups offer their members 'a breathing space for the acquisition of confidence', as they slowly extricate themselves from emotional dependence on their families.

2. As for 'gangs proper', defined as those with a leader, definite membership, persistence in time, a den, initiation procedure, and criminal objectives, Scott found very few. Out of a total of 151 boys known to have committed group offences, only 17 were classified as belonging to structured gangs. 'It is indeed difficult,' adds Scott, 'to find good examples of gangs, nor do the few that are found conform with the picture of healthy devilment, adventqrousness, pride of leadership or loyal lieutenancy, that is often painted.' In fact those members of 'gangs proper' whocome before the courts are described as having 'a gross antisocial character defect', and as coming from homes where the emotional atmosphere had been 'obviously disturbed and detrimental.' I shall have cause to return to this observation later.

3. Loosely structured or diffuse groups amounted to 86% of the total, and are themselves subdivided by Scott into three:
(a) fleeting, casual delinquent associations, consisting mainly of immature 10- to 13-year-olds;
(b) groups of friends and siblings who were not much concerned with delinquency;
(c) loose, antisocial groups of unhappy and disturbed children who were involved in more serious forms of delinquency.

It is my general impression that, although the boys studied are said to be between the ages of eight and 17, Scott is really talking about the sort of groups formed by pre-adolescents, by boys of 12 and 13. This is borne out by

Scott himself who gives the average age of the various types of group. Furthermore, the delinquent activities even of the 'gangs proper' could not by any stretch of the imagination be characterised as those of violent gangs.

Pre-adolescent gangs are the subject of AR Crane's (1958) study, which provides a useful corrective to the general opinion which equates gang membership with future delinquent behaviour. The data was collected in both England and Australia from student teachers who came predominantly from aspiring lower middle and working class homes. As many as nine-tenths of the men and some two-fifths of the women reported that they had belonged to at least one gang between their eighth and 14th year. Moreover, 'socially disapproved activity' was part of the repertoire of every one of the boys' gangs, while the most common disapproved activity among the girls was scandal-mongering. Such findings make it clear that pre-adolescent gangs 'are not confined to subnormal environments, nor to those where recreational outlets are lacking.' Ganging in the lives of these students had been a passing phase which they had all left behind them by the age of 14. Far from being 'the growing point of the delinquent sub-culture', Crane argues that the pre-adolescent gang can be a training ground for morality, that gang membership can be 'an important bridge between the kinship-based status conferred on the child by the family and the achievement based status conferred by society at large.' We are here reminded that ganging is a very common phenomenon especially among boys, that delinquency is by no means confined to those who are legally labelled 'delinquents', and that the type of gang Crane is describing and which Yablonsky calls the social gang is in no need of treatment. These are perhaps commonplace observations but still worth noting in a book where violence and abnormality are such recurrent themes.

TR Fyvel (1963) would have us believe that the Teddy boys made a cult of violence in the mid 1950s, that they 'introduced an element of violent lawlessness' (p.61). In a lively form of reportage, Fyvel claims that the Teddy boys were organised in gangs to defend their territories, that they indulged in 'a sort of stylised warfare' with others wearing the same uniform, and that they cultivated 'a fashion for carrying improvised offensive weapons.' Recently, this view of the Teddy boy movement has been questioned. Downes (1968, p.65) argues that 'people reached for the nearest cliché and made it fit: gang warfare.' Further, he contends (1966, p.120) that Fyvel in his impressionistic account of the Teddy boys uses the word 'gang' loosely, in a context where it appears 'to have emotive rather than structural significance, connoting delinquency and violence by large groups of working-class adolescents.' Whatever the truth of the matter, and I tend to support Downes's interpretation, there is no doubt that the Teddy boys of Notting Hill and South London were a different species from the razor gangs of Glasgow in the 1930s. Fyvel writes (p.66):

> The older gangs were basically a product of poverty, of mass unemployment and degraded slum life ... The gang leaders were not adolescents but older men, who were often also notorious criminals. The gangs were strictly confined to certain areas; their ascendancy rested on primitive brute force ... the cloth-capped pre-war gangs of Sheffield and Glasgow were a survival from a cruder past and could be dealt with as such ...

A general picture is beginning to emerge in which the absence of structured gangs in England in the fifties and sixties is the most striking feature. Added support for such a view comes from FH McClintock's (1963) detailed study of crimes of violence in London which contains a note on young offenders and hooliganism. Having examined the figures for 1950, 1957 and 1960, he found, contrary to general opinion, no evidence that numerous gangs of youths existed who were armed with offensive weapons and who roamed the streets in aggressive and menacing attitudes. The majority of offensive weapon charges resulted from boys being arrested in connection with property offences and then being found to possess an offensive weapon. Only a very small percentage of the total cases of hooliganism resulted from pitched battles between gangs, and 'there was little evidence to suggest that such groups were sufficiently distinct or permanent to be regarded as gangs, either in the neighbourhood, or by the participants themselves' (p.245). Even in those cases where injury was sustained, it was inflicted in the vast majority of cases with the attacker's fist or foot, not with a weapon. A final major difference between the situation in London and Glasgow among young offenders is contained in McClintock's finding that 'the few cases in which females were injured had resulted from their coming to the assistance of their male companions who were the objects of the attack' (p.244). No girl had herself been the object of violence.

John Spencer's (1964) later work is in part concerned with the 'Espressos', an exceptionally difficult group of roughly 30 girls and boys, most of whom were in late adolescence, and who lived on a new housing estate near Bristol. The group 'were not a closely knit and well-organised gang on the American metropolitan pattern' (p.164), but they did exhibit behaviour which was highly disruptive to the local community. They liked to think that they 'took over' the local cinema at weekends; they rounded off an evening with a bout of policeman-baiting. They indulged in such acts of bravado and then rejoiced when the press accorded them the notice for which they craved. Yet these young people, for all their destructive and rowdy activities, 'were very far from being a single gang with a sanctioned mode of behaviour and a hierarchy of roles, or a series of such gangs ... ' (p.186). The Espressos appear to be a typical example of Scott's last category: a loose, antisocial group of unhappy and disturbed youngsters.

Colin Fletcher (1964) was himself a member of two Merseyside gangs from 1954 to 1958. He describes how during this period 'beat invaded the gangs and changed them beyond all recognition'. Before the advent of the new style of music, Liverpool's slums had certainly contained gangs which were based on territory, on 'a strict geographical delineation'. Each gang had its hard core of brothers or 'life-long' friends, among whom 'barnies or punch-ups were common but regulated. We fought for our status, not for fun.' As gang leader 'the most reliable, tough, and fair boy' was chosen by the boys, to whom girls were secondary, mere 'notches on the gang's belt'.

All this changed with the arrival of rock 'n' roll, with the growth of a 'youth culture'. Musical groups began to be formed within the gangs and these became the new status symbol. 'What mattered now was not how many boys a gang could muster for a Friday night fight but how well their group played on Saturday night ... In a very small space of time the boy fighting came to be regarded as just a man without a woman.'

Fletcher maintains that beat killed the gangs in a matter of months; unfortunately, no such process took place in Glasgow, where, if anything, 'teenage culture' has been fused with gang culture and has not replaced it.

Another of the very few first-hand accounts of adolescent groups in England is provided by Michael Farrant's (1965) MA thesis. His participant observation study of the nature and structure of three adolescent groups is set in 'Subville', a fictitious name given to a housing estate on the boundary of a city in southern England. The author's most important conclusion, for my purpose, is that the three groups studied were nothing more than leadership nuclei of what he terms 'quasi groups'. These 'quasi groups', likened by Farrant to Yablonsky's 'near group', were loosely knit, amorphous gatherings of boys who joined and left at will. At times the 'quasi group' could consist of as many as 40 members, including the original nucleus, but once this size, the 'quasi group' suffered from heightened emotionalism, fantasy and instability.

Although two of the three groups were certainly delinquent and occasionally violent, although they highly prized skill in fighting and acts of vandalism, they could not be accurately described as gangs. Even the oldest and most delinquent group lacked the structure, organisation and integration normally associated with gang culture. And nowhere is their difference from a violent, fighting gang more apparent than in the general absence of both sexual exploitation of the girls by the boys and of offensive weapon carrying.

David Downes's (1966) own study in subcultural theory, *The Delinquent Solution*, ends with a survey of delinquency in Stepney and Poplar (two boroughs in the East End of London), and the subject of gangs is touched upon. The approach employed by Downes was informal rather than participant observation and, by simply hanging around, he formed the impression that in the area the adolescent groups 'responsible for the bulk of delinquency were simply small cliques whose members committed illegal acts sometimes collectively, sometimes in pairs, sometimes individually, in some cases regularly, in others only rarely. Delinquency was no more the central requirement for membership than the experience of sexual intercourse ... Average group size was 4-5, with a few individuals on the periphery. While these street-corner groups persisted over time, and invariably possessed a dominant personality, all the other features commonly attributed to the delinquent 'gang' were absent: i.e. leadership, role allocation, hierarchical structure, consensus on membership, uniform, and name.' (p.199).

Fighting or conflict-oriented gangs were not found but were only heard of by repute. The delinquent groups of Stepney and Poplar, then, were 'fluid, street-corner cliques, averse to any form of structure and organisation.' In this they conform precisely to the familiar English pattern. For Downes, as for other English investigators, 'the issue now at stake is not what gangs there are, but why none – or very few – exist.'

One, but only one, of these very unusual groups which come close to the sterotyped image of the gang, is reported by Peter Willmott (1966) among the adolescent boys he studied in Bethnal Green, again in the East End of London. They exhibited a callousness about injury inflicted on others and their main motive for violence and hooliganism was, according to Wilimott, 'a desire to strike at society' for its consistent rejection of them as failures. The majority of boys living in the same area, however, belonged to casual and informal peer groups, which the boys themselves called mobs, rather than to highly organised gangs. The members of these peer groups were 'roughly equal in status', and the groups had neither definite leaders nor hierarchial structure. Here again, we are presented with the same pattern as that outlined by Downes, and both authors report that systematic lighting or battling between the mobs was a rarity, although the boys indulged in a cult of manly toughness and aggression. For these youngsters, AK Cohen's theory of status frustration[31] is thought to have little relevance: bored they certainly were at school, discontented at work, but they were not openly rebellious. As for those boys whose group formation most resembled that of a gang proper, Wilimott suggests that we may have to examine their psychological rather than sociological condition.

One study remains to be included: Stan Cohen's (1967) analysis of the Mods and Rockers disturbances at resorts on the south-east coast of England in the period 1963 to 1966. The picture of riots and gang warfare which was presented by the mass media could not be substantiated:

> There was initially nothing like the gang rivalry supposed to characterise the American type of conflict gang caricatured in West Side Story, in fact there was nothing like a gang ... The groups were merely loose collectivities or crowds within which there was occasionally some more structured grouping, based on territorial loyalty e.g. 'The Walthamstow Boys', 'The Lot from Eltham'. Constant repetition of the gang image made these collectivities see themselves as gangs and behave in a gang fashion, (p.128)

In complete contrast to the impression created by television and the press, the amount of malicious damage and serious violence was in fact negligible. Cohen's contention is supported by Paul Barker's (1964) survey of 44 Margate offenders, only one of whom was charged with causing bodily harm as well as carrying a weapon: far and away the most typical offence was for 'threatening behaviour'.

What Stan Cohen did find, and this is the kernel of his argument, was 'enough evidence to suggest that the development of this behaviour was not independent of the reaction it provoked'. His thesis is that the punitive response of the community in general to the initial event, and the absurd overreaction of the mass media and the Magistrates in particular ('these sawdust Caesars who can only find courage like rats hunting in packs') set in motion an amplifying process -'a cumulative sequence which serves to fulfil the expectations created by the earlier events.' The gang stereotype was invoked to justify the tough, punitive measures taken by the police and the courts.

All the available evidence, then, points to the conclusion that there is no English equivalent of the Glasgow gang I have described: I shall have to look elsewhere for a parallel. In the past, in the 1930s, 1940s and perhaps also in the early 1950s, as Spinley (1953) and Fletcher (1964) testify, there were gangs of a more organised type; but even these seemed to have lacked the essential attributes of a Glasgow team or a 'bopping' gang from New York – the idealisation of violence, weapon carrying, definite leadership, gang structure etc. Nowadays, however, 'it can be safely asserted that the structured gang is unknown in this country.' (Downes, 1966, p.122)

A note of caution should be sounded here, for Downes's argument is based on scanty evidence, as he himself admits. Half of the authors reviewed above deal with the topic of gangs in passing, as a side-issue. And, though the others address themselves exclusively to the problem of gangs, they have all produced articles (with the exception of Farrant) rather than comprehensive treatises. Relevant research is as rare and as short-lived as the English gang appears to be. Gibbens and Ahrenfeldt (1966) report in fact that a research project into gangs had to be abandoned because no gang could be found: 'Gangs are always present in the next district, or they existed last year; never here and now. This mirage effect may be an important characteristic' (p.83)

The very reasons given for the non-existence of gangs in England emphasise the differences between Glasgow and the other cities of Great Britain in the mid-1960s. 'We have slums', writes Downes, 'but they are not teeming slums.' Two additional reasons are later advanced: full juvenile employment and the absence of second-generation immigrant adolescents. Glasgow, on the other hand, suffers from all three conditions – teeming slums, juvenile unemployment, and second-generation immigrant (Irish and, to a much lesser (extent, Pakistani) adolescents; these, taken together with other factors, to which I now turn, may in part explain the unique character within a British context, of the city's gangs.

Research into the modern Glasgow gang

In the previous section I have been complaining about the paucity of research into gangs in England. The situation is much worse in Scotland where there has been virtually none. One of the most serious social problems facing the community of Glasgow has been strangely and almost totally neglected by academics. Indeed one of my manifest motives for undertaking this study was, by acquiring some hard information on the Glasgow gang, to suggest that the phenomenon is a fit subject for scientific research.

Having completed the fieldwork, the problem then became one of finding any piece of work on Glasgow gangs with which to compare my findings. For instance, one of the most painstaking, statistical studies on juvenile delinquency in the city has been produced by Ferguson (1952). His conclusions on the connection between overcrowding and delinquency, on 'the added risk of delinquency represented by the presence in the home of a relative who had been convicted' remain valuable: but the subject of gangs is nowhere mentioned, the word 'gang' does not appear in the text at all. Similarly, Stott's (1961) survey of Glasgow boys put on probation, though involved with the interrelationship between maladjustment and delinquency like much of his later work (1964, 1966), makes no reference to a gang problem.

One investigation, however, into the leisure time pursuits of young people aged 15 to 19 in the west of Scotland deals tangentially with what the author, Pearl Jephcott (1967), refers to as 'Trouble with a capital T.' One of the three districts chosen for study was Drumchapel, a large housing estate with a population in 1964 of over 40,000, situated on the north-west boundary of Glasgow. Jephcott stresses the abnormal structure of this population in that the adults barely outnumbered those under 21, and the 15 to 19 age group 'formed about 16% of the total which was nearly twice the national proportion or that for Glasgow as a whole.'

The large formless groups described by Jephcott were so loose in structure that they hardly merited the term gang:

> The Drumchapel Bucks were said to number about 300 youngsters if hangers-on and girlfriends, Baby and Lady Bucks, were included. A gang's five or six key individuals, young fellows in their late teens and early twenties, were described as louts and deadbeats, 'right bampots' ... They were feared as ready to do *anything* to gain an immediate satisfaction and their private ends. (p.96)

Jephcott returns twice to the theme of the real core of serious trouble-makers, the 'hard men': 'In their case Trouble appeared to be associated with psychological disturbance which, it was noted, had been spotted way back by their contemporaries.' And again, ' ... they were cold-blooded, "He'd knife his grandmother for a bottle of Vordo." These instigators of serious Trouble were feared as unlike ordinary people.' Such supporting evidence, slight though it is, and based on interviews with the 'average', law-abiding adolescents of the district, provides some grounds for believing that the gang I joined was not atypical of the species.

Further information can be obtained from the articles on stabbings written by surgeons at two of the city's leading hospitals. It is in itself remarkable that these articles were produced and the reason appears to have been the concern of all members of the hospital staffs over the number and serious nature of knife wounds. Stalker (1966) reports that his hospital in 1964 treated 959 cases of assault, including stabbings, in the casualty department; a further 42 stabbing cases had to be admitted to the wards. He continues: ' ... surprisingly few of these serious offences were the basis of legal proceedings. This probably results from fear of retribution on the part of victims, although several of these appeared to be purely innocent parties.'

The second article, by Batey and MacBain (1967), deals only with the stabbing cases admitted to their hospital, a total of 147 in the four-year period 1962 to 1965. With regard to the age of the injured, 'nearly 40% of the patients were under 20 ... and over 65% were below 30.' They also call attention to the change from the weapon used by the gangs of the 1930s: 'The razor, which usually only disfigured, now seems to be replaced by the knife, which is potentially more dangerous and causes wounds which more often require expensive and time-consuming inpatient care.' It is a mark of the seriousness of the situation in Glasgow that the modern gang has in this respect eclipsed its predecessor, and that doctors can write of weapons which *only* disfigure.

The only other source of data is a report of the Scottish branch of the Institute for the Study and Treatment of Delinquency (1970). This is concerned with the study of the 860 offenders charged in Glasgow with the carrying of offensive weapons in 1965, the peak year for this offence in the city. In the majority of cases 'the weapon found to be offensive was some kind of knife. ... Other weapons found included knuckledusters, kukris, razors, sharpened steel combs, hammers, axes, a sword, a pistol, metal bars, a garden fork, scissors, belts and chisels.' (p.265). The Glasgow working party responsible for the report were not able to determine directly the gang membership of the accused, but nevertheless, two of the conclusions which were reached are relevant here. Firstly, the peak age for this type of offence was 16 to 17; secondly, weapon-carrying was much more widespread in the old housing areas to the east of the city centre than anywhere else in Glasgow. The latter finding casts doubt on the widely held belief that the gangs are mainly concentrated in the new housing estates, a view fostered by the mass media, including an otherwise perceptive article by Richard Boston (1968). My own experience would suggest the opposite, namely, that the main gangs are still centred in the old slum areas, and that gang traditions have been transferred to the new estates which proved to be first-rate breeding grounds for gang activity. Support for this explanation comes from the work of Cloward and Ohlin (1960) in New York: 'Former gang members displaced by slum-clearance projects to outer areas carry their conflict subculture with them and seek to establish their old reputations in the new areas.' (p.30)

To my knowledge, that concludes the sum total of work (apart from highly inaccurate newspaper articles), which in any way pertains to the modern Glasgow gang. Two interim reports have recently been produced by Gail Armstrong and Mary Wilson (1970, 1971) on their research in Easterhouse, but little of their findings is publicly available beyond what Stan Cohen (1971, pp.246-8) has to say.

As for the official statistics on crime and violence in Scotland, John Mack (1968) argues that there has been a substantial rise, the greater part of which has been carried by the 17 to 24 age-group. The crime rate of the 14- to 16-year olds has also increased 'alarmingly' (70% in Scotland, 60% in England and Wales in the years 1966 and 1967). According to Mack, the bulk of these additions to the annual Scottish crime figures 'appears to be the result of casual aggression, running fights, apparently motiveless violence on the part of the young and not-so-young males, and, of course, the use of fatally dangerous weapons.'

In case it is inferred that Glasgow is responsible for this increase, the facts are that the city's share of all Scottish crimes has been decreasing from 38% in 1938 to 32% in 1967. But if the more serious crimes of violence (murder, attempted murder, and culpable homicide) are taken separately, Glasgow's share has been increasing from 30% in the period 1954 to 1957 to 42% in the years 1964 to 1967. Two points emerge from these figures. Firstly, other areas of Scotland have their own very serious problems of crime, including violent crime. This is underlined by Shields and Duncan (1964, p.50) who give the rates for crimes of violence per 1,000 population for the year 1961-2. Glasgow heads the list of the cities of Scotland with a rate of 0·89 (the figure for Edinburgh is 0·13); but amongst the burghs, Ayr has a rate of 0·96, while Paisley has the highest rate of all, 1·41. Secondly, it remains true that Glasgow, with one-fifth of the population of Scotland, accounts for just less than half of the crimes of violence.

In Chapter 18 I selected two structural conditions in Glasgow which are conducive to ganging: long traditions of slum housing and violence. But the list does not end there. During the last decade unemployment in Glasgow ran at almost twice the rate as that for Britain as a whole. And increasingly, fears of a return to the massive unemployment of 1931, when in Glasgow alone 130,000 men were out of work, have spread along Clydeside. By December 1971 more than 42,000 Glaswegians (or 7·5 per cent) were registered as unemployed.[32]

Moreover, it has been estimated (by the Glasgow Council on Alcoholism) that the local rate for alcoholic dependence is two to three times as high as in equivalent cities in England; that Glasgow has one-tenth of all the alcoholics in Great Britain (in round figures between 40,000 and 50,000 people). The local traditions of hard drinking, and the figures for those charged with being drunk and incapable, have been commented upon by many observers for almost a century. Sillitoe, for example, in his chief constable's report for 1932 devotes a section to the 'pernicious influence' of cheap red wine, which was purchased by the gill for 3d. or 6d. in public houses by both men and women, who then added half a pint of beer to it. More recent reports (1968, 1969) of the Chief Constable have concerned themselves with the problems of juvenile drunkenness and the increasing number of persons under 18 who frequent pubs.

The list of measurable pathologies could be extended because we are confronted in John McQuaid's (1968, p.45) words, 'with the coincidence not of two but of half-a-dozen anomalies converging on a relatively small, well-defined population.' The same author refers to what he calls 'the south-west complex', and in another article (1970, p.154) 'the sociopathic singularity of the region'. For McQuaid, this singularity comprises not only the factors I have already mentioned, but also 'a high general death rate, very high incidence of lung cancer and arteriosclerotic and degenerative heart disease, both among the highest in Europe. . .' The return of infantile rickets in Glasgow (Arneil and Crosbie, 1963; Arneil, 1964) is only another sympton of the same complex.

The city's high rates of slum housing and unemployment, of delinquency and violent crime, of alcoholism and disease, are not discrete areas of deprivation but inter-connecting and cumulative forms of inequality.[33] And it is from this 'inter-locking network of inequalities' that the subculture of gangs in Glasgow has grown. This subculture shows in the starkest possible way how poverty, inferior education, the lack of even minimum opportunities, and a steadily deteriorating economic situation all combine to produce feelings of frustration, rage and powerlessness.

But why do so many adolescent boys in Glasgow choose the violent gang as their form of adaptation to such a plethora of social and environmental adversities? Why do they become street fighters rather than drug addicts or political activists? Why do they not retreat into social despair or fatalistic acceptance of the *status quo*? I would speculate that there are two answers to such crucial questions, posed by Cloward and Ohlin (1960, p.32). Firstly, there is a strong subcultural emphasis on self-assertion and on a rebellious independence against authority as the means of attaining masculinity.

Glasgow's long history of industrial militancy, culminating in the 1971 'work-in' at Upper Clyde Shipbuilders, is evidence of an active, even aggressive response in times of crisis. Secondly, economic hardship, suffered by generations of Glaswegians, has narrowed down the possibilities of action. A sense of desperation (cf. Matza, 1964) is created amongst boys who find some forms of action (work, apprenticeships, all forms of higher education) closed to them, while other forms (apathy, hard-line drugs) are excluded by the subculture as being the very antithesis of manliness. The only alternative, and one hallowed in the traditions of Glasgow slum life, is to respond with violence. The large urban centres in England with histories of violence have prospered since the war in ways which leave Glasgow a grey, depressed area in comparison.

The Glasgow gang boy feels that he is being pushed around, that he has no control over the social conditions which predetermine his future and yet he is expected to act like a man who is in charge of the situation. 'Some dramatic reassurance that he can still make things happen is necessary' (Matza, 1964, p.189). That reassurance, I suggest, is likely to take the form of gang fighting, because over the last hundred years in Glasgow acts of extreme and unpredictable violence have become invested with an aura which transcends mere brutality. The leading exponent of such violence, the gang leader, is accorded the title of King, no less. It is only in this social context that the most disturbed personality can come to the fore; through his prowess in explosive acts of violence he is able to capture the leadership of the gang.

Only a radical new policy of regional redevelopment can hope to combat this deeply ingrained malaise of social and economic problems in west central Scotland. Government intervention is needed urgently to provide jobs, capital investment, housing, and additional educational and medical facilities. Nothing less than a really comprehensive policy of social action on a regional basis is called for; and yet the tragedy lies in the indifference of successive Governments who, decade after decade, leave desperate situations to fester. The lesson of Ulster has not yet been learned.

20
American research into gangs

THERE IS NO dearth of research into gangs in the United States nor of comprehensive reviews of that research; so instead of examining in detail the vast literature which has been produced there, I propose to give a very short summary of the theoretical ideas associated with the most influential thinkers in this field: Albert K Cohen, Richard Cloward and Lloyd Ohlin, Walter B Miller and David Matza. The Glasgow gang will then be described under a number of headings and its characteristics compared with those of gangs which have been studied in America since the early days of Thrasher. Finally, I shall discuss a few general points which have arisen directly from my own research.

Very briefly, Cohen's (1955) theory in *Delinquent Boys: The Culture of the Gang* is that lower working-class boys in American society are ill prepared by virtue of their socialisation to compete with their middle-class counterparts in the race for position and success in an intensely competitive society. At school, for example, they are judged and found wanting by middle-class standards of behaviour and performance, by 'the middle-class measuring rod'. Because they are denied status by respectable society, they suffer loss of self-respect, experience feelings of guilt, shame and resentment, become 'status frustrated', and so have to cope with a psychological problem of adjustment. One of a number of possible solutions is for them to join together in a delinquent subculture with others who share the same problems, and 'jointly to establish new norms, new criteria of status which define as meritorious the characteristics they *do* possess, the kinds of conduct of which they *are* capable.' (Cohen, 1955, p.66, italics as in original.)

The delinquent subculture is typified by Cohen as non-utilitarian (stealing 'for the hell of it', without thought of gain or profit), malicious (enjoying 'the discomfiture of others, a delight in the defiance of taboos ... ') and negativistic (rules of conduct are taken from middle-class society but turned upside down so that the very behaviour proscribed by the dominant culture is espoused by the boys). The function of the delinquent subculture is that it encourages the boy to 'break clean with middle-class morality' and legitimises aggression against the sources of his frustration. An essential link in Cohen's argument is that delinquent subcultures are collective or *group* solutions to the social and psychological problems experienced by boys who have not been able to thrust aside completely the middle-class criteria which they had earlier internalised and which now proclaim them as failures. The gang boys deal with the consequent anxiety by employing the mechanism of 'reaction-formation', whereby they over-react in 'irrational, malicious, unaccountable hostility to the enemy within the gates as well as without: the norms of the respectable middle-class society' (p.133). The wealth of empirical research, stimulated by the publication of Cohen's book, has not been supportive of his original ideas and a mass of evidence has been collected (by Gordon, Short, Cartwright and Strodtbeck, Martin Gold and others) which seriously questions the hypothesis that gang members reject middle-class values.

Cloward and Ohlin's (1960) starting-point in *Delinquency and Opportunity: A Theory of Delinquent Gangs* is their belief that lower-class boys form delinquent subcultures *not* to solve internal, psychological problems of adjustment as Cohen claims, but in response to external problems of social injustice. The delinquent boy, for Cloward and Ohlin, is one who blames society or the larger social system rather than himself for his failure. The briefest outline of the theory would run as follows: delinquent subcultures emerge because of the strain and alienation felt by working-class youths who aspire to the same cultural goals of success as the rest of American society while being confronted by the differential availability of the legitimate means of achieving these success goals. In Cloward and Ohlin's words (1960, p.86) there is a 'disparity between what lower-class youth are led to want and what is actually available to them ... '. Consequently, they react by adopting illegitimate means of reaching the same goal of economic affluence. However, illegitimate channels to advancement differ in accessibility in the same way that legitimate channels do, with stable, integrated neighbourhoods offering far more opportunities for professional criminal careers than socially disorganised areas. The authors hypothesise the existence of three distinctive types of delinquent subculture found among adolescent males in lower-class areas of large urban cities. First is the *criminal subculture* – 'a type of gang which is devoted to theft, extortion, and other illegal means of securing income.' Such gangs flourish in stable working-class areas where boys are able to learn, like apprentices, the criminal role from adults who are involved in organised crime and who act as success-models. The second is the *conflict subculture* 'a type of gang in which the manipulation of violence predominates as a way of winning status.' Boys living in unintegrated neighbourhoods resort through frustration to street fighting and gang battles because *both* the conventional *and* the criminal roads to success are closed to them. The third is the *retreatist subculture* – 'a type of gang in which the consumption of drugs is stressed.' Boys who have become alienated from conventional roles and who have not succeeded in gaining status in either criminal or conflict gangs are the 'double failures' who retreat into drug use. Unfortunately for this elaborate typology, extensive empirical research in Chicago (Short and Strodtbeck, 1965, p.13) has found great difficulty in locating a full-blown criminal gang or more than one drug-using group, a finding which 'casts doubt on the generality of these phenomena, if not on their existence.' Other researchers, in London (Downes, 1966), in Paris (Vaz, 1962 and Monod, 1967), and in Cordoba, in Argentina (de Fleur, 1967), have experienced similar difficulties in verifying the existence of the three distinct forms of subculture.

Walter B Miller (1958), a cultural anthropologist, has raised even more fundamental objections to the motives imputed to delinquents by Cohen in an influential paper, 'Lower Class Culture as a Generating Milieu of Gang Delinquency'. Miller refuses to accept, that the norms of working-class gang boys are merely an inversion or repudiation of middle-class standards; for him, 'the cultural system which exerts the most direct influence on behaviour is that of the lower class community itself – a long-established, distinctively patterned tradition with an integrity of its own' (1958, p.6). In other words, Miller would explain the gang delinquency of deprived youngsters more in terms of their *absolute* position in the social system rather than their position *relative* to other more favourably placed sections of the community (Short and Strodtbeck, 1965, p.7). Certain features or 'focal concerns' of lower-class culture are said to facilitate the emergence of delinquency: getting into and staying out of trouble, being a 'tough guy', outsmarting or 'conning' others, searching for excitement or thrills, considering one's life in the control of fate, destiny, or luck, and finally, being ambivalent about independence are all 'areas or issues which command widespread and persistent attention and a high degree of emotional involvement.' For the adolescent male, reared in such a community, socialised in a 'female-based household', and bereft of the stable economic support of an adult male, the single-sex street-corner gang is of particular importance because it provides 'the first real opportunity to learn essential aspects of the male role in the context of peers facing similar problems of sex-role identification.' The thesis seems to be that the boys have so deeply internalised lower class culture, which is itself intrinsically criminogenic, that predominantly middle-class institutions like the school have no effect upon their behaviour. Michael Power's (1967, 1972) research in Tower Hamlets (to be discussed in the final chapter) shows that this suspect conclusion of Miller's is simply not valid in a British context. Note also Charles Valentine's (1968, p.44) provocative opinion that the six focal concerns reveal more about the anxieties and projections of middle-class scholars like Miller than they do about the cultural patterns of the poor: 'Where could one find a better brief inventory of unresolved value conflicts underlying the confusion and anomie of middle-class life in America than the many ambiguities and ambivalences associated with legality, masculinity, shrewdness, boredom, luck, and autonomy?'

More recently, David Matza in a number of papers and books has produced a forceful and attractive alternative to the perspectives already described. The typical delinquent, in Matza's writings, is neither totally opposed nor committed to the dominant normative system and is in no fundamental way dissimilar to other adolescent youths: 'The juvenile delinquent would appear to be at least partially committed to the dominant social order in that he frequently exhibits guilt or shame when he violates its proscriptions, accords approval to certain conforming figures, and distinguishes between appropriate and inappropriate targets for his deviance' (1957, p.666). In order to assuage their guilt, delinquents employ rationalisations or justifications for their deviant behaviour both before and after the delinquent act. Examples of these 'techniques of neutralization' are the denial of responsibility ('I didn't mean it'), the denial of injury ('I didn't really hurt anybody'), the denial of the victim ('those queers/Pakistanis had it coming to them'), the condemnation of the condemners ('the corrupt police always pick on me'), and the appeal to higher loyalties ('the gang forced me to do it'). By using such techniques, the boys bend or stretch the rules rather than break them, they strike 'tangential or glancing blows' at middle-class standards rather than create an opposing ideology.

Next, Matza and Sykes (1961) argue that the values of the delinquent – the search for kicks, the disdain for work, and the demonstration of masculinity through aggression – are remarkably similar to the values of the gentleman of leisure. Delinquent values are far less deviant than commonly portrayed and are merely exaggerated forms of 'subterranean values' which are present in the leisure activities of the dominant culture: The delinquent may not stand as an alien in the body of society but may represent instead a disturbing reflection or a caricature' (1961, p.717).

In his two books *Delinquency and Drift* (1964), and *Becoming Deviant* (1969), Matza develops these ideas into a more comprehensive theory of delinquency which depicts the delinquent as vacillating between criminal and conventional roles, 'an actor neither compelled nor committed to deeds nor freely choosing them ... ' (1964, p.28). He engages in crime only 'casually, intermittently, and transiently', and it is this state of drift, defined as the 'episodic release from moral constraint', which allows, but does not compel, the boy to commit delinquent acts. Individually and privately, the majority of delinquent boys remain uncommitted to their misdeeds, but in the company of the gang 'a system of shared misunderstandings, based on miscues' leads them to believe that the others have in fact decided to become criminals.

In his second book, Matza moves even further away from an acceptance of any sort of determinism and protests against any theory which conceives of man as object instead of subject, 'as merely reactive and denying that he is the author of action ... ' (1969, p.7). According to Matza, delinquents *choose* to become deviant even if their circumstances predispose them towards crime. Carson and Wiles (1971, p.57) believe that Matza has reached the point where 'he rejects the total, harsh determinism of previous sociological explanations with their emphasis upon irresistible, if largely unidentifiable "causes", and at the same time, resists the final sociological nihilism of accepting the complete centrality of will in human affairs.'

All the theories discussed so far, Cohen's reaction formation, Cloward and Ohlin's theory of differential opportunity systems, and Miller's autonomous traditions, have one feature in common – an inability to stand up to empirical research, and Matza's notion of drift is no exception, as Michael Hindelang's (1970) study demonstrates.

A further danger concerns the whole scale transference to this country of concepts developed in the United States. The combined researches of Veness (1962), Downes (1966), Willmott (1966) and Hargreaves (1967) suggest, for example, that explanations of delinquency which rely on the concept of status frustration are not appropriate in an English context. David Downes (1966, pp.230-31) found 'an almost monolithic conformity to the traditional working class value-system, and little discontent with working class status, especially in the occupational field.' Unlike those of their counterparts in America, the aspirations of young people in the lower socio-economic strata of English society seem to be severely limited but realistic.

Such divergence is not altogether surprising when one considers the important historical and structural differences in education, race, economics and politics, between the two countries. What is intriguing is that, in spite of these major differences, the closest parallel to the Young Team remains the account of the gangs of New York as presented by Yablonsky, with whom my only disagreements are points of detail rather than of substance.

Yablonsky (1967, p.169ff.) classifies all gangs into three types: social gangs are based upon 'feelings of mutual attraction' among boys who band together to enjoy social interaction in socially acceptable activities; delinquent gangs are comprised of emotionally stable youths whose essential objective is *profit* through stealing or assault; violent gangs are 'primarily organised for emotional gratification, and violence is the theme around which all activities centre.' The Young Team belongs to this last category and its main characteristics are summarised under the following headings:

Structure and Membership

Like most students of juvenile gangs, I make a gross distinction between two types of membership, core and marginal. The Young Team consisted of a small hard core of seven to eight boys, often only four to five, and of a much larger peripheral membership of at the most, 20 to 25. The more violent boy, in Yablonsky's terms, the more 'sociopathic', tends to be the core member, and the less pathologically disturbed boy tends to be a fringe member. These are not meant to be rigid diagnostic categories, but merely rough classifications which overlap and shade into one another. In the Young Team, Baggy, for example, was either the most marginal of the core members or the most central of the marginals.

Membership had little formal or permanent character. No initiation ceremony or test was demanded of me or anyone else. Boys joined by 'being around', by standing at the gang's corner or by drinking in the gang's pub. If there had not been this casual attitude to membership, I doubt if I could have gained admission as easily as I did, even with the help of Tim's introduction. While their involvement with the gang lasted, boys moved in and out as they pleased. Group membership, in Fisher's (1962, p.255) phrase, was not static but dynamic; and this fluid situation has been commented upon time after time in the United States, witness Short and Strodtbeck (1965, p.207): 'Boys come and go for days or weeks at a time, and unless they occupy a particularly strong leadership or other important role in the group, they are hardly missed.' In Glasgow, boys, even leaders, terminated their connection with the gang by simply quitting, by not turning up – and this was acceptable, as it was in New York: 'A youth can terminate "belonging" by simply saying "I quit".' (Yablonsky, 1967, p.175).

The leading gangs in the area had a hierarchical structure based upon five age gradings. Boys progressed up the ladder from the Baby to the Toddler Team, to the Tiny, to the Young Team and then on to the Heavy Team. These age divisions were not always clear-cut, as some boys, like Tim's brother John, found themselves in the ambiguous position of being members of both the Young Team and the Heavy Team: they were trying to leave the former but had not yet been fully integrated in the latter. As far as I am aware, such vertical divisions have not been noted before in British research on gangs, but they are commonplace in America. Short (1963), for example, in his new introduction to Thrasher's classic study, refers to 'networks of gang "nations" comprised of Senior, Junior, Midget (sometimes even down to Pee Wee!).'

One of the most important effects, of course, of this integration of different age levels of offenders, is the perpetuation of the conflict subculture, as

Cloward and Ohlin (1960) emphasised. What happens in such communities is that boys 'select their role models from the next oldest age group, with a consequent tendency for the traditions of street life, including its delinquent patterns, to be transmitted relatively intact.' (Kobrin, 1962, p.389).

Leadership

In The Young Team it was not the strongest or the tallest or the most intelligent boys who became leaders, but the most disturbed, the most violent boys, those with lowest impulse control. To use the gang's terms, such boys were the 'mentalest' or the 'mental heids', the 'psychies', and the 'gemmies'. Prowess in violence - spontaneous, irrational, unprovoked violence - marked out the leader and at the same time served to terrify his followers. The power of the local King did not stem from his personal charisma or magnetic personality, but from the speed of his forehead and his feet. Dick Stevenson and Tim exercised leadership through the use, or more often the threatened use, of physical assault. In this respect the popular conception of the gang leader is correct: fear of sheer brute force, not influence, controlled the gang. Tim maintained absolute hegemony, his rule was autocratic, he was dictatorial and demanding.

And the leader's image was built up by the fantasy of the gang; stories of shooting and stabbing policemen, of stealing hand grenades and guns, of diving through glass panels, were told without contradiction. The core leaders, and to a far lesser extent the gang, lived in a fantasy world of which they seemed to be in need. Tim claimed a following of a hundred boys and together they 'ruled' the city: he did not strike me as consciously lying, for his self-image and prestige demanded at least as many members. Yablonsky asked members of a New York gang, the Balkans, to estimate the size of their group, and answers varied from 80 to 5,000. 'Such "illusionary members" were identified essentially to satisfy the leaders' needs to "possess" a large membership.' (1967, p.230)

The research literature, however, is split from top to bottom over the essential quality of gang leadership. On the one side banners reading 'psychopath' or 'sociopath' are flourished, and on the other, cutting remarks are passed about 'easy generalizations of emotional disturbance'. What is so frequently glossed over is that both sets of explanations, emanating as they do from very different data, are possible and can co-exist peaceably.

Let us enter the jungle of disputed opinions on this matter. Thrasher (1927, p.355) believed that the gang leader, 'even at the height of his power, is not an absolute monarch, but plays his part through his response to the wishes of his followers, and this is illustrated in the crude sort of democracy which is almost universal in such groups'. This traditional view of the well-adjusted, tough, 'natural' leader is continued in the work of William Whyte (1955) and his portrayal of Doc, the leader of the Norton Street gang in the Italian slum of 'Cornerville' in the heart of 'Eastern City'. Early on, Doc speaks of how he took over the leadership of the gang from Nutsy by thrashing him in a fist fight. 'So after that I was the leader and he was my lieutenant ... Nutsy was a cocky kid before I beat him up ... After that he seemed to lose his pride. I would talk to him and try to get him to buck up.' A few sentences later, Doc is saying to the author: 'But I wasn't such a tough kid, Bill. I was always sorry after I walloped them.'

The gangs described by Thrasher and Whyte are simply not of the same genre as the violent Young Team; compare, for example, Doc's behaviour with Tim's general lack of remorse and his hammer assault on Big Dim for challenging his leadership. In many vital ways, the Norton Street gang does not provide a proper comparison; they were a stable group of older men in their twenties who could hardly be called delinquent, and who continued to participate in the group after marriage. Moreover, there is only one reference to gang fighting in the whole book (p.6). So Whyte's observations that he never saw the leaders 'exert their authority through physical force' (p.12), and his comments on the leader's dependability and fair-mindedness (p.259ff.) have very limited relevance to the present discussion.

Others more involved with delinquent corner groups and fighting gangs, like WB Miller (1957, pp.402-3), still maintain that leadership patterns vary 'both according to the nature of the activity and the presence or absence in the area of certain "key" youngsters.' Leadership in WB Miller's groups was 'based primarily on special personal qualities and abilities of different boys.' So the leaders changed as the gang prepared for a baseball game, a dance, or a 'rumble'. Certainly, among his Junior Outlaws (1961), there was no autocratic despot who both made and enforced decisions for the group.

In the writings of Short on adolescent gangs in Chicago the contrasts between this position and that of Yablonsky and myself are first brought out into the open. Short (1963, p.xxxviii) believes that one of the basic skills of a gang leader is the ability to get along with people, and that this explains his better job record. The debate is continued in a footnote: 'This, quite in contrast to the view advanced by Yablonsky that gang leaders are the most seriously emotionally disturbed boys. Our data suggest that the latter more often are fringe members who often attempt to achieve leadership by aggressive means or by involving the group in conflict with other gangs in order to create leadership opportunities.' Short and Strodtbeck (1965, p.195) develop this argument in a later book, where the 'overwhelming preponderance' of the actions of conflict gang leaders is said to be 'co-ordinating and nurturant'. Among the gangs they observed, leadership was not exercised arbitrarily and the internal status hierarchy was not maintained by 'aggressive dominance-seeking by leaders'.

Similarly, the Sherifs (1964, p.160ff.) must have been studying groups of adolescents who differ in kind from their Glasgow counterparts, when they found fit to emphasise: *'Too frequently, the leader-follower relations are viewed as simple "dominance-submission", with the result that the followers' roles and their ties to the group are completely misunderstood.* [Italics as in original.] Influence rather than sheer physical force, which is demoted to a 'relatively minor role', allowed the Sherifs' leaders to maintain their power. Leaders were expected to be the exemplars of group activities: indeed, one of the boys was 'chastised by his fellows for being so foolish as to carry a weapon with him ... ' (p.179). In Glasgow, boys including myself were 'chastised' for not carrying weapons.

LR Jansyn (1966, p.610) follows in the footsteps of Short and Strodtbeck by asserting that among the Dons, leadership 'appears to go to boys who are held in high regard by the members'. And Lincoln Keiser (1969, p.45) associates the Vice Lords of Chicago with the same school of thought when he reports that one and the same person could assume the identities of both leader and follower at different times. Leaders rule by means of influence not force, and Vice Lords follow them 'because they like them, or respect them, or because they think they will gain something by doing so, but not because they fear them.'

This image of the gang leader is the dominant one in British work as well. To Turner and Spencer (1955, p.55), the leader is 'the member whose ability most adequately fulfils the current demands of the group.' To Mays (1954, pp.108-9), the gang leader is the most admired personality: 'He is someone they all look up to and like.' In fact any list of the characteristics supposedly linked with leadership – greater emotional maturity, insight, responsibility, sensitivity and so on (Evans, 1962, pp.56-7) – only summarises all the qualities which Tim Malloy and Dick Stevenson lacked.

Faced with such a mass of contrary evidence, is there any corroboration of my experience? There is always Yablonsky, of course; but, luckily, there are other sources of support. Earlier workers in New York, like Crawford, Malamud, and Dumpson (1950, pp.11-12), characterised each street club as 'a miniature autocracy', led by boys who usually ran their clubs 'dictatorially'. There is also a close parallel in the study of the New York City Youth Board (1960, p.52ff.), but an even closer one in Howard Polsky's (1962) analysis of the informal peer group culture of a residential treatment centre, which he calls 'Cottage Six'. There the leaders exerted power through intimidation and physical domination; but once they had consolidated their position in the institution, they had less need of overt aggression.[34] Polsky (p.78) captures the essence of the relationship I observed between leader and follower in the Young Team in these lines: 'The delinquent leader does not need to establish his dominance every moment. He exudes aggression; it is implicit in every gesture. Past aggression results in the expectation, more effective than action, that if the occasion arose, Davis could conquer any opponent.' And the defence mechanism, employed by Tim and the other core leaders to deal with their anxiety about their aggression, is caught in Polsky's (p.79) description of Davis, one of the leaders: ' ... he constantly rationalised his aggression by projecting onto others his insecurities and inadequacies. *They* always wanted to attack *him*, so he literally beat them to the punch.' [Italics as in original.]

Mattick and Caplan (1967, pp.114-19) provide further confirmation of the existence on the streets of Chicago of a leadership style 'associated with concentration of power, dicatorial methods, authoritarian personality, and tyrannical behaviour.' Although they state that such boys are not found nearly so often 'as the popular literature in the field would lead us to believe', they do trace the history of one leader 'who worked from an extremely narrow base of physical prowess and delinquent behaviour.' This 'do-nothing' leader was manoeuvred into a 'do-something' situation and his subsequent failure allowed more capable youngsters to emerge as leaders in their own right.

In Yablonsky's (1967, p.242) opinion, gang leaders are 'essentially self-appointed', and one of their vital functions is 'to serve as a symbol of idealised violence'. In the eyes of the other boys, the leader 'has "heart", and will pull a trigger, swing a bat, or wield a knife without any expression of fear or, most important, regret'. Another paragraph of his could almost be a profile of Dick Stevenson:

> The core sociopath in the violent gang is generally the leader. Contrary to many widely held misconceptions that these leaders could become 'captains of industry if only their energies were redirected,' the gang leader appears as a socially ineffectual youth incapable of transferring his leadership ability and functioning to more demanding social groups. The low-level expectations of the violent gang, with its minimal social requirements, is appropriate to the leader's ability. Given his undersocialised personality attributes, he could only be a leader of a violent gang. . . The violent gang leader obsessively needs the gang, and provides it with its basic cohesive force. In a gang of some 30 boys there may be five or six core leaders who desperately rely on the gang to build and maintain their rep. (p.236)

The similarity between Yablonsky's violent gang and Tim's Young Team is clearly brought out in this passage.

Style of leadership, then, like gang structure, can vary among adolescent gangs from the most dictatorial to the most democratic. Kobrin (1961, p.693) observed, 'in an ethnic working-class neighbourhood of a large city' in the United States, three sub-groups within the Eagles, each with its own very different leadership pattern. He studied the evolution of the gang until 'the head of the toughest and most aggressive faction captured the leadership of the entire group.' Bloch and Niederhoffer (1958, pp.201-16), in their analysis of the power structure of the Pirates in New York, showed how the presence in one gang of four leaders – Paulie, the strategist; Lulu, the tactician; Solly, the Diplomat; and Blackie, the procurer and scapegoat permitted flexibility and avoided clashes. All sorts of leadership patterns can exist: my task has been to place the Glasgow gang firmly at the dictatorial end of the continuum.

Role Allocation

In Glasgow there was little differentiation in the horizontal structure of the gang. Young Teams, Tiny and Toddler Teams were ruled by a leader-aff', Heavy Teams by a 'King'. This latter office was frequently kept within one family and passed from father to son or from elder to younger brother: it was not assumed only when a gang battle was pending, but was permanent. Apart from the leadership role, there were indefinite follower or membership roles filled by the 'punters'; the two exceptions were Big Fry, the gang wit, and Davie Wilson, the scapegoat.

In comparison with American juvenile gangs, such role allocation is minimal. A common situation in such gangs is for each one to have its president, vice-president, war counsellor, and 'light-up' man who takes charge of the club's arsenal of weapons (see, for example, Crawford, Malamud and Dumpson, 1950, p.11). Keiser's (1969, p.17) Vice Lords had seven named officers, but the palm in this regard must go to one group, reported by Delaney (1954, p.40) in Philadelphia, which had no less than 12 distinct officers with 'such descriptive titles as ... chief of war intelligence, spokesman, and commander of tactical operations.'

Group Cohesion

Core members of the Young Team formed no warm, loving hetero sexual relationships: the bonds of friendship which linked them to each other and which linked them with the ordinary members of the gang were equally tenuous.

Group cohesion was low, inter personal relationships were shallow and superficial. Core members operated like loners in a crowd and both they and marginal members flitted in and out of the group like shadows, without commitment to the group. There was no *esprit de corps*, no camaraderie, no mutual kindness. Strangers, like myself, could attach themselves to such a loose grouping of boys without having to handle deep or ripening relationships. Only one homosexual attachment was in evidence, between Tim and Big Dave, but the inescapable ambience of aggression prevented the expression of tender feelings on anyone's part.

The libidinal ties, which are said by Freud (1922, p.54) to be *the* characteristic of a group, were not conspicuously present among the Young Team. The boys did hold collections to help pay the fines of fellow members, they handed money and drink to those just released from custody, and they presented £30 to the mother of one of their murdered leaders. But they also quarrelled over who should take the King to hospital to have his stomach pumped, and on another occasion no one was prepared to render Beano that service except myself. Dick had stabbed members of his own gang, one seriously, and Tim had hit Big Dim on the head with a hammer. Tim and Big Dave had stabbed two relatives of a core member of the gang at a party. Besides this, the Young Team and the Heavy Team had had a brawling match, and numerous 'square-goes' had been fought between members of the same gang. This absence of solidarity is graphically summed up in the phrase of one American delinquent quoted by the Schwendingers (1967, p.98): 'It's fuck your buddy week, fifty-two weeks of the year.'

Observers of gangs are divided into the same two camps on this issue, as they were over gang leadership. Thrasher (1927, p.57) includes *esprit de corps*, solidarity and morale in his definition of the gang, and claims (p.278) these to be characteristics even of the diffuse type of gang. 'This manifests itself in many forms of self-sacrifice. If a member is in serious danger the rest will spare no pains to save his life.' (p.290).

AK Cohen (1955, p.31), who like Cloward and Ohlin (1960) is strangely silent on the subject of gang leadership, stresses the group autonomy of the gang, which is 'a separate, distinct and often irresistible focus of attraction, loyalty and solidarity.'

WB Miller (1958) considers that for many an adolescent male, reared in a female-based household, the gang 'is the most stable and solidary primary group he has ever belonged to ... The activity patterns of the group require a high level of intra-group solidarity.' It is, however, the article by WB Miller (1961) and his associates on the aggressive acts of the Junior Outlaws which shows how fundamentally Miller's gang in Boston differs from mine in

Glasgow, or Yablonsky's in New York. This meticulous study of the targets, form and intensity of the Junior Outlaws' aggression makes clear that intragroup fighting is not in itself an indication of weak solidarity. Internal dissensions among the Outlaws are rather 'the result of violations of a specific and precisely defined set of standards', a code which is comparable to that 'of the Arthurian knights or Samurai warriors.' The 'ideal' corner boy for a Junior Outlaw is athletic, faithful, dependable, modest, smart, honest, sensitive, 'smooth' and 'physically strong, but careful not to take unfair advantage of this strength in dealing with fellow group members.' Although 'seventy per cent of the aggressive actions of all types, from good-natured ribbing to outright physical attack, were directed at fellow group members', in not one of the 95 physically aggressive acts was a weapon of any description employed. The Junior Outlaws appeared to have directed most of their aggressive actions at one another and still enjoyed 'harmonious' inter-personal relations, but they were no violent gang.

LR Jansyn (1966), after observing for over two years the variations in the group activities of the Dons, a severely delinquent street corner group in Chicago, concluded that two-thirds of the membership was constant and of these the nine core members of the gang had a very high attendance rate. His interpretation of these findings is that solidarity is important to the boys, and that it has a tendency to decline until it reaches a level where it becomes threatening to them. Then, Jansyn says, 'there is a spurt of group activity which generates interest and increases attendance and solidarity.' In the Young Team and the Heavy Team it was the sudden reappearance of the leaders from detention which galvanised the gangs into action. Without the 'top men' the gang disintegrated.

The Vice Lords of Chicago (Keiser, 1969, p.38ff.), a tough and at times violent, adolescent negro gang, accepted that in times of real need 'mutual help, both material and physical, is a binding obligation.' Their ideology of brotherhood was expressed in a wine drinking ritual, where the first of the wine was poured on the ground in a symbolic libation to absent friends who had been killed or who were in jail. The bottle was then passed round everyone in the group. 'Man, we're just like brothers.' (pp.53-4).

In England, John Spencer (1950, p.117) feels that 'the essence of the gang is the intense sense of loyalty to the group and the feeling of solidarity which exists among its members.' Mays (1954, p.107 and p.116) talks of group solidarity temporarily overriding individual conscience and of 'fundamental group loyalties'. Turner and Spencer (1955, p.54) do, however, quote Emmanual Miller's reservations about the solidarity of the gang. What internally united the two gangs which Miller studied 'was the fact that each one of them needed some form of psychological outlet which could only be found through the temporary aggregation.'

No better introduction could be found for Yablonsky's views on group cohesion. He was one of the first to cast doubt on the traditional view of the internal cohesion of the gang by introducing his concept of the 'near-group' (1959). To begin with, he emphasises that the element of co-operativeness, which was central to Whyte's gang and others like it, is totally absent from the modern violent gang. He then explains the violent gang in terms of a 'near-group', which stands midway on a continuum between mobs and cohesive groups, as can be seen from his diagram:

Organisation Factors
(Cohesion, Norm, Role Definition)

Least Defined		Most Defined
MOB	NEAR GROUP	GROUP
Youth Riot Lynch Mob	Violent Gang	Social Gang Delinquent Gang

Of the 15 characteristics of the 'near-group', or 'the compensatory paranoid pseudo-community', listed by Yablonsky (1967, pp.251-2), the most relevant for our purpose at present are: the sociopathic, self-appointed nature of the leadership, the individualised roles which are defined to fit the emotional needs of the participant, the limited consensus on norms, and the decrease in group cohesiveness 'as one moves from the centre of the collectivity to the periphery'.

Pfautz (1961) amongst others, has strongly criticised the introduction of this neologism 'near group', suggesting that the violent adolescent gang is better viewed as 'an expressive social movement' in the general theoretical traditions of 'collective behaviour'. But the Meyerhoffs (1964) found a use for the concept when describing several groups of deviant and non-deviant middle-class youths in a suburb of Los Angeles. Their behaviour conformed precisely to Yablonsky's description of a 'near-group' – with the sole exception of disturbed leadership. The Meyerhoffs are concerned to indicate 'the point by point similarity' between their findings and Yablonsky's 'regardless of the conceptual framework he uses in describing them'.

The New York City Youth Board (1960, p.30) provides further support for Yablonsky's views on low group cohesion with their references to 'intra-group disharmony and lack of camaraderie.' Gerrard (1964, p.361) talks of 'the intense but fragile quality of gang cohesion', while Gannon (1967, p.123) reports that the majority of gang workers would describe the group cohesion of the modern New York gang as loosely-knit. The 'episodic and highly situational character' of most delinquent acts illustrates for Empey (1967, p.34) the group's lack of cohesion. The literature is indeed replete with examples of spontaneous rather than planned delinquencies, and Empey's idea certainly tallies with my experience.

Finally, Klein and Crawford (1967) make an interesting distinction between internal sources of cohesion which are generally considered to be weak, and external pressures which give the gang whatever tenuous cohesiveness it achieves. Examples of the former are minimal group goals, unstable membership, lack of group norms, little role differentiation and even gang names which change too often for lasting identity. 'An exception is to be found among gangs with a long history, for gang tradition does seem to be a major internal source of cohesiveness.' The main external pressures are environmental frustrations, threats from rival groups, the police, and lack of acceptance by adults generally.

Norms

By the norms of a group Hargreaves (1967, p.8) means 'that which defines the behaviour which is expected or desired by the group as a whole. We may regard these norms as the behavioural expression of the *values* of the group.' The Sherifs (1964, p.166) explain the term by saying that group members arrive at common definitions of what is good and desirable, how a 'good' member should and should not treat his fellows and outsiders.

The Young Team claimed to have five main norms, although they did not collate them as I have done here:

1. The first rule, and one noted by all gang observers, was 'no grassing' to the authorities.
2. Internal gang fights were to be settled by 'square-goes'; weapons were to be used only on rival gangs. Keiser (1969, p.14) notes: 'In feuds between branches Vice Lords state that fighting should be limited to fists, although other weapons are sometimes used. In wars between clubs, in contrast, there are no limitations set on the legitimate use of weapons.'
3. To ensure that the gang always had 'blades' available, members were expected to take turns in being armed; and those who had no convictions for offensive weapon carrying were supposed to have weapons with them for the others. Ordinary gang members were to

render this service to their leaders.
4. All boys were to indulge in acts of violence. To be charged with assault was honourable: to be convicted of theft or housebreaking was a disgrace, especially if the offence was committed in the gang's own neighbourhood.
5. Gang members should not stab girls nor should they lie in wait for boys in the closes of their homes.

The only sanction for deviation from these norms was violence or the threat of it. The insistence that boys who broke the rules would be chibbed, itself contravened the second norm, but no illogicality was noticed by the core members. The sanction for disobeying the call to be violent remained violence.

The behaviour of the boys, especially of the leaders, negated each and every one of the principles by which they claimed to live their lives. Tim, for instance, had more convictions for dishonesty than for physical assault. The same was true of Dick Stevenson; and both boys had gone 'on the creep', and had assaulted their own members with weapons. The marginals, including myself, evaded the duty of carrying arms and took as little part in violent action as they could get away with. There was no question of there being 'latitudes of acceptable behaviour', which varied according to the importance of the activity to the group, or according to the standing of the member, as the Sherifs (1964, pp.178-80) argue. The more significant the activity, the more frequent were the breaches of the norm; and far from the latitude for the leader being narrowest in such a situation, he acted contrary to the norms more often than anyone else.

The influence of group norms on most gang members is thought by Short and Strodtbeck (1965, pp.206-7) to be 'tenuous and largely situational', but Klein and Crawford (1967, p.68) best summarise my attitude: 'group norms are relatively non-existent in the gang world except as myths which are exploded upon test.' The examples they quote are loyalty and mutual support, norms which are frequently not upheld. Matza (1964, p.157) is right when he argues that 'loyalty is a basic issue ... partially because its adherents are so regularly disloyal.' One of the techniques of neutralisation proposed by Matza and Sykes (1957, p.665) refers to the sharp line delinquents often draw between those who can be victimised and those who cannot. Indeed, under the fourth norm, the Glasgow boys felt it more morally reprehensible to steal 'from yir ain people'; and yet their delinquent forages showed that they were not bound by their own scruples. Klein and Crawford are probably nearer the truth when they assert that the only norm which is acted upon is the 'acceptance of a wide variety of illegal acts.'

Values

The main objects valued by the Young Team were territory, the title of 'gemmie', drink, drugs, status, 'patter', clothes, and, of course, sex. As all of these topics have been treated in detail in earlier chapters, I shall only add the briefest comments.

Like most American adolescent gangs described by observers, the Young Team attached immense importance to territory and used the same word 'turf' for it. It was the locality in which a boy lived, rather than his religion or race, which determined what gang he belonged to. The gang was therefore a mixed group of Catholics and Protestants, of third generation Irish immigrants, of Celts, and Lowland Scots.

All adolescent groups of boys, delinquent and non-delinquent alike, are concerned to prove their masculinity. But the Glasgow gang boy's desire to be a 'gemmie', a 'hardman', or a 'chib-man' entails far more than the 'readiness for physical combat' observed by Kobrin (1961, p.688), or the 'toughness' described by Walter B Miller (1958). The 'gemmie' ideology is more in line with what many other American gangs call 'heart', which is defined by Harrison Salisbury (1959, p.31) as a 'devil-may-care disregard for self and consequences'. The Glasgow concept contains this element of disregard for personal risk and adds to it the carrying and the use of weapons. The 'chib-man' is the ideal corner boy; and it was by using weapons that the Young Team sought to boost their tenuous masculinity. Tenuous, because beneath the air of bravado, I detected, like Miller (1958), 'powerful dependency cravings'. The boys were caught in the trap of being 'afraid of fighting other gangs but more afraid of not fighting them.'

This concentration upon toughness is, according to Miller, one of the six focal concerns which characterise 'lower class culture', by which he refers to that segment of the American population which we in Britain call the rough working class. These focal concerns (over trouble, toughness, smartness, excitement, fate and autonomy) appear to me to be very similar to the dominant emphases in the working-class culture of Maryhill. Miller further suggests that the adolescent street corner gangs in Boston not only share the focal concerns of the lower class community from which they spring, but that they are, in addition, concerned with 'belonging' and with 'status'. It is to the second of these that I now turn.

The gang's fondness of publicity, and more generally their preoccupation with status, can best be described in three ways. Firstly, there was an internal status hierarchy, an intra-group pecking order, where the crucial determinant of prestige was readiness to commit violence. There existed a second status hierarchy among the major violent gangs in the city, where the gang's position was determined by its history of violence in the way that Short (1968, p.20) details. Kobrin (1961, p.690) remarks on 'the tendency of the oldest dominant group, after it had established itself, to attract followers from an area wider than the local neighbourhood.' The Maryhill Fleet's ability to attract members from a distance of 22 miles is a good example of just this process. The third aspect of status concerns the practice which allowed low status members of the Heavy Team or members of the Young Team to initiate aggressive activity in order to win prestige for themselves and so involve the senior boys in their struggle. 'These fights are consciously sought out and searched for in an attempt to build a reputation where none existed before and the boys are referred to as "looking for trouble because they are coming up".' (Werthman, quoted by S Cohen, 1970, p.15).

Another focal concern of 'lower class culture' is smartness, which involves 'a dominant emphasis ... on ingenious aggressive repartee,' (Miller, 1958). This is the same attribute as the Young Team's fancy for 'brilliant patter'. The boys had in many ways a language of their own, an argot, as Monod (1967, p.150ff.) calls it in his analysis of juvenile gangs in Paris. The value of this special language is that it strengthens both the identity and the affiliation of the group members. Argot, for Monod, 'is a way of thinking as well as speaking' and he also claims to have recorded argotic dreams. Monod, in a felicitous phrase, interprets clothes 'as an argot way of dressing. Style of dress may be seen as a nonverbal means of communication.' The particular form of dress favoured by the Young Team and other Glasgow gangs heightened their visibility and made identification easier both for members of the subculture and for the police. Wilkins (1961, p.26) argues that the results of such obvious symbols of communication are to increase the solidarity of the group, but also to make 'formal negative sanctions, rejection and limitation of access' easier to apply.

Another commodity valued by the gang was sex. Girls were sexual objects to the boys who were unable to enter into deep relationships with them. Rather, their heterosexual relations were based on physical dominance and exploitation; their girlfriends were *at* the scene, but not quite *of* it. Tim, it is true, had been involved with one girl for 15 months and his elder brother, Mick, had been courting a girl for four years. One must remember, however, their long periods in custody; the gang also spoke of these liaisons as the exceptions which proved the rule. In Yablonsky's words (1967, p.219), sex for the violent gang boy 'is an itch that is scratched when the opportunity arises.'

The boys' attitude towards sex was an odd combination of puritanism and permissiveness. They did not make love to their girl friends at parties but had no objection to joining a public 'line-up': the sexual status of the girl determined their actions. There was, however, no elaborate sex code such as that described by Whyte (1943) in 'Cornerville', where women were classified into 'good girls' (virgins) and three categories of non-virgins, and where there was an appropriate form of behaviour supported by social sanctions for each category. Although self-imposed restrictions on their sexual behaviour were in evidence at parties, sexual intercourse did take place before and after in closes and by the canal bank. No contraceptives were used by the boys or by the girls, and no additional status accrued to a boy who became an illegitimate father. Short and Strodtbeck's (1965, pp.27-46) study of parenthood among the Chiefs, a delinquent negro gang in Chicago, similarly indicated that it was sex and not paternity which was linked with status.

Educational, Occupational and Social Background

The Young Team had the smell of failure about it. Although they were only 15 and 16 years of age, the boys knew themselves to be educational, occupational and social failures; they knew they were at the bottom of the heap. I wish to stress that the deterministic and fatalistic view of the Young Team's future does not emanate from me but from the boys themselves. *They* were the ones who saw themselves hemmed in by poverty, unemployment, the subculture of violence, and the indifference or hostility of the community at large. *They* were the ones who pictured themselves, accurately, as the inmates of prisons and young offenders' institutions in the years to come and *they* were the ones who could envisage no alternative. They felt that the educational and occupational spheres were rigged against them, and that the major decisions of their lives would be taken for them. In their own eyes, they were the victims of circumstance, powerless puppets manipulated by forces beyond their control. The Young Team believed their world to be one of inevitable conflict, blocked opportunities and non-existent choice, and they would have hotly disputed Matza's claim that one *actively* chooses to become delinquent.

LJ Taylor (1968, p.102) hypothesises that the sense of powerlessness, (which the Young Team experienced), may lead boys to commit vandalism and other non-utilitarian acts which are not aimed 'at securing power but at destroying or mutilating the uncontrollable world.' All the boys scorned their schools and hated the external trappings of education – uniforms, school bags, books. The schools' response to the behaviour of the core members, who, admittedly, could not have been easy to teach, was corporal punishment and expulsion. The boys were then left to roam the streets, unable to find work as they were under age. It was as though society had resolved to give them all the time in the world to become committed to the gang culture. If they had not been expelled, or 'temporarily excluded' as the authorities called it, they would have left school at the earliest possible moment, as the other boys had done or were planning to do. They were the products of junior secondary schools or of the lowest streams in comprehensive schools; none of them contemplated any form of further education.

Kobrin (1951, p.660) and later AK Cohen (1955) interpreted the burglaries of schools, 'in which the delinquent escapade is sometimes crowned, as it were, by defecating upon the school principal's desk', as acts of defiance and contempt, as a rejection of middle-class norms. This explanation does not fit the attitude of the Glasgow boys, nor does David Downes's (1966, p.237ff.) characterisation of the English delinquents' reaction to school as one of 'pupil inertia, boredom, and passivity, with periodic outbursts of what Webb termed "spontaneity, irrepressibility and rule-breaking".' The Young Team's bitter feelings against education were more a reflection, in Bloch and Niederhoffer's (1958, p.167) words, 'of hatred directed against the one institution that shatters their dream, insisting every day: "You are not men but school boys. School boys you must remain until you are seventeen. Only then can you escape from school".' It is an unequal battle, for the values of the peer group are so much more attractive than teacher expectations. Michael Farrant (1965, p.86) provides a good example of the power of the peer group when he relates how members of the most delinquent group he studied passed up opportunities to earn extra money (by doing overtime) in order to be with the others.

It was not possible to collect systematic information about the boys' work records, but it was still clear that in terms of occupational status they were the flotsam and jetsam of industry. And they were likely to remain so, for the values they espoused, especially their love of just 'dossin', militated against their chances of holding down a good job. Rivera and Short (1967, p.89) report that in Chicago boys will refuse or quit jobs which interfere with gang life and that 'the long hours on the corner with customary pursuits of wine, women, and "rep" are involved in tardiness and absenteeism which contribute to job failure.' The point has been emphasised by writers on gangs from Thrasher (1927) to Short and Strodtbeck (1965, p.230).

The gang was well aware of its social status: they called themselves the 'slummies' and tried to take some inverted pride from the fact. Nearly all of them had spent at least their earliest days in slum property and just over half of them were now living in relatively new accommodation. The move had inaugurated no change in their behaviour, nor would anyone familiar with Ferguson and Pettigrew's (1954) study (of Glasgow slum families rehoused for upwards of ten years) have expected it to.

The concept of social disability has already been introduced in Chapter 11. Many other students of gangs have noted the limited horizons of gang boys, their desire but inability to break out of their surroundings. Doc, the leader of the Norton Street gang (Whyte, 1955, p.256), felt that his followers were to all intents and purposes restricted to 'a radius of about three hundred yards'. Far from this lack of social ability increasing group interaction, as Whyte reported, Gordon (1967, p.62) holds that social disability adversely affects 'the rewards of interpersonal relations'. This inability of the boys to relate to each other strikes me as a more accurate but partial explanation of the Young Team's lack of internal cohesion. Gordon continues his argument: 'As conceived, the components of social disability are abstractions derived from previously recognised psychological states, some of which at least would be regarded as pathological.'

A Subculture of Violence

A picture of the Young Team has now been built up and they appear as a loose grouping of socially ineffectual youths, whose gang is 'more a vehicle for its members' fantasies and desires for status than a well-oiled criminal machine' or a well-integrated fighting machine.

The previous pages have shown that the Glasgow gang has no counterpart in England, and has very little in common with the gangs described by Thrasher, Whyte, and WB Miller. The vital difference is between gangs dominated by delinquency and those dominated by violence, and the main features of each are well listed by Hardman (1967, p.24). Bordua (1961, p.136) neatly points out that, in the writing of modern theorists who pay scant attention to the quality of adventure in many illegal acts, it does not seem much fun any more to be a gang delinquent: 'Thrasher's boys enjoyed themselves being chased by the police, shooting dice, skipping school, rolling drunks... Cohen's boys and Cloward and Ohlin's boys are driven by grim economic and psychic necessity into rebellion.'

Is there an all-embracing concept to combine the various psychological and sociological factors I have described as characteristic of the Young Team? Wolfgang and Ferracuti (1967) provide one in their concept of a subculture of violence, but before discussing it I want to assess the role played by violence in the life of the Glasgow gang.

John Spencer (1964, p.167) emphasises the dangers in a work of this kind of forgetting the commonplace and recording the unusual; and no topic is more likely to be exaggerated out of all proportion than that of violence, the 'darling of the publicist'. Care has been taken to avoid falling into this trap, and an attempt has been made to see the boys' violence within the context of their total behaviour.

English criminologists constantly refer to the 'cultural normality' of *theft* among adolescent boys in certain working-class areas. One can almost talk of the 'cultural normality' of *violence* among their counterparts in Glasgow. Violence, for the Young Team, was not only a standard reaction to frustration, a standard solution to trivial as well as serious problems, it was a way of life. At times their violence was spontaneous and gratuitous; like Yablonsky's (1967, p.94) Balkans, they talked about past, present and future violence. Pfautz (1961, p.172) may be right in arguing that there is little 'technique' to violence, but the Young Team had their own words for weapons and fighting, a specialised vocabulary which revealed their basic interests, as Cavan (1962, p.171ff.) illustrates with reference to American gangs. For the Glasgow boys, violence was a matter of conforming to the norms of their subculture; it was also a matter of history, for violence is a vital tradition among certain sectors of Glasgow's population, and the boys were inheritors of traditions of gang warfare which have been traced back for almost a hundred years.

The boys' manifest motives for their violence were that they were defending their territory, that they were in need of protection, that they were avenging a slight on their girlfriends, that they didn't like the look of the victim's face, that he was a Protestant, a Catholic, a Pakistani etc. Together with Yablonsky, I would hypothesise that their latent motives were the projection of internal conflicts and hostilities, the 'demonstration of easily achieved power', and the acquisition of local notoriety, prestige and respect which these boys could only win through violence.

There is no implication in the above that the boys were continually and solely engaged in acts of violence. Just as delinquency is not the only act of delinquent gangs, so violence is not the only type of behaviour even in violent gangs, not all members participate in violence, nor are those who do equally committed to its use.

How does this compare with Wolfgang and Ferracuti's thesis? Seven propositions are advanced (1967, pp.158-61) to explain the subculture of violence, and in a truncated form they are:

> 1. No subculture can be totally different from or totally in conflict with the society of which it is a part. 'A subculture of violence is not entirely an expression of violence, for there must be interlocking value elements shared with the dominant culture.'
> 2. Members of the subculture are not required to express violence in all situations. Members 'do not engage in violence continuously, oth-

erwise normal social functioning would be virtually impossible. We are merely suggesting that ... the carrying of knives ... becomes a common symbol of willingness to participate in violence, to expect violence, and to be ready for its retaliation.'

3. The willingness to resort to violence in a variety of situations emphasises the penetrating and diffuse character of this culture theme.

4. The ethos of violence is most prominent in a limited age group, ranging from late adolescence to middle age.

5. The counter-norm is non-violence. 'The juvenile who fails to live up to the conflict gang's requirements is pushed outside the group.'

6. Both the use of violence and the development of favourable attitudes towards its use are learned responses. 'Not all persons exposed – even equally exposed – to the presence of a subculture of violence absorb and share in the values in equal portions.' Here, differential personality variables are taken into account in an attempt to explain why so many boys who are exposed to the same stimuli do not exhibit a violent response.

7. As the use of violence is not viewed as illicit conduct, the users have no guilt feelings. 'Violence can become a part of the life style, the theme of solving difficult problems ... '

Only the fifth proposition does not fit the situation I have been describing. In the Glasgow gang, violation of the norm is met with violence or the threat of it, not ostracism. The thesis, then, is thought to apply to the gang culture in Glasgow, where there exists a shared system of norms, beliefs and values set apart from the dominant nonviolent culture and which expects or requires the use of violence in many types of social relationships. The subculture of violence is passed on from generation to generation because members share 'not only the tenement's plumbing but also its system of values.' (p.298).

Wolfgang and Ferracuti indicate the presence of subcultures of extreme violence in Columbia, in Mexico, in certain isolated communities in Italy, and in negro ghettoes in the United States. The statistical and illustrative material provided by the two authors on these subcultures demonstrates that the Glasgow equivalent is of comparatively minor proportions and severity. To give one example, in 1969 more than twice as many people were murdered in Dallas, Texas, which has a population of just under one million, than in the whole of Great Britain with 56 million.

After I had completed the fieldwork for this study, I began reading the literature on gang delinquency. The most important impression I gained from this review was that many theoretical propositions have the stamp and outlook of the outsider, especially of the middle-class observer, who classifies delinquent behaviour from a safe distance. Two propositions, in particular, struck me as being the interpretations of theorists on the outside of a gang, looking in: short-run hedonism and non-utilitarian delinquency.

According to AK Cohen (1955,p.30), one of the leading characteristics of delinquent gangs and of the social class from which they come, is short-run hedonism, which is defined as having 'little interest in long-run goals, in planning activities and budgeting time ... the pinch of the present is a more potent stimulus than the threat or promise of the future.' This general unwillingness to defer gratification is seen in Freudian terms by Kate Friedlander (1947, pp.69-70), as the delinquent's failure to advance from the pleasure-pain principle to the reality principle. Mary Morse (1965, p.75) reports that 'a hand-to-mouth philosophy governed the lives' of the unattached youths studied in England; and similarly, David Downes (1966, p.206) found the strain of short-run hedonism very marked in the life of the group he observed in Poplar. This feature of delinquent life has been remarked upon by many observers on both sides of the Atlantic; and 'an over-evaluation of the immediate goals as opposed to remote or deferred ones' is even quoted approvingly by Eysenck (1970, p.54) as one of the ten characteristics of the psychopath, although the qualification is added that none of the attitudes, taken alone, would be crucial.

How accurately can this concept be applied to the Young Team? Tim's standard reaction to being asked about the future was to reply: 'Ye only think aboot the noo, the present.' And certainly his behaviour on weekend leave from the approved school would strengthen the belief that he did not consider long-term consequences. But this would be to misunderstand and misinterpret his behaviour. From Tim's fatalistic viewpoint, the future held nothing for him but senior approved school or borstal and then prison; and so far he has not been proved wrong. He felt himself powerless to prevent this progression (cf. LJ Taylor, 1968), which would take place whatever he did. In the immediate future he had 36 hours leave before being obliged to return for a month to the 'boredom' of the approved school. In these circumstances Tim thought that the only sensible course of action was to 'create all merry hell' while he could. This decision stemmed *not* from an inability to postpone immediate pleasure for the sake of future freedom, but from a realistic appraisal of that future which he considered to be predetermined.

SM Miller and Riessman (1961) have already questioned the appropriateness of the concept of deferred gratification to understanding the essence of the working-class subculture, and have instanced the 'acting-out' of prosperous, middle-class students in America who defer little in the way of gratification during their college days. Similarly, one could point to the vandalism in this country of students during 'rag' days, to the excesses of rugby clubs on tour and so on.

A much more sophisticated interpretation of short-run hedonism is offered by Short and Strodtbeck (1965, p.248ff), who prefer the term 'aleatory risks' because they are of the opinion that the 'abandon in actions suggested by the term *hedonism* is misleading.' Their argument is that boys indulge in violence, for example, because 'the rewards and probabilities associated with risk taking appear to outweigh the disadvantages. In a very special way they gamble and, sometimes, lose.' (p.251).

Elliot Liebow (1967, pp.64-9), however, comes closer to my position than anyone else. The working man at Tally's Corner who squanders a week's pay in two days does so, not because 'like an animal or a child, he is "present-time oriented", unaware of or unconcerned with his future. He does so precisely because he is aware of the future and the hopelessness of it all.' Examples are given of short-run hedonism among people of all classes whenever they are uncertain about the future: sexual licence during wartime, spending of savings in times of inflation. Liebow rightly concludes that 'there is no mystically intrinsic connection between "present-time orientation" and lower class persons.' The delinquent boy is simply reacting to the future as he sees it, reacting in a way common to all of us in times of stress or uncertainty. The concept of short-run hedonism has hardened into a formula which obscures more than it illuminates.

AK Cohen (1955, pp.25-7) also stressed the non-utilitarian character of much gang activity and in particular stealing, by which he meant that boys stole not for gain and profit but for the fun of it. 'There is no accounting in rational and utilitarian terms for the effort expended and the danger run in stealing things which are often discarded, destroyed or casually given away.' The motivation for such behaviour is said to lie in the thrill of stealing itself, in the glory and prowess attached to stealing, rather than in the value of the stolen object.

Was such non-utilitarian theft the characteristic mode of stealing in the Glasgow gang? Is this to be expected in a slum area? The boys were skilful and practised thieves who had mastered the techniques at an earlier stage of their delinquent careers. Stealing was thought by them to be a more appropriate activity for 11 and 12-year-olds, fighting for boys of 14 and over. They gloried in memories of primary school trips to outlying districts where their expertise had allegedly acquired them anything they desired; they talked about these thefts as though they were games. But during my period of involvement with them, they stole half-pound bars of chocolate because they were hungry, they stole cigarettes, clothes, and drink for parties because they could not afford them, they stole knives and weapons for 'protection'. They stole, then, mainly for reasons of parental neglect and simple poverty, the latter of which David Downes (1966, p.202) found to be still a real force for crime among the Poplar group, the bulk of whose delinquencies was classified as non-utilitarian. If they stole more than they needed or objects they did not want, the boys did not discard the goods but sold them to local 'punters', the mark of the semi-professional theft subculture according to Cohen and Short (1958).

Many of their other activities, however, could be properly categorised as non-utilitarian: the bouts of window-smashing, the rowdyism in cinemas, the beheading of tailors' dummies, the ubiquitous spraying of gang slogans. Such behaviour falls under the heading of what Martin (1961, p.73) calls wanton vandalism, where it seems to be entirely irrelevant who the owners of the damaged property are. Not all their window smashing, though, was as meaningless as the local press reported, for they chose this means of retaliating against those local shopkeepers who had written a public letter to Members of Parliament, demanding action against the Glasgow gangs. Martin (p.77) terms this vindictive vandalism where 'the chief motivation appears to be the desire ... to express the antagonism and hatred they feel toward special individuals...' WB Miller (1966, p.110) claims that most of the damage caused by violent gangs in 'Midcity' was directed against the property of people who had angered them and, in saying that little vandalism could be classified as uncontrolled or senseless, he is supported by Stan Cohen (1968). The Young Team, therefore, was capable of both utilitarian and non-utilitarian delinquent acts. The same boys could steal objects for profit, for their own consumption, and for 'the hell of it' all in the one day. They committed thefts as the need and the mood of the moment took them without regard for the neat classifications of sociologists.

The existence of rational, calculated, utilitarian behaviour among delinquent gangs has been pointed out by many reviewers of Cohen's work, including Kitsuse and Dietrick (1959, p.213). Fewer commentators have reported gangs who indulged regularly in both types of behaviour, although Mannheim (1965, p.512) thought it 'likely that within . . . the same gang delinquent acts may occur of both a utilitarian and a non-utilitarian nature and that even the same individual may indulge today in acts of the first and tomorrow in acts of the second type, according to his mood and the specific situation in which he finds himself.'

Now I want to drag into the open an argument which has been alluded to a number of times during this book but which has not yet been dealt with directly. Were the core members of the gang pathologically or psychologically disturbed or not? I have already made it clear that I thought they were, and I continue to think so despite the fashionable approach which seeks to avoid assumptions that the behaviour of delinquents is irrational, pathological, and of no meaning to them.

Examining delinquency, or deviance generally, from the actor's point of view often floods the interpretation of the delinquent act with meaning. Becker's (1963, p.14) view that 'deviance is not a quality that lies in behaviour itself, but in the interaction between the person who commits an act and those who respond to it' has added an invaluable corrective to earlier work on deviance. The interactionist perspective, as it has been called, has concentrated not so much on the deviant act itself as on the consequences which result from other people applying rules and sanctions to someone they define as an offender.

Hand-in-hand with this study of the transaction that takes place between society and the rule-breaker has gone a movement 'to question and criticise a conception of pathology, and increasingly, to purge it from the discipline of sociology.' (Matza, 1969, p.42.) Many harsh comments have been written on pathological explanations of deviance, some students of delinquency even claiming that they do not deserve to be called explanations at all as they only restate the problem in different words and that it would be more honest to substitute the simple term 'anti-social behaviour' for the value-laden concept of 'psychopathology'. A few of these sources are quoted to give the flavour of their argument. Becker (1963, p.5ff.) objects to the medical metaphor involved in identifying deviance as something essentially pathological because it prevents us 'from seeing the judgement itself as a crucial part of the phenomenon.' Geis (1965, p.17) quotes Kimball Young's view that to call a gang member psychopathic is to leave the full causation of his conduct untouched, while the Sherifs (1964, passim) are so opposed to the 'futile luxury' of denouncing individuals or groups as morbid and pathological that they repeat their dissent on six occasions in one book. Stan Cohen (1970, p.7) also feels that 'violence tends to be seen through the distorting lens of pathology.'

Faced with such virulent opposition, why do I persist with an unpopular interpretation? I shall examine a number of gang incidents to help clarify my position. I am not saying that all gang members or that the leaders invariably exhibited pathological tendencies. Some of the Young Team's behaviour, for example, which was publicly labelled irrational was very meaningful to them; two cases are in point here. Firstly, the press gave great coverage to the fate of a café-owner who had had his shop wrecked by a gang. Amidst headlines of 'aimless violence' and 'pointless destruction', no one reported that the serving staff had brought the trouble upon themselves by tipping the food ordered by the boys on to the floor. The other incident involved the assault of a bus conductor, and again the mass media treated that case as one of senseless violence. The conductor had muttered insults under his breath as the gang had boarded the bus; he had then rolled the boys' change along the floor because, as he said, he refused to touch the hands of young thugs. Although many passengers witnessed this provocation, it was never reported by the press. These two examples are important because they increased the boys' resentment at being treated like dirt and their sense of injustice at the sensational and highly inaccurate headlines which stereotyped their behaviour.

However, there remains a small group of very violent actions which is not susceptible to such an explanation. The attack upon the two labourers in the pub during my first encounter with the gang (see Chapter 3) provides an instance of this type of behaviour. The boys responsible for the assault could think of no motive of any kind to explain their actions and nor could I. They were neither drunk nor drugged; the attack was an explosion of irrational, spontaneous violence which was an end in itself. Many investigators tend to dismiss such attacks on spectators or innocent bystanders because they happen so occasionally. An example can be found in Reiser's (1969) analysis of the Vice Lords, which concludes with the autobiography of one of the boys called Cupid. 'Jumping on innocent people' (p.67) is obviously important to the boy because he refers to it three times; one of these occasions describes a stranger being 'stomped' to death, another a man being shot in the leg. These incidents are passed over in silence by the author who includes no discussion of the personality of the boys. This is not satisfactory. Although outbursts of irrational violence by core members of the Young Team were not frequent, they assumed an importance within the gang out of all proportion to their number. As will be readily understood, it does not take many outbreaks of uncontrollable fury to terrorise one's followers.

Not only were the marginals terrified by the core members of the gang, but the leaders were disturbed by aspects of their own behaviour for which they could find no rational explanation. It is important to emphasise that certain acts are not being classified as pathological simply because they did not coincide with my conception of 'normality': they were not thought to be normal by the actors or by any of the spectators. The epithets attached to the gang (mental, crackpot), the names assumed by individuals (the Mad Mexican, Big Sick), and the expressions used to describe the behaviour in question (going radio, throwing a maddie, running a psychey) were not chosen by me but by the boys themselves. The terminology used does not fit David Matza's idea that delinquents prefer to 'go crazy' rather than be considered insane. Matza(1964, p.84) argues that this idea of being sick, mixed up or mental seems incongruous with the delinquent's traditional self-image of manly toughness and precocious independence:

> The preference among delinquents is to expand the more traditional notion of insanity. 'Goin' crazy' is somehow more manly than being sick, and thus the company of delinquents prefer that formulation and the extenuating circumstances implicit in it. 'I lost my temper. I was crazy with anger.' *Temporarily*, he did not know the nature of what he was doing. *Temporarily*, he could not distinguish between right and wrong. [Italics as in original.]

The core members of the Young Team, however, were worried about their psychological make-up, they were afraid that they were mentally ill; these were not half-digested psychological explanations of their conduct which they had picked up at court or from their probation officer, but deep anxieties about their mental health.

Nor are we in the situation Matza (1969, p.64) describes where 'what is deemed pathological by the professional server in the mental institution may seem normal enough in the client's subculture.' Not even in a subculture of violence were the rages of the gang leaders considered normal. Barmen, billiard-hall attendants, local residents generally viewed the core members of the gang as dangerous, moody, touchy boys who were not to be interfered with. As Hans Toch (1969, p.195) says, there are people in a subculture of violence who take to violence with more alacrity and enthusiasm than their neighbours:

> It is these individuals, who meet the norm 'thou shalt be violent' much more than halfway, who best personify the sociopsychological model of subculturally induced violence. For it is these persons whose needs are most felicitously responded to by the license to destroy which they feel is furnished them. And ultimately, these persons carry violence to such an extreme that even their subcultural co-religionaries may classify them as violence-prone.

Becker (1963, p.20) has produced a typology of deviant behaviour and it is one of the categories which is peripheral to his main argument – the pure deviant type – which is our concern here. The pure deviant type of behaviour is defined as that which disobeys the rule and is perceived by everyone, including the actor, as doing so. 'He may brand himself as deviant because of what he has done and punish himself in one way or another for his behaviour.' (p.31). The core members were aware that from time to time they crossed a different sort of barrier from the normal infraction of social rules. Motiveless violence, they knew, placed them in a special category and it was they who labelled themselves as outsiders, as youngsters in need of psychological help and advice. The pathological definitions of their behaviour were not foisted upon them by the agents of social control but were their own descriptions of their own behaviour.

Were there any other indications of disturbed behaviour besides the occasional explosions of fury? The boys displayed no guilt feelings, they had no remorse; they were social inadequates, their interpersonal relationships were never anything but shallow; there was a calculated and sadistic cruelty about some of their actions (they lay in wait for opponents whom they wanted to 'rip', and not just disfigure); they committed acts of wanton vandalism; and they exhibited a variety of anxieties and phobias. The list tallies very closely with Yablonsky's (1967, pp.181-2) profile of the sociopath.

Other isolated incidents lead me to the same conclusion. Fergie was known to the gang as the 'heid-banger', but he was not the only boy observed in that activity. The core members also smashed the window of a clothes store and then ceremonially beheaded the tailor's dummies. Big Dave Mailoy spoke of lacerating the carcasses of animals at a meat market as a childhood pastime. And when I say that nearly all the boys were nail-biters, I do so in the knowledge that there is 'no justification for regarding the habit as a sign of any kind of pathology – as Kanner put it, it is an "everyday problem of the everyday child".' (Rutter, Tizard, and Whitmore, 1970, p.216). However, there is nail-biting and nail-biting, and I have seen very few 'everyday' children gouge at their fingers until they bleed. Such a habit suggests to me a high degree of tension and anxiety.

The symptoms which have been enumerated, serious though some of them are, still do not induce me to call the core members psychopaths because that term 'has now had so much currency that it has been rubbed almost smooth of meaning', as Clark (1965) wrote in another context. Instead, I am claiming that certain aspects of their behaviour had pathological overtones. Call it what you will, their behaviour at times disturbed all those associated with it – actors, victims and spectators. These sporadic outbursts must not be ignored as irrelevant or inconvenient; they are stubborn, awkward facts which do not fit most fashionable theories. In my view, a comprehensive theory will be evolved only when sociologists pay more than cursory attention to the personality of the boys concerned. No one who has read the earlier chapter on

Glasgow housing, violence and unemployment can claim that the sociological or structural conditions have not been granted their true prominence. Similarly, no one should play down the importance of individual personality variables. Both types of explanation have to be combined to do justice to the facts as I observed them.

Although in round numbers many boys in the Maryhill area were members (of one kind or another) of their local gangs, they constituted only a minority of the total population at risk. Most boys living in the same housing conditions managed to stay out of serious trouble and had no need of the gang. A very small group of boys, of whom Tom Nolan (see Chapter 3) is a good example, would associate with the gang whenever they had a temporary need for violent behaviour. The majority of boys, though mocked and even assaulted at times, found other solutions to their problems which did not involve joining a violent gang. Sheldon Glueck (1959, p.247) is making the same point when he writes: ' ... even in the worst possible delinquency area of the urban slums, the great majority of boys somehow manage not to become delinquents ... '.

Psychologists and sociologists have been engaged for over half a century in a tug-of-war over the psychological condition of the gang member. Again, the same two battle lines, as I have mentioned with reference to gang leadership, are drawn up. The view of the early sociologists, exemplified in the work of Thrasher (1927, p.172), was that gang boys are 'ordinarily wholesome ... they are not morbid or psychopathic' The picture he conveys is of essentially well-adjusted, healthy boys seeking romantic adventure and excitement in the 'drab hideousness' of the slum. Miller's (1961, p.298) Junior Outlaws follow in this tradition because they 'could scarcely be characterised as abnormal. On the contrary, they appear as an organised, efficient, and dynamically balanced system, performing stabilizing and integrative functions for both the group and its members.'

Many writers, like the Sherifs (1964, p.66) and Cloward and Ohlin (1960, p.10), believe that severely disturbed individuals cannot be tolerated in a group and are therefore excluded. They find support in Fritz Redl's (1956, pp.64-5) observation that the unreliability and irresponsibility of such boys cause their estrangement from the group. One severely psychotic boy, Davie Wilson, who is now in a mental institution, was ostracised by the Young Team. But the organisation of a violent gang is such that core members with less serious symptoms than Davie Wilson can be accommodated within its fold.

This is not a view which is held only by students of gangs like Yablonsky and myself. It is corroborated in the writings of Crawford (1950, p.140) and his associates, who felt that their project lacked a psychiatrist to work with 'severely disturbed' gang boys. The New York City Youth Board (1960) talks of the 'morbid psychology' of core members, while Bloch and Niederhoffer (1958, p.148) fear that 'the frequency of psychopathies and emotional disturbances among young offenders may be reaching significant proportions.' Wolman (1951, p.181) concludes that among groups of youngsters in Israel 'only maladjusted adolescents are inclined to belong to gangs, which seem to be a symptom of infantile regression in the late teens.' The gangs of nine cities in the United States were studied by Saul Bernstein (1964, pp.37-8), who reports that the problem of the 'gang psycho' or the 'gang war butch' was prevalent in every one of them, and that Los Angeles gang workers identified 14% of all gang members as belonging to this category. Harrison Salisbury (1959, p.33) describes the leader of the conflict gang as a 'deeply disturbed, homicidal individual' and records (p.184) that boys chose weapons to disfigure as well as injure the person attacked. Howard Polsky (1962, p.26) quotes several other American investigators who have noted 'extreme psychotic behaviour in gang members', while Gordon's (1967, p.48ff.) review of the literature on personality and delinquency favours the conclusion that delinquents do suffer from personality disturbances.

In England, the work of Spinley (1953, p.77) and of Scott (1956, pp.11-13) can also be cited in support of the importance of psychological factors; Scott claims, for example, that leaders of 'gangs proper' frequently suffer from a gross antisocial character defect which seems to obliterate their sense of guilt. One of the main conclusions drawn by Morris (1957, p.168) from his analysis of crime and delinquency in Croydon was that 'in each occupational group there is a hard core of "psychiatric delinquency" related to serious emotional disturbance in the family, or mental ill health, which accounts for between one-fifth and one-quarter of all the cases.' Morris stresses that personality factors in the individual family must be added to economic or cultural explanations of 'psychiatric delinquency'. And Spencer (1964) always refers to the Espressos as a disturbed and insecure group of young people.

Many other studies could be quoted in support of or in opposition to the idea that gang members exhibit psychological abnormalities, but the mere counting of heads will not settle the issue. The sociological and the psychological explanations seem to clash at every point, yet a resolution, along the lines suggested by Mays (1963, p.226ff), is possible. Authors like Thrasher, Whyte, Miller, Short, AK Cohen, the Sherifs, and Matza are really engaged in explaining the conduct of boys who would be called marginals by Yablonsky and myself. Mays's (1954, p.25) work in Liverpool is concerned mainly with this type of boy, the 'average lad from a bad neighbourhood who does what all the others do, not because he suffers acute emotional conflict, but because he dreads to be thought different; the boy, in a phrase, who succumbs, however temporarily, to the social infection of a delinquent area.'

The offences of the young Liverpudlians are innocuous when compared with those of the core members of a violent gang, who are boys suffering from severe personal and psychological difficulties. In this case, 'the causal complex is rooted in the psychology of the individual offender'; in the former case, 'the delinquency is largely a function of the local environment'. (Mays, 1963, p.226.)

Finally, British observers should take note of the recent history of gang activity in the United States. Saul Bernstein concluded in 1964 that the highly structured gang was on the decline in all of the nine cities he visited. Groups had become smaller, quieter, less formal; the boys called the new groupings 'clusters' and were frequently to be seen 'without obvious symbols such as jackets' (p.34). Geis (1965, p.48) quotes one former member of a fighting gang as saying: 'It is almost square to go down (to fight). It don't have the kicks it used to. Some of the shrimps take to it, but it ain't what it used to be. It's cliché, man.' The growing emphasis on 'coolness' has also been observed by Gannon (1967, p.119ff.), who reports that in New York the tightly structured gangs of the 1950s have 'splintered into smaller cliques numbering from three to fifteen members', whose most common form of conflict is defensive fighting and 'individual skirmishes, spontaneous fighting, and "japping" attacks' rather than full-scale, planned rumbles. And Keiser (1969, pp.9-11) records the remarkable developments over a ten-year period of the Vice Lord Nation from a 'bopping' gang to a social club, complete with membership cards 'printed with the Vice Lords' insignia - a top hat, cane, and white gloves.' The Lords finally opened a business office, had their club legally recognised, and started a restaurant. A very different movement from this fascinating example of self-help in Chicago has been witnessed among New York gangs by Geis (1965, p.49) - the movement towards the use of narcotic drugs.

The early months of 1972 saw a reversal of this trend with the sudden resurgence of violent youth gangs in New York, Los Angeles, Chicago and Philadelphia. Some newspaper articles claimed that the new gangs, now armed with guns rather than with knives or bicycle chains, were offshoots from earlier protest movements, like the Black Panthers, which had lost momentum. Other commentators concentrated on the growing number of attacks on drug pushers, arguing that the reappearance of the gangs was in some way connected with strong opposition to hard drugs among young adolescents in districts like the Bronx. It remains to be seen whether this pattern of behaviour will be followed in Glasgow.

21
Treatment and prevention

DURING THE PUBLIC outcry over the violence of the gangs in Glasgow, the following suggestions were made in a letter which was typical of many to be published in a local newspaper:

> That all convicted prisoners, regardless of age or sex, be maintained in purgatorial, dungeon conditions, shackled and subsisting upon a meagre, vitamin-deficient diet and moreover overlooked by armed guards authorised to kill if necessary.
>
> As a further salutary measure the more serious offenders might well prove invaluable in the furtherance of laboratory research in place of unfortunate and mercilessly exploited animals.

Such sentiments were not confined to a few eccentrics: the convener of the Glasgow police committee was reported in the press as saying: 'The psychiatrists and the so-called enlightened do-gooders have had their day. I am moving in with older methods – the hammer instead of the kid-glove.' One city councillor recommended the introduction of a curfew, another the creation of ghettoes for families of convicted criminals, and a municipal candidate advocated the return of the stocks to George Square.

However much one may sympathise with the sincerity of those who hold such views and agree with their abhorrence of violent crime, the subject of control and cure must be approached dispassionately. A sceptical review of the successes and failures of various forms of treatment is of more value than an emotional reaction. The report of the Cadogan Committee, to the effect that violent offenders who were given corporal punishment committed *more* acts of violence than violent criminals who were treated in a different manner, should give those in favour of birching cause for thought.

First of all, Hargreave's (1967, p.x) point that 'the primary function of the social researcher is to make a diagnosis, not prescribe a cure' must be answered. It is unscientific to move directly from descriptive to prescriptive writing but, like Skinner, I have found a purely descriptive system to be highly unpopular. The constant pressure for solutions from people still working with delinquents, and the growing demand for a greater social return from academic research have forced me to add some ideas, however unoriginal and banal, on prevention and treatment. I shall restrict myself to areas where I can claim some first-hand knowledge by, for example, writing of approved schools rather than of the educational system in general. For once, though, I can agree with the Sherifs (1964, p.301) who object to the aloofness of most researchers to action programmes.

The discouraging truth, however, is that the programmes designed to prevent juvenile delinquency, the most extensive being American, have largely been failures. The famous Cambridge-Somerville Youth Study (Powers and Witmer, 1950), started in 1935, traced the careers of a group of 325 'treatment' boys and of a similar number of carefully matched 'controls'. Both the original study and a follow-up report (McCord and McCord, 1959) of the boys into adulthood found that as many of the treatment group had been convicted of offences as of the control group, and that the crimes had been equally serious.

Projects designed specifically to control the delinquency of street-corner gangs have had no greater success. WB Miller (1962) has thoroughly evaluated the efficacy of the 'Midcity' project, which was directed at the community and the family, as well as the gang. The intensive care of professionally trained detached workers, who were sent out into the streets to redirect the energies of a group of seven gangs into constructive channels, proved to have 'negligible impact' on the number of their crimes and court appearances. Even the drop in court appearances after the age of 20 could not be attributed to a delayed effect of the project, as a group of similar gangs who had *not* received attention from the detached workers showed an almost identical decrease.

There is, then, no simple solution, no panacea. But if my diagnosis of the Glasgow gang is correct, if the violent gang is, as Yablonsky (1967, p.284) claims, 'a pathological entity requiring elimination', action in the short term at least is clear. For the immediate protection of society, the core members of the gang need to be arrested and imprisoned. The members of the Young Team realised that such a move would prove to be the death knell of the gang as a fighting force. The removal of the seriously disturbed leaders would permit orthodox group work to begin with the marginals.

The very suggestion that the gang should be broken up is anathema to most group workers. Thrasher (1927, p.496) thinks the idea to be typical of the police who always assume that the gang must be suppressed: 'They fail to understand that boyish energies, like tics, suppressed at one place are sure to break out at some other. And when the breaking-up of the gang has been accomplished, there is usually no attempt to provide substitute activities for the boys.' The Sherifs (1964, p.313) feel that the adult who disperses the members of a group, or who forbids them to associate is deluding himself, 'perhaps creating a more cohesive unit, and usually sending its problems elsewhere.'

According to Spencer (1964, p.48): 'Merely to eliminate the gang is too simple an answer to the problem. Such a policy, moreover, fails to take account of the emotional security which the gang provides for its members in a confused and often hostile environment.' The proposal being recommended here is not so drastic; it is recognised that the gang can be a positive force for good in the lives of its members, but only after the core members have been withdrawn from circulation. The fringe members, who are by far the majority, will not be thrust into isolation but will remain members of a supportive peer group where they can continue, with help, to overcome whatever emotional, social or occupational problems confront them.

'Removal or "breaking-up" seems necessary', writes Scott (1956, p.22), 'when one or more very disturbed boys are holding a group together only by terrorism ... '. This is my position. If there are different types of gangs and different types of members within one gang, then uniform treatment should not be expected. Yablonsky (1967, p.261) has made it clear that working with a violent gang solidifies its structure in a way that only magnifies the problem. 'The validity of such anti-social patterns as gang warfare, territory, and peace meetings should be challenged and discouraged rather than accepted and in some cases aggrandised and given legitimacy.' Yablonsky's experience in calling peace meetings was that he was *reinforcing* rather than *modifying* the definition and organisation of the violent gangs involved, by accepting the fantasy world of the leaders and by conferring on them all the prestige and status they craved. Although this research took place in New York in the mid-1950s, massive publicity was accorded the truce and amnesty arranged among Easterhouse gangs in 1968 by the well-intentioned efforts of Frankie Vaughan. Richard Boston (1968, p.121) was the only one to suggest that involving the boys as *gangs* rather than as *individuals* may be giving a structure and organisation to what was previously loosely grouped and unorganised.

It is easy to suggest that the leaders should be arrested and imprisoned: it is quite another matter to propose what kind of therapy should then be employed. It is clear that the present form of treatment offered by the approved school service is inadequate and inappropriate to the needs of core offenders. In recent years the success rate for boys (usually calculated as the percentage who are not reconvicted within three years of release) has declined steadily in Scotland and in the rest of Great Britain (Rose, 1967, p.86) to a figure of 43%. In negative terms, 57% were reconvicted and that total does not include those who were not caught. Wilkinson (1964) estimates that the failure rate is much higher, between 65 and 75%. Moreover, the official definition of cure, three years without reconviction, is very different from a psychological definition which would stress changes in basic attitudes, the establishment of stable personal relationships, and the ability to hold down a job. The further offences of 149 boys released consecutively from one approved school were examined by Scott (1964) and, though the quality of these offences was not considered serious, their quantity was. And 'the consequences for the offenders in terms of further legal action were very serious'. Rose (1959, p.270) in a study of a borstal where failure rates are generally higher than in approved schools, noted that boys who were leaders of large groups were almost all reconvicted. Barbara Wootton (1959, p.69) puts the point succinctly: 'We have to face the disagreeable paradox that experience of what are intended to be reformative institutions actually increases the probability of future lapses into criminality: it has, for example, been shown that a previous residence in an approved school is one of the best predictors of recidivism among borstal boys.' In a very real sense approved schools are incubators of crime.

When one considers the large sums of money that are spent every year on keeping a boy in an approved school, why are the success rates so low? To try to answer this question, I shall discuss boys' approved schools in general; most of my remarks apply to the system as a whole rather than to the particular school to which I was attached. My criticism is levelled not at the headmasters and staff of these schools but at the physical conditions in which they have to work. The schools, despite their reputation, are not supposed to be places of punishment; they are open institutions for the education and training of young boys, the majority of whom have been convicted of theft. A sizeable minority have committed no criminal offence but have been found in need of care, protection, or control or they have truanted persistently from school. From the psychological point of view, however, there is little to distinguish between these categories of youngsters.

Approved schools are only now moving out of an era where the humiliation of the boys was institutionalised; for example, absconders, no matter what their age or physical size, were forced to wear short trousers and their hair was shaved. Tim's first experience of the institution was to be stripped and given a shower. His own clothes were then taken away and he was dressed in school togs which were considered suitable by the staff, but which were thought to be a punishment by a boy who was acutely conscious of modern fashion. From that first moment on, he enjoyed no privacy until he was released. The school had no place for the boys to be on their own, no lockers for their private possessions. All incoming letters were read, as were a number of those written by the boys to their parents and girlfriends. Attendance at Sunday Mass was compulsory and a fetish was made of bed-making in that only one particular military style was acceptable. Thirty boys slept in one dormitory which was so small that beds had to be placed down the middle passage of the room and those round the wall were so close together that they almost touched. If a boy was found to be a bed-wetter, a sock was tied to the end of his bed so that the night supervisor might identify him and send him to the toilet at regular intervals.

During his stay in the school the boy was unlikely to form the impression that the building was run by psychiatrists or psychologists. At the time Tim was an approved school boy, there were 26 such schools in Scotland and four clinical psychologists attached to the service. This meant that a psychologist spent less than a day a week in any one school and, when a school had a complement of over 100 boys, only a handful could be interviewed, and none treated. In addition to this provision, a psychiatrist came to the school for an hour or so every week. Fritz Redl (1945, p.375) has warned that, even when psychotherapeutic sessions are far more frequent, boys in an institution are stored in what he calls a group psychological climate: 'Several times a week the youngster is taken out of this climate for an hour or a half, is exposed to the influence of a psychiatrist in interview contact and is from there sent back to a place where every wall oozes gang psychological defence.'

Great Britain also maintains the illogical position of having banned corporal punishment in prisons and borstals but of retaining it in approved schools and remand homes. What has been found ineffective and brutalizing in the case of adults is still administered to young boys. In Scotland a specially approved tawse or leather strap may be applied three times on each hand or six times on the posterior over ordinary cloth trousers of boys of 14 and older. Tim received his fair share of punishment without any noticeable improvement in his subsequent conduct.

When a boy was released, and replaced in the very environment which caused the original court order to be made, he was supervised for a period of two years. But this was the weakest point of a weak system because the aftercare officers were so overloaded with cases that they rushed from one crisis situation to another.

The staffing problem was so acute that even people like myself, with irrelevant qualifications in Classics, were welcomed. The boys made it clear that neither the teachers nor the social welfare officers could act as role-models or objects of emulation because they considered our work a 'doss'. They could only identify with members of the staff like the farmer and the bricklayer who were seen to do a hard, 'manly' job. No additional or specialised training was considered necessary for headmasters, teachers, instructors, or housemasters; but all were expected to work long hours in the evenings and at weekends for little financial reward. Such conditions of employment exacerbated the task of trying to establish relationships with difficult boys. The pattern of duties dictated that every three weeks a man worked for a normal week, spent the weekend on duty at the school, and then commenced a new week's work as though nothing unusual had happened. It was not surprising that from time to time men's tempers frayed. The staff-pupil ratio approached 1:8. In Denmark, where the incidence of juvenile crime is decreasing, the ratio is 1:2. Howard Polsky (1962, p.15) describes how the custodial institution he studied in the United States had 195 pupils and an adult staff of 150, 55 of whom were professionally trained workers.

The facts which have been presented are not just of historical interest now that approved schools have become 'residential establishments' in Scotland and 'community homes' in England. The Social Work (Scotland) Act (1968) has inaugurated radical change by abolishing Juvenile Courts and introducing Children's Panels, and by bringing all sections of the social services into one department under a Director of Social Work. But little has changed in approved schools since the late 1960s apart from their name, and my fear is that the opportunity for fundamental change will be missed. It is no advance simply to rename the solitary confinement room an 'intensive care unit' (cf. David May, 1971, p.366).

A more serious and well-established criticism, which applies to nearly all our residential establishments for young offenders, remains to be made. Treatment is subordinated to the task of containing and controlling the boys, and the day to day running of the institution assumes paramount importance. Long-term planning, evaluation of past work, and research are luxuries which the empirical demands of the job cannot afford. As Howard Polsky (1962, p.149) phrases it, 'the issue of control takes precedence over abstract therapeutic norms', and as a result a gap opens up between the rules of the official system and of the subterranean, inmate, peer group culture. Howard Jones (1960, p.2) calls the latter a hidden world, a 'social and psychological environment to which the inmate has to relate, and by which he is being shaped.' Even first-rate institutions, like the one analysed by Polsky (pp.6-7), can 'create, maintain, and transmit a separate deviant subculture that supports values and a social system that are counter to those of the institution itself and in substantial part negate even the most intensive and skilful individual therapeutic efforts.'

The boys' lives become dominated not by the lectures, exhortations, and advice of teachers, social workers and psychiatrists, but by their own social system which is so pervasive that 'widespread accommodation' to its negative aspects is made by the staff. Tim, for example, in the approved school quickly asserted his authority among the other boys, and the gang culture of the streets was transmitted to the institution. Just as quickly, the staff realised that he was a force to be reckoned with and unwittingly hit upon the collective solution of according him positions of responsibility and special privileges. By seeking to contain Tim's challenge, the staff covertly acknowledged the superiority of the boys' system of values. Similarly, Polsky's (p.134) cottage parents 'reinforced the delinquent subculture by manipulating the boys' social hierarchy, wooing the leadership, and dominating weak members.'

Empey and Rabow's (1961) crucial criterion for any treatment programme is 'not what an individual does while in it, but what he does while he is *not* in it.' By this standard, Tim's behaviour on weekend leave would suggest that approved school training is neither too lenient nor too severe but irrelevant. What are the alternatives for the core offender? Since the Second World War, renewed interest has been shown in treating delinquents in therapeutic communities. The concept is itself much older and had been put into practice by such charismatic leaders as Homer Lane (Bazeley, 1928), August Aichhorn (1925), and Anton Makarenko (1951) amongst many others. More recent examples of the same approach can be found in the work of Shields (1962), Craft (1965) or Briggs (1972), but this is not the place for a detailed description of the approach. More to our purpose is the finding reported by Whiteley (1968) that the traditional, permissive regime of the type advocated by Maxwell Jones (1968) is ineffective with the aggressive type of psychopath.

What appears to be more successful is Dr Stump's (1968) attempt at Herstedvester near Copenhagen to rehabilitate dangerous and habitual criminals. In a much more structured environment, Stürup's primary objective in treatment is the security of society. When this has been established, the inmate is thrown back upon himself, he is left to plan his own future, while the staff assist him by examining his plans critically. Not only does the chronic criminal become a collaborator in his own treatment, he becomes his own therapist. No adequate account of detailed principles of treatment can be given in a few lines but the approach is in many ways similar to that employed in Synanon which is described in Yablonsky's book, *The Tunnel Back*, (1965). Here newcomers enter voluntarily into a 'total therapeutic' community where proof of the desire to reorientate their lives is the basis for being accepted. In such an environment no hidden inmate subculture develops because, in Synanon sessions, the norm is to 'grass', with the result that all the participants become brutally frank about their own and their neighbours' deviance, and everyone is involved in the success or failure of other members.

The ideas behind such self-help movements, of which Alcoholics Anonymous is a prime example, have been carried further forward by Hans Toch (1969), who involved violent offenders and policemen in a study of their own violent behaviour. Such self-analysis is reminiscent of the street corner research of Schwitzgebel (1964), who paid delinquents one to two dollars an hour for talking about themselves into a tape-recorder. Although this technique was at first dismissed as naive, the author claimed that in a short time the boys became co-workers with the experimenters in finding new ways to change their behaviour and that at the end of nine months they were committing significantly fewer crimes. The act of participating in the study of their own behaviour seems to have been the crucial factor in modifying it and Toch now corroborates this claim with respect to violent offenders. The theoretical foundation for most of this recent work has been Donald Cressey's (1955, p.119) plea for the introduction of criminals into group therapy to help change the behaviour of other criminals. The crux of the argument is that 'a group in which criminal A joins with some noncriminals to change criminal B is probably most effective in changing criminal A, not B ... '. The great value of this school of thought is that the offender has some say over the initiation and development of his treatment; it is opposed to the philosophy of those who submit aggressive offenders to brain surgery, like the Japanese and British doctors who, according to Gibbens (1970), perform the operation of amygdalotomy.

Sufficient experimentation has taken place to help us decide what type of therapeutic community is most appropriate for the treatment of the core members of the gang. But what of the marginals? A far less drastic and costly method of treating them is available. Detached workers, who are employed so extensively in the United States and who have been used on a limited scale in England, could be introduced to the streets of Glasgow. My main reason for advocating such a measure is that at present there is no organisation and no professional group whose specific task it is to cater for the needs of gang boys. When faced with the job of controlling or treating a gang, the existing agencies concentrate on solving their own problems and often react in an aggressive or indifferent manner. The police, for example, find their own masculinity challenged by the constant physical threat of the gang and take the necessary steps to reassure themselves. Teachers, with 30 other pupils in need of their attention, use corporal punishment to keep their heads above water; and probation officers devote themselves to more co-operative cases. Someone, and I suggest a detached worker, must take a new approach which would make the boys stop and think; someone must assume responsibility for gang boys who presently fall into 'the various bits of no-man's land which exist between the different fields of care'. (Morse, 1965, p.96.)

What is the role of the detached worker? Briefly, he is a social worker who is assigned to an area where his job is to locate, contact, and establish a relationship with the local gang in order to change it. The worker becomes a bridge between the boys and main social agencies which affect their lives – the police, the courts, the school, the youth employment service. This technique was first employed by the Chicago Area Project (Kobrin, 1959) in the 1930s and by 1957 it was 'a major feature of over twenty-five delinquency control programmes in about a dozen large American cities'. (Miller, 1957, p.406.) Little reference will be made to detached work with adolescents in England, as it is concerned more with unattached youth (Morse, 1965; Goetschius and Tash, 1967, and Cyril Smith's work in Manchester) than with delinquent or violent gangs.

The decades of experience in using this method have pin-pointed the primary benefits for American researchers. To Cloward and Ohlin (1960, p.176) 'the advent of the street-gang worker symbolised the end of social rejection and the beginning of social accommodation'. If the gang achieves status by having a detached worker assigned to it, then the authors logically expect that the gang will not have to resort to violence to achieve the same end. In Short and Strodtbeck's (1965, p.197) opinion, gang leaders indulge in less aggression as a 'quid pro quo for services performed by the worker' as well as for the additional status they acquire. Cooper (1967, p.185) describes an intriguing extension of the technique in Chicago, where not only are local adults paid $50 a month for assisting the detached worker in keeping a check on fringe members, but also boys from the very groups to which the worker has been allocated are made 'Field Assistants' at $10 a month or 'Consultants' at $20. The reward for a year's co-operation is promotion to the position of 'Senior Consultants' at $30. It sounds like another practical illustration of Cressey's principle, enunciated earlier; and, furthermore, as Geis (1965, p.27) remarks, engaging a gang member to help in the treatment of other members gives him a job about which he is knowledgeable, and is an enterprise which is 'more likely to succeed than attempts to portray dull jobs as attractive.'

Considerable success was claimed for the technique by Crawford, Malamud and Dumpson (1950, p.78), and by the New York City Youth Board (1960). More recently, however, critics like Kantor and Bennett (1968) and especially Malcolm Klein (1971) have pointed out that persuasive accounts of the method are no substitute for convincing objective demonstration of its effectiveness; and Miller's careful evaluation of the 'Midcity' project makes dispiriting reading for those of us who favour the adoption of a similar approach in Glasgow. On the other hand, we are in the happy position of being able to profit from the experience and the errors of previous programmes, such as the Group Guidance Project in Los Angeles where the intervention programmes, based on group work, inadvertently led to greater recruitment, cohesiveness and violence among the gangs (Klein, 1971, p.137). Yablonsky (1967, p.258ff.) makes a similarly trenchant attack upon the traditional detached worker's goal, the one aimed at in the 'Midcity' project, of redirecting the gang from destructive to constructive activities. In respect of a violent gang, this aim only serves to structure and organise into a group a diffuse collectivity of boys, thus producing what Yablonsky calls 'the group-fulfilling prophecy'. But if we have already removed the core members from the group, could we not self-consciously apply this technique to the remainder of the gang, and form the marginals into a conventional peer group which would then be amenable to normal social group work practice? The Meyerhoffs (1964) report that this very suggestion has been implemented in Los Angeles with success. This would promote the detached worker from the more straightforward task, to which he is relegated by David Downes (1968, p.69), of collecting basic information on groups in his local area.

Another lesson learned by Youth Boards in New York and in Boston has been the necessity to saturate a given area with workers rather than to single out one group of gangs for treatment. Miller's (1957, p.399) experience was that groups in areas adjacent to those which were part of the programme increased their violence in order to be awarded the social cachet of a gang worker.

The infusion into the community of a new style of worker with a new role can have particular advantages. Miller (1957) found that adolescents, who manifested an established set of attitudes towards familiar authority figures, did not know how to react to the non-evaluative, non-judgmental approach of the street worker: 'They were unable to fall back on known ways of acting and reacting.' Detached workers are usually mature, professionally-trained adults, guided and supported in the United States by a research team who constantly evaluate progress; the combination has also generated new theoretical perspectives. Mary Morse (1965, p.196) is confident that the presence of an understanding adult who becomes a significant person in the lives of unattached youngsters is one of the best services which they could be offered. The job is exacting and dangerous; one New York worker was murdered in 1963 (Bernstein, 1964, p.54). The personal qualities listed as essential attributes of the successful detached worker 'present a catalogue of virtues little short of those requisite for canonization' (Geis, 1965, p.57). But, to my mind, a team of detached workers could have an immense impact on the gang subculture of Glasgow. A cost-effectiveness approach to the evaluation of street gang work (Adams, 1967) demonstrated that the expense of institutional treatment was several times that of employing detached workers.

Another form of treatment applicable to marginal gang members is the

Provo experiment (Empey & Rabow, 1961), which concentrates on making the boys anxious about the ultimate utility of their delinquent system. The boys live at home and spend a few hours each day at the programme centre, which is really a day approved school of the type suggested by Rose (1967, p.203). This experiment has the two advantages of preventing the creation of an inmate system and of costing one-tenth of institutional treatment. Instead of rewarding delinquents for 'conformance to norms which concentrate upon effective custody as an end in itself, instead of devoting time to athletics or remedial education, only realistic and lasting changes in the boy's behaviour, particularly in his work habits, are considered criteria for release. A boy in the Provo experiment as in Synanon achieves status by being willing to confront other boys, in a daily group meeting, with their delinquent behaviour. The boy remains in the programme until he begins to make crucial decisions about his own future. 'In a reformatory a boy cannot help but see the official system as doing things to him in which he has no say: locking him up, testing him, feeding him, making his decisions.' Only when the boy has given evidence of having reformed himself and of being willing to reform others is he released.

Possible methods of treatment for the core and marginal offender have been outlined as means of controlling the immediate situation. Of course, Pfautz (1961, p.174) is right in concluding that neither therapy nor the 'ad hoc accolade' of a detached worker project will solve the basic social roots of the problem. 'The target for preventive action', as Cloward and Ohlin (1960, p.211) write, 'should be defined not as the individual or group that exhibits the delinquent pattern, but as the social setting that gives rise to delinquency.' In Glasgow terms, that means a stepping up of the slum clearance programme, and action on a national level to end the city's sordid mass of substandard housing. If Wolfgang and Ferracuti's (1967, p.299ff.) concept of a subculture of violence is appropriate to Glasgow, then social planning on a massive scale will also be necessary because 'renewal programmes that simply shift the location of the subculture from one part of a city to another do not destroy the subculture'. When confronted with engrained traditions of violence, a detached worker programme is viewed by the two authors as nothing more than a holding action or containment policy; they argue that to break into the vicious circle the representatives of the subculture of violence must be 'disrupted, dispersed, disorganised' to prevent aggressive attitudes being supported by one generation and imitated by another.

Government action is needed to tackle the whole complex of pathologies in west central Scotland and not just housing or unemployment. Such global measures are not, however, the subject of this chapter, the remainder of which is more concerned with short-term projects, like earlier diagnosis and prevention, which would have a more immediate effect upon violent gang delinquency. There is nothing novel in what follows; the ideas have been current since the early writings of Burt (1925) and Thrasher (1927, p.552), who were complaining even then that society spent 'far too much thought and money upon the problem of repressing the finished product of the delinquent career.' Society could be forgiven for its tardiness in acting if children suddenly took to delinquency at the age of 12 or 14. But Kate Friedlander (1947, p.112) has underlined the general truth that delinquent acts are preceded by periods of unruly behaviour; she further contends that future antisocial conduct can be predicted from the inability of children of six or seven to conform to ordinary methods of discipline suitable for their age.

This would suggest, as so many commentators have observed, that the school and particularly the primary school could act as a forward observation post to detect delinquency at the earliest possible moment. The Northtown worker in the Mary Morse (1965, p.147) study was convinced that the teachers and the headmistress were able to identify potential troublemakers in the first year of the secondary school, while Jephcott's (1967) research in Drumchapel indicates that future gang leaders were spotted not only by their teachers at an early age but also by their fellow pupils. DJ West's preliminary report (1969, p.143) and subsequent articles (1970, 1971) on the longitudinal Cambridge Study in Delinquent Development suggests that boys of 11 'are able to identify with surprising clarity the more deviant and troublesome individuals in their class'; the study also provides evidence that, on the basis of teachers' and psychiatric social workers' assessments, 'a substantial proportion of persistently anti-social juveniles can be picked out by their behaviour well before the age of 10 ... ' (p.140). Gibson and Hanson (1969, p.321), members of West's team of investigators, have convincingly demonstrated that ' ... at the end of a boy's career in a primary school, his main characteristics of social behaviour are well known to both his classmates and teachers' and that 'peer rating is indeed a powerfully predictive technique.' Amongst American researchers, Kobrin (1961, p.691) reports that 'at the ages of nine and ten, the five boys who came to constitute the core clique, out of which the Eagles as a street gang ultimately emerged, were known in the neighbourhood by residents, agency workers, and teachers as a particularly troublesome and incorrigible lot.' There would appear to be within the community a pool of knowledge about potential offenders which is not tapped.

That boys who become core members of teenage gangs can be identified at an early age is a vital pointer to action; but most predictive devices which have been developed have had less success with spotting the more 'normal' juvenile delinquent. To begin with, prediction tables or scales are subject to two kinds of error: they omit children who become delinquents and include others who do not. In addition, they raise issues of principle; Wilkins (1961, p.30) poses the pertinent question: 'To what extent is it ethical to seek the necessary information from persons who have not violated society's norms?' Two opposing attitudes are taken by criminologists: one view, supported by the Gluecks in the United States and by Morris in this country, is that there is a crying need for 'character prophylaxis' or 'preventive medicine of personality' (S Glueck, 1959, p.1005). Morris (1957, p.196) favours an extension of the periodic medical examination of school children 'to include some form of psychiatric interview with the child and the mother ... Nervous disorders in children cannot be less important than flat feet or carious teeth.' Supporters of the alternative position are both astonished and troubled by the recent efforts of the Gluecks (E Glueck, 1966) to identify potential delinquents at two to three years of age. Stan Cohen (1971, p.11), protesting against 'the dehumanizing tendency of the social sciences', quotes as an example the serious American proposal to give psychological tests to the total population of sixyear-olds to uncover their potential for future criminal behaviour. Less objection is usually made to Stott's (1960, 1971) Bristol Social Adjustment Guide and to the very simple preliminary combing-out procedure which he has developed. But those who are opposed to all screening methods may take heart from the considered opinion, based upon empirical research, of Cyril Burt (1965, p.375): 'No psychological tests or techniques, no interview by a psychologist or a clinical psychologist, can yield such trustworthy assessments or such sound predictions as those of an experienced teacher who has watched and studied his pupils' behaviour and development, year after year.' This glowing tribute to the intuitive wisdom of the experienced teacher must be set against other empirical evidence such as that presented by Phillipson (1971, p.242) who reports that, in an investigation into the differential rates of delinquency between schools in a London borough, primary school headmasters showed no ability to pick out the future delinquents.

With regard to earlier treatment as opposed to diagnosis, Kate Friedlander (1947, p.219) estimates that the best prospects of success are with children between the ages of seven and ten, and the McCords (1959, p.94) conclude from their analysis of the Cambridge-Somerville Youth Study that intensive contact with the child, 'particularly if begun when the child is under 10 or by a female after the boy has reached adolescence', would be more effective than the techniques which were employed.

Benjamin Bloom (1964, p.231) sums up the debate: 'If school dropouts, delinquent behaviour and frustration with the educational requirements of a society can be predicted long in advance, can we sit idly by and watch the prophecies come true? If remedial actions and therapy are less effective at later stages in the individual's development, can we satisfy a social conscience by indulging in such activities when it is far too late?' Bloom's thesis is that the increased ability to predict delinquency places new reponsibilities on the school and on society. It is my own view that these responsibilities are being neglected or even ignored.

An example of gross irresponsibility is readily available: the refusal of the Inner London Education Authority and teachers' organisations to allow Power and his colleagues (1967, 1972 and Phillipson 1971) to pursue their research. Power observes that, in the past, efforts to explain juvenile delinquency have concentrated either on the personality of the offender, his family, or on the neighbourhood to the exclusion of one important factor: the secondary school the offender attends. Basing his study in Tower Hamlets, an almost exclusively working-class borough of London, Power discovered wide variation in delinquency rates between the 20 secondary modern schools serving the area in the period 1958 to 1963. Some schools showed consistently high rates of delinquency throughout the period, while others retained very low rates, and even after a major reorganisation of the schools in 1963, the association between delinquency rates and school attended remained very close for the next five years. Further investigation revealed that these differences were not simply a reflection of the delinquency rates in the catchment areas of the schools, nor could they be explained by variations in local police practice or 'by any outside environmental factor that it has been possible to identify' (Power, 1972, p.122). The all-important conclusion the researchers were forced to reach was that, among a number of overtly similar schools, some were preventing their pupils becoming delinquent while others were apparently putting them at risk of it. But the vital information needed by teachers and administrators, as to what features of the 'good' schools enabled them to protect their boys from delinquency is missing because access to the schools was and continues to be refused. So the most promising research into juvenile delinquency in this country is brought to a halt at the very point where the community has most to gain from its continuance.

The gang culture of Glasgow has proved so resilient over the years that no single measure or group of measures is likely to be effective in isolation. The 'synergism' concept, defined by Miller (1962, p.190) as 'the simultaneous and concerted application of multiple and diverse programs on different levels' holds out the best hope of success – despite Miller's own reservations. If one accepts Beeley's (1959, p.227) axiom that the causes of delinquency are 'complex rather than simple, plural rather than singular, concurrent and/or contributory rather than exclusive', then it follows that no one treatment will be foolproof. Most investigators (see, for example, the Sherifs, 1964, p.308ff.) plead for action on at least three levels, on three interacting sets of influences: the individual or group, the immediate neighbourhood, and the larger social setting.

The following points of attack on the problem are more a personal statement of interests (mainly educational) than a comprehensive list and are acknowledged as being more relevant to marginal rather than core gang members.

1. The Plowden Committee's recommendations which favoured positive discrimination for selected primary schools in educational priority areas (EPA's) should be extended and implemented. Action research (involving five experimental area projects which were mounted as a result of the Plowden report) has confirmed that the EPA *is* a viable notion, that preschooling is an economical and efficient method of raising standards, and that community schools (studying a community curriculum and supported by deep parental involvement of the kind achieved by Eric Midwinter in Liverpool) can revitalise even the most rundown urban area (Halsey, 1972). The original Plowden recommendations could be improved in two ways: by accepting the findings of the Swansea project in compensatory education which argues strongly that intervention should be geared to *individuals* rather than to areas or schools; and by extending positive discrimination to selected *secondary* as well as primary pupils for the reasons given by Phillipson (1971, p.245). I am arguing here for extra educational facilities to be given to those children who are identified as being in the greatest need. But how many people in England are aware that many of these children, far from enjoying additional benefits, are not receiving even normal educational provision? In 1969, in certain readily identifiable areas of Glasgow, 7,500 children were subject to part-time education. In Drumchapel, three nursery schools catered for 150 of the 2,500 children under five (Jephcott, 1967, p.25). At present the most deprived children receive the least schooling.

2. Such a major investment in preschool facilities, in EPA's etc., would be expensive. However, by redeploying our educational resources, alternative strategies become available to us at no extra charge to the taxpayer. Firstly, the teachers, who are the most costly item in the educational budget, could be redistributed within the system. Recently, Alan Little has asked the question: by what act of God

is the teacher-pupil ratio one to eight in universities, one to 12 in sixth forms, one to 18 in secondary schools generally, and one to 27 in primary schools? These ratios should be reversed or at least modified in order to bring help to schools and children with special difficulties. Secondly, promotion within the teaching profession could be tied to those teachers who have worked successfully in the more deprived areas, as John Mays has been advocating for 20 years (Mays, 1954, p.156ff).

3. More vigilance must be paid by school authorities to the problem of truancy. The ISTD (1970) report on the carrying of offensive weapons notes the long history of truancy among 78% of the intake of approved schools, regardless of the reason for the boy's committal. The close relationship between delinquency and truancy has long been established, and TG Tennent (1971) reviews 25 studies of British and American origin all of which suggest a significant correlation between school non-attendance and later delinquency. In view of such knowledge, one reads with surprise Catherine Lindsay's (1970, p.118) study of two comprehensive schools in Glasgow which uncovered the fact that 20% of the delinquents had truancy records, compared with 8% of the non-delinquents, 'but no higher a percentage of them had been under the supervision of the default officer.' And yet when one thinks of the curriculum of the non-academic boy in such schools, one could almost consider truancy a healthy response, if it were not for Tyerman's (1968) evidence of the high proportion of maladjusted children among truants.

4. Many schools have already introduced into the curriculum classes in parenthood and elementary child psychology, but fewer study violence and aggression, although texts like Colin Ward's *Violence* (1970) are now available. Bettleheim (1966) criticises the American educational system which 'proceeds as if these tendencies exist neither in society nor in man'. We provide few outlets for the violence of children and do not equip them to deal with their own violence. Toch's claim, that involving the violent in a study of their own behaviour may succeed in modifying it, is relevant here.

5. The practice of expelling 'difficult' boys even for a temporary period should be abandoned.

6. Glasgow's pioneering venture of attaching social workers to secondary schools should be extended to primary schools where one might have expected them to have been introduced in the first place. The school welfare officers, as they have been called, provide 'a

school-focused, school-based service' (Auld, 1967, p.174) for the detection and prevention of delinquency. Their contacts with the local community should bring help at an earlier stage to the type of young girl whose promiscuous relationships with adolescent gangs earn them the title of 'cows'. The Young Team associated with three such girls whose behaviour was notorious in the neighbourhood but unknown to the schools they attended.

7. The training of teachers should stress that social work is a profession with its own body of theory and practical skills and not 'a combination of the provision of moral uplift and free shoes' (Phillipson, 1971, p.254). Despite repeated calls for student and practising teachers to be given the ability to detect the symptoms of maladjustment and delinquency, reports still suggest that their level of information on these topics is low and, more seriously, that 'there are aspects of their perceptions of delinquency as a problem which are likely to reinforce the pattern of delinquency between schools' (Phillipson, p.252).

8. Part of New York's Mobilization for Youth project is a 'Homework Helper' programme, in which peripheral gang members attending secondary school are paid to help primary school children. The gang boy acquires recognition as well as money, while the child 'reaps the advantages of a relationship with a role model much closer to him in age and interests than his regular day teacher' (Bibb, 1967, p.179).

9. A police juvenile liaison scheme should be introduced into Glasgow. Since the invention of the idea by the Liverpool police force in 1949 and its adoption by the Greenock police in 1956, similar schemes have been launched by over 20 forces in England and six in Scotland (Mack, 1968). The Glasgow police have yet to employ this method of preventing juvenile delinquency by establishing liaison with parents, school teachers, social workers, and youth club leaders. The scheme in Greenock concentrates on the eight to 14 age bracket, with the accent on those eight- to 11-year-olds (Mack, 1963), who have committed an offence or who are potential delinquents. JB Mays (1965) calculates that the JLO system has had a high record of successes in Liverpool, and more detailed evaluations, carried out by Mack (1968) on the schemes operating in Scotland, and by M Taylor (1971) on the scheme in West Ham, support this view, though Rose and Hamilton's (1970) study of an experimental scheme in Blackburn found no evidence that supervision reduced the recidi-

vism rate to a significant degree. I agree with Mack, however, that the main justification for liaison schemes may be their effect on police-public relations. The public image of the police would be greatly improved by the emergence of a body of officers in plain clothes working in a preventive and social capacity. 'Juvenile liaison brings the police closer to the parents as well as the children. It personalises authority, gives it a kindlier face, makes the agencies of social control more approachable and less fearsome.' (Mack, 1963, p.374.) The scheme is an advance on the Glasgow practice of bringing trivial cases involving youngsters before the Superintendent's Court (Ferguson, 1952). But prior to training juvenile liaison officers, the Glasgow police would understandably prefer to fill the 500 vacancies in the force (Chief Constable's Report, 1968, 1969).

10. Society must provide socially acceptable outlets for aggression, adventure and excitement. The traditional youth club's staple diet of ping-pong, Coca-Cola and five-a-side football will not cure the gang boy's thirst for thrills. Mary Morse (1965, p.74) comments that many young people rejected their local youth clubs 'because the services were so inadequate that only the maladjusted could have enjoyed or tolerated them.' The Young Team attended their youth club once or twice a week but only to relieve their boredom for a few hours. A club run on the lines of the Barge Club as depicted by Spencer (1950) or of the hot-rod clubs initiated by the police in California (Salisbury, 1959) may be more successful in deflecting and captivating the attention of the marginal gang member.

11. There is a critical need to provide adequate, compulsory Further Education for boys like the members of the Young Team, who at the ages of 15 and 16 found themselves both unskilled and unemployed. They hated and rejected school, but they might well have responded far more positively to concrete technical training tied to realistic job opportunities. But, of course, even the best detached workers, youth clubs and Further Education in the world cannot compensate for the despair created by a long period of high unemployment and economic stagnation. As automation continues to increase redundancies among the most unskilled, we run the risk (through the failure of the present system of Further Education) of creating a large group of young people who are not only unemployed but unemployable: ' ... the streets of our urban slums are slowly filling with young men *who have no prospect of finding manhood through work: who are coming of age in a society which neither wants them nor needs them.*' (R

Cloward, quoted by Downes, 1966, p.264. Italics as in original.)
12. From the 1920s to the present day, successive groups of sociologists, known as the Chicago School, have combined theoretical speculation with experimental action programmes. The result has been that Chicago has become a centre for gang research, for gang information, for theory which is firmly based on empirical investigation, and for remedial action. In contrast, we know next to nothing about Glasgow's social problems. The city should therefore establish a Research Centre, and part of its responsibility would be the training, supervision and evaluation of a detached worked programme. Sean Darner's (1970) proposal that Glasgow Corporation should set up a centre for urban research springs from the same desire to tackle the city's social problems in a systematic way.

'We have gangs not because we do not know how to prevent them but because we do not have enough interest or energy to do the things we know will bring an end to delinquency. We do not lack knowledge. We lack the will.' Harrison Salisbury (1959, p.197) perhaps overstates the case when writing of New York gangs. In Glasgow we have neither the knowledge nor the will.

I have sought to describe, and to a lesser extent to interpret, the activities of one Glasgow gang in their terms and in their territory. It is only a beginning and not an end in itself: the Glasgow gang awaits definitive study. Earlier research into delinquency in the city was criticised by JB Mays (1954, p.22) because it did not show us what it feels like to be a young delinquent in Glasgow: 'We require added information ... so that these youngsters who are treated as facts and figures come alive to imagination as well as to intellectual understanding.' This book has been an attempt to present the daily lives of a group of adolescent delinquents with appreciation and empathy; it has been an attempt to 'place upon the bare bones of statistics the flesh and blood and spirit of recognisable humanity.'

Glossary

FOR THE BENEFIT of those who do not understand the Glasgow dialect or gang slang, I here translate the principal abbreviations and corruptions into standard English. Some of the following words are more fully explained in Eric Partridge's (1961) *Dictionary of Slang and Unconventional English* (London: Routledge and Kegan Paul), and even more in the same author's (1950) *Dictionary of the Underworld* (London: Routledge and Kegan Paul). A few words, like 'boggin', 'malky', 'huckle', etc., seem to be peculiar to Glasgow.

aboot	about
afore	before
afrighted aff	afraid off
ag-ain	again
Ah	I
ain	own
alane	alone
an' 'at	and that
an' aw	and all
auld	old
aw	all
awae	away
baith	both
bam-pot	fool, 'mug'
bass, as in 'ya bass'	bastard
ba'le	battle
beamer, to have a beamer	one's cheeks are red with embarrassment
beef (verb)	to have sexual intercourse with
bender	see under 'edger'
bent-shot	homosexual
bevie (noun and verb)	drink
bevied (past participle)	drunk
boggin'	pejorative adjective used to describe any thing the boys didn't like or understand
blocked up	'high' with drugs
boa'le	bottle

Glossary

boax	box
boaygang's	pronunciation of 'boy'
bookie	turf accountant
buroo	bureau – Ministry of Social Security
bummin'	boasting
busies	the police. A busy in Partridge (1950) is explained as 'a detective', the word being used to distinguish him from 'flattie', the ordinary policeman
bust (verb)	burst, 'split open', punch
caird	card
cairt	to arrest and put into a Black Maria
cawed	called
can	approved school jargon, but used far more widely, for 'toilet'
cannae	cannot
to chat up, or to pa'er up	to indulge in badinage, frequently of a pseudo-flattering nature
chib (noun)	a weapon
(verb, transitive)	to strike with a weapon
chip (verb)	throw, toss, cf. 'pap'
chuckies	small stones, i.e. testicles
claes	clothes
clatty	'stourie', dirty, 'manky'
claw (verb)	pull, drag, catch hold of
coarner	corner
cop, as in 'cop yir whack'	to get one's deserts, to be put in one's place by physical force
cow	a promiscuous girl who performs with a 'lineup' of boys
crack up (verb)	to go mad, 'throw a maddie'
crap-bags	cowards
croass	cross
dabs	fingerprints
dae (verb)	to do
dain' (present participle)	doing
daen't	don't
deid	dead

dig up	'pull up', pick someone out of a crowd
dittery-lookin'	stupid appearance
doon	down
dossin'	lazing about, loafing
dubbed up	locked up, confined
dug	dog
edge, as in 'keeping the edge up'	keeping a look-out
edger, as in 'bending edger'	approved school term to denote a boy who is prepared to welcome homosexual advances from members of staff in order to curry favour with them
efter	after
'em	them
esactly	exactly
fae	from
feart	afraid
fit	foot
fitba'	football
froak	frock
fur	for
gallous	flashy, sharp, hard, the way a 'spiv' or 'hard man' would act. This word appears at least twice in JM Synge's *Playboy of the Western World*: 'Father Reilly's after reading it in gallous Latin' (Michael, in Act III), and 'there's a great gap between a gallous story and a dirty deed' (Pegeen, in Act III)
gammy	withered
gear	clothes
geared up	dressed to kill
gee	give
gemme	game
gemmie	'a hardman'
git	get
Glesga	Glaswegians' pronunciation of Glasgow
glessies	glasses, spectacles

Glossary

goaney	going to
goat	got
goofies	pills, drugs
grass (verb)	to inform on, to squeal
greetin'	crying
groovy (noun)	scar
'Grove	Larchgrove remand home in Glasgow
grun'	ground
gu'er	gutter
to guy the course	run away, make off
ha'e	have
hander (verb)	to go to the aid of
handit	handed (past participle of verb 'to hand'), used to designate the number of boys in a gang
haud o', as in 'to get a haud o''	to get a hold of
haufer	halfer, i.e. the boy with whom you share your tobacco, etc.
haun'	hand
haw maws	rhyming slang for baws, i.e. balls or testicles
heid	head
heid-banger	someone who allegedly hits his head against walls, and so thought to be mad
hid	had
hing	hang
hing-oot	defined by Tim as a girl 'who's done it so often, her cunt's hingin' oot'
hink	I think
hissel'	himself
hiv'	have
hob-nobs	rhyming slang for snobs
hoosey, housey, provey	approved school
huckle (verb)	to apprehend, arrest
hunner	hundred
huvtae, as in 'huvtae cases'	situation where partners 'have to' get married because the girl is pregnant
ither	other
intae	into

jaiket	jacket
jist	just
joab	job
jump (verb)	to leap out from hiding and attack, to pounce upon; American equivalent is 'mugging'
Karflick	Catholic
Kerry	carry
kerry-oot	carry-out, i.e. beer etc., taken in carrier bag from a pub
kin (verb)	can
knock	steal
lae or le'e	leave
len as in 'take a len' o''	to make a fool of
loaked	locked
loat	lot
loast	lost
lumber	a girl escorted home from a dance
ma	my
Ma	mother, so 'ma Ma' is 'my Mother'
mair	more
maist	most
milky	chib, weapon
masel'	myself
ma'er	matter
merried	married
mither	Mother
mix, as in to put the mix in'	to contrive a quarrel, to cause a fight by intrigue
mooth	mouth
'mon!	come on!
morra', as in 'ra morra''	tomorrow
mulk	milk
nabbed	caught, arrested
nae	no
naeb'dy	nobody
noo	now

Glossary

no'	not
nu	no
nuthin'	nothing
oaffice	office
oan	on
oaneytime	anytime
oaneywae	anyway
oaneywan	anyone
oarder	order
oor	our
'oors	hours
oot	out
ower	over
Pakies	Pakistanis; word used pejoratively of all coloured people
pap (noun)	breast
pap (verb)	to throw, pitch, or 'chip'
pa'er (noun)	patter, conversation
pa'er up (verb)	to 'chat up', pay court to a young girl, to wheedle with plausible speech
peter	police cell, prison cell
piece	sandwich
pied	paid
pineapple	rhyming slang for chapel
pit (noun)	bed
pit (verb)	put
pi'in (present participle)	putting
pitch	territory, area, equivalent of New York gang word 'turf
poakit	pocket
polis	police
poun'	pound
psychey (noun and adjective)	someone the gang thought to be mentally disturbed, who needed psychological help
puddin'	pudding
puggled	drunk
punter	1. resetter of stolen goods 2. a gang member

puss	face
pussyin' aroun'	playing about, mostly used in a sexual context
queer-hawk	'odd-ball', 'mental case', sometimes used to describe a homosexual
ra	the
rake	to search, rifle the pockets of, cf. American expression 'to roll'
rakin'	searching
rid	red
rid neck	to flush with embarrassment
riddie, as in 'big riddie'	to blush, to have cheeks red with embarrassment
roun'	round
sannies	sandshoes, plimsolls
screw (verb)	to break into, to burgle
screw (noun)	prison officer, police constable or approved school staff member
screw, as in 'screw the nut'	to become sensible, to 'get wise' to oneself, to pull oneself together
screw, as in 'screw-taps'	screw-tops, bottles of beer
Selly	Celtic Football Club
selt	past participle of verb 'to sell'
set, as in 'to set aboot'	to attack, to assault someone
Setirday	Saturday
shoap	shop
Shug	Glasgow pronunciation of Hugh
sleekit	sly, cunning
snide	'boggin'' as used in phrase 'snide gear', i.e. clothes that are out of fashion, contemptible, inferior
soaft	soft
soart	sort
soart, as in 'to soart oot'	to put someone in his place, to cut him down to size
some'dy	somebody

Glossary

square-go	a fight without weapons
staun'	stand
steamin'	drunk
stoap	stop
stoatin'	staggering (because of drink)
stomik	stomach
stuck, as in 'to get stuck intae'	to attack with head, fist and foot
sur	sir
tae	to
techey	technical
telt	past participle of verb 'to tell'
thae	those
thaem	them
thegither	together
thir	their
thir's	there is
thoat	thought
thoosans	thousands
thruple	triple, three times
'tic	Celtic Football Club
Tim, as in 'a Tim'	Roman Catholic
Tim Malloy	a Glasgow expression for a Catholic youth
toaffie	1. as in toaffie-nose, snobbish
	2. as in 'gettin'yir toaffie', 'gettin'yir hole', i.e having sexual intercourse
toap	top
toon	town
touch	to come up to the same standard as
trannies	diminutive for transistor radios
tumble, as in 'take a tumble tae yirsel''	to waken up to the true facts, to face reality; cf. 'to screw the nut'
Uncle John	rhyming slang for pawnbroker
ur	are
urnae, as in 'Ah'm urnae'	I am not
uzz	us
wa'	wall (plural wa's)

211

wae	way
wan	one
wance	once
wank	masturbate
wean	baby
weil	well
whaur	where
whit	what
wi'	with
wi'oot	without
wid	would
wide, as in 'to come wide'	to get the better of, to outsmart
winchin'	1. 'necking'
	2. courting
windaes	windows
wir (verb)	were
wir (possessive adjective)	our
wis	was
wisnae	was not
wull	will
wummin	woman
ye yersel'	you yourself
yir	your
yon	diminutive for 'yonder'; otherwise 'that'
youse	you (plural)

Annotations

1   Boys in approved schools were at that time officially allowed 42 days leave each year.
2   See Glossary, page 206.
3   The Scottish equivalent of an English secondary modern.
4   Several gangs in Glasgow adopted the name 'Tongs' out of respect for the Calton Tongs. (cf. Yablonsky, L., 1967, p. 103). While recording the invasion of Morningside Heights in New York by the Dragons, he comments: 'Many gangs thus assumed the Dragon name simply for prestige purposes, even though they had no clear affiliation.'
5   A phrase used in a letter to me by John Mack, formerly Director of Social Studies at Glasgow.
6   The novel of Glasgow street-gangs in the 1940s *Cut and Run* by Bill McGhee (Corgi edition, 1963) includes on p.108 the phrase, 'Ah don't gie a "donald".' Here, by abbreviation and rhyme, a quite different meaning is being conveyed.
7   'Tea leaf' for 'thief' is one of the examples of rhyming slang with which Julian Franklyn (1960) deals. Of all the examples used by the gang only this one, together with 'brass nail' and 'hit and miss' are included in Franklyn's book.
8   This was the gang expression for an open razor which has no lock of any kind. What the boys mean by the expression, I think, is that the blade of the razor can be pushed back against the holder and held in a 'locked' position.
9   An exactly similar incident is reported by Walter Bernstein in his article *The Cherubs are Rumbling* to be found in James F Short, jnr., (1968, p.28). The butt of the 'joke' in the American context is one of the 'weak kids' in the gang, a dope addict.
10   Werthman and Piliavin (1967, pp.61-2) describe the relationship between gang members and policemen as an ecological struggle over who has final control of the gang's corner for 'the very places that are defended like homes by gang members also constitute places of work or "beats" to the police, and the home-like uses to which gang members put the streets are often perceived as threats to the patrolman's task of maintaining the conventional rules that ordinarily govern behavior on them.'
11   The Glasgow Police inform me that no such group exists within the force. Yet again, this phrase proves to be a figment of Tim's imagination, or of the

collective imagination of the subculture to which he belongs.
12 As elsewhere, when reports are quoted, all names etc. have been altered, but other details are unchanged.
13 Polmont Borstal, near Falkirk.
14 Why the boys should use this English term in preference to the Scottish one of 'serious assault' I can only conjecture. Perhaps the use of the English term in crime films and books is the explanation.
15 The Chinese gangs in the United States, the Tongs, after which the Calton Tongs are named, are 'as American as chop suey' according to Thrasher (1927, pp.208ff.):

> Contrary to general belief, the tongs are an American product. They did not come to us from China. They originated in California and Nevada during the early Gold Rush, and had their inception in the theory that might makes right.
>
> The meaning of the word tong is 'protective society'. For a yearly fee, one tong will guarantee protection to its members against any enemies they may happen to have in a rival tong ... It began as a benevolent association or a trade union or a social club. Then tong men found they could make money by intensive organization, plus hatchets. The idea spread through the years and the tongs grew because even the most peaceable Chinese would rather perish at the hands of fellow-countrymen than be saved by asking the white man to interfere.

Now why a group of Glasgow teenagers from the Calton district should settle upon this name as the name of their gang was a mystery to the boys of Maryhill. One plausible explanation appeared in an article on Glasgow gangs in the *Daily Telegraph Magazine* (Friday, 4 October 1968). Billy, a self-styled founder member of the Tongs, is explaining how the gang was formed: 'We saw a film The Terror of the Tongs. It was about a Chinese secret society. When we came out we just started breaking windows and shouting : "Tongs! Tongs, ya bass!" After that all the kids started teaming up.'
16 The gang members share this primitive belief with some staff members of approved schools. My main objection is not to the idea itself, but to its power to create the very turmoil it purports to prophesy.
17 Cf. James F Short, jnr., (1968, p.20):

> Members of such [i.e. conflict] gangs often evidence great pride when the mass media take note of their activities, even though the

notices usually are derogatory. A prominent member of one such gang in Chicago compiled a scrapbook filled with newspaper articles featuring his gang. The scrapbook was embellished with 'art work' featuring guns, dynamite, 'brass knucks', money, a skull and crossed pool cues (!), and a motto – 'Lords of Lovers!'

18   The *Evening Times*, Glasgow, 1 September 1936.
19   Larchgrove remand home in Glasgow.
20   Throughout the text the word 'want' when spoken by Tim or one of the boys is to be imagined as rhyming with 'pant'.
21   Short & Strodtbeck (1965, p.218) comment upon the reluctance or inability of the Chicago gang boy to escape from his own environment:

> The range of gang boys' physical movements is severely restricted. They are ill at ease when outside their 'area', in part because of fear that they may infringe on a rival gang's territory, but in part due also to a more general lack of social assurance ...

The authors go on to hypothesise a fundamental lack of social skills on the part of gang boys, a 'social disability'.
22   The expression is explained by Julian Franklyn (1960, p.42), as rhyming slang for 'tail', and so, prostitute.
23   There were 120 blocks, housing, I estimate, under 40,000 people in 1968. See The Corporation of the City of Glasgow, Housing Management Department Annual Report, 1968.
24   Figure based on the Annual Report (1968) of the Housing Management Department of the Corporation of the City of Glasgow. Like Catherine Lindsay (1970), I worked on the basis of an average 3.5 persons per household.
25   Report by a Joint Working Party on Community Problems, appointed by the Corporation of the City of Glasgow and the Secretary of State for Scotland, 1969.
26   Figures extracted from the 1966 Sample Census by the Shelter Organisation. See Shelter in Scotland, Facts Sheet (1).
27   Overcrowding was defined in the census as the number of persons living at a density of more than 1.5 persons per room.
28   Report by a Sub-Committee of the Scottish Housing Advisory Committee HMSO, Edinburgh, 1967.
29   For figures, see Corporation of the City of Glasgow, Housing Management Department, Annual Report, 1968.

30 Sillitoe, P. (1955) *Cloak without Dagger*, London: Cassell. This book, an *Evening Citizen* series in January 1955, and the fictional novel *No Mean City* and its sequel *No Bad Money* provide most of the information on the subject.
31 For an explanation, see the beginning of Chapter 20.
32 *Department of Employment Gazette*, vol. LXXIX, no.12, December 1971, p.1183.
33 I am particularly grateful to David Downes for his suggestions at this point.
34 The evidence presented by others besides Polsky makes me question Downes's (1966, p.88) suggestion that the autocracy of the cottage was 'a reflex of institutionalisation'.

Bibliography

Adams, S. (1967), 'A Cost Approach to the Assessment of Gang Rehabilitation Techniques', *J. Research in Crime and Delinq.*, vol. 4, no.1, 166-182.

Aichhorn, A. (1925), *Wayward Youth*, London: Imago.

Arneil, GC, & Crosbie JC. (1963), 'Infantile Rickets returns to Glasgow', *The Lancet* vol. 2, 423-5.

Arneil, GC. (1964), 'Rickets returns in British Children', Practitioner, vol. 192, May 1964, 652-5.

Auld, MH. (1967), 'Attaching Social Workers to Schools – I'. In Craft M, Raynor, J & Cohen L. (eds.), *Linking Home and School*, London: Longmans.

Baittle, B. (1961), 'Psychiatric Aspects of the Development of a Street Corner Group: An Exploratory Study', *Amer. J. Orthopsych*, vol. 31, no.4, 703-11.

Baker, BD. (1958), 'The Glasgow Overspill Problem'. In Miller, R & Tivy, J (eds.), *The Glasgow Region*, Glasgow

Barker, P. (1964), 'The Margate Offenders: A Survey'. In Raison, T. (ed.) (1966), *Youth in New Society*, London: Rupert Hart-Davis.

Batey, NR & MacBain GC. (1967), 'Injury By Stabbing', *Scot. Med. J.*, 12, 251-5.

Bazeley, ET. (1928), *Homer Lane and the Little Commonwealth*, London: New Education Book Club.

Becher, HS. (1958), 'Problems of Inference and Proof in Participant Observation', *Amer. Sociol. Rev.*, vol. 23, 652-60.
(1963), *Outsiders*, New York: Free Press of Glencoe.
(1967), 'Whose Side Are We On?', *Social Problems*, vol. 14, no.3, 239-7.

Belley, AL. (1959), 'A Sociopsychological Theory of Crime and Delinquency'. In Glueck, S. (ed.), *The Problem of Delinquency*, Cambridge, Mass.: Riverside Press.

Bermant, CI. (1964), *Jericho Sleep Alone*, London: Chapman and Hall.

Bernstein, S. (1964), *Youth on the Streets*, New York: Association Press.

Bernstein, W. (1968), 'The Cherubs are Rumbling'. In Short, J.F (ed.), *Gang Delinquency and Delinquent Subcultures*, New York: Harper and Row.

Bettleheim, B. (1966), 'Violence: A Neglected Mode of Behavior', *Annals*, 364, March, 19-27.

Bibb, M. (1967), 'Gang-Related Services of Mobilization for Youth'. In Klein, MW (ed.), *Juvenile Gangs in Context*, New Jersey: Prentice-Hall.

Bibliography

Bloch, HA & Neiderhoffer, A. (1958), *The Gang: A Study in Adolescent Behavior*, New York: Philosophical Library.

Bloom, BS. (1964), *Stability and Change in Human Characteristics*, New York: John Wiley.

Bordua, DJ. (1961), 'Delinquent Subcultures: Sociological Interpretations of Gang Delinquency', *Annals*, vol. CCCXXXVIII, November 1961, 120-36. (1967), 'Recent Trends: Deviant Behavior and Social Control', *Annals*, 369, 147-63.

Boston, R. (1968), 'The Glasgow Gangs', *New Society*; 1 August, 149-51.

Brennan, T. (1959), *Reshaping a City*, Glasgow: House of Grant.

Briggs, DL (1972), 'A Transitional Therapeutic Community for Young, Violent Offenders', *Howard J.*, vol. XIII, no. 3, 171-184.

NBurt, C. (1925), *The Young Delinquent*, London: University of London Press. (1965), 'Factorial Studies of Personality and their Bearing on the Work of the Teacher', *Brit. J. Educ. Psychol.*, 1965, 35, 368-78.

Carson, WG & Wiles, P. (eds.) (1971), *Crime and Delinquency in Britain*, London: Martin Robertson.

Cavan, RS. (1962), *Juvenile Delinquency*, New York: JB Lippincott.

Clark, DH. (1965), 'The Therapeutic Community – Concept, Practice and Future', *Brit. J. Psychiat.*, 111, no. 479, 947-54.

Cloward, RA & Ohlin, LE. (1960), *Delinquency and Opportunity*, Glencoe, Ill.: The Free Press.

Cohen AK. (1955), *Delinquent Boys: the culture of the gang*, Glencoe, Ill.: The Free Press.

Cohen AK & Short, JF, jnr. (1958), 'Research in Delinquent Subcultures', *J. of Social Issues*, 14, 20-37.

Cohen, S. (1967), 'Mods, Rockers and the Rest: Community Reactions to Juvenile Delinquency', *Howard J.*, 12, 121-30.
(1968), 'Who are the Vandals'. Three articles on the politics, nature, and control of vandalism in *New Society*, 12 December, no. 324, 872-8.
(1970),'Research into group violence and vandalism among adolescents'. Paper given at Fourth National Conference on Research and Teaching in Criminology, Institute of Criminology, University of Cambridge.
(ed.) (1971), *Images of Deviance*, Harmondsworth: Penguin Books.

Cooper, CN. (1967), 'The Chicago YMCA Detached Workers: Current Status of an Action Program'. In Klein, MW (ed.), *Juvenile Gangs in Context*, New Jersey: Prentice-Hall.

Craft, M. (1965), 'A Follow-up Study of Disturbed Juvenile Delinquents', *Brit. J. Crimin.*, vol. 5, no.1, 55-62.

Crane AR. (1958), 'The Development of Moral Values in Children – Pre-adolescent Gangs and the Moral Development of Children', *Brit. J. Educ. Psych.*, XXVIII, 201-8.

Crawford PL, Malamud, DI & Dumpson, JR. (1950), *Working with Teenage Gangs*, New York: Welfare Council of New York City.

Cressey, DR. (1955), 'Changing Criminals: the Application of the Theory of Differential Association', *Amer. J. Sociol.*, vol. 61, September, 116-20.

Cullingworth, JB. (1968), *A Profile of Glasgow Housing*, 1965 University of Glasgow Social and Economic Studies, Occasional Papers, No.8, Edinburgh: Oliver and Boyd.

Damer, S. (1970), 'Missing facts on life in Glasgow'. Article in *Glasgow Herald*, Tuesday, 6 January.

Defleur, LB. (1967), 'Delinquent Gangs in Cross-Cultural Perspective: the case of Cordoba', *J. Research in Crime and Delinq.*, vol. 4, no.1, 132-41.

Delaney, LT. (1954), 'Establishing Relations with Anti-Social Groups and an Analysis of their Structure', *Brit. J. Delinq.*, vol. 5, no.1, July, 34-45.

Downes, DM. (1966), *The Delinquent Solution*, London: Routledge & Kegan Paul.

(1968), 'The Gang Myth'. In *The Formative Years*, London: BBC.

Dumpson, JR. (1959), 'An Approach to Antisocial Street Gangs'. In Glueck, S. (ed.), *The Problem of Delinquency*, Cambridge, Mass.: Riverside Press.

Eisenstadt, SN. (1951), 'Delinquent Group-Formation among Immigrant Youth', *Brit. J. Delinq.*, vol. 2, no.1, 34-45.

Empey, LT & Rabow, J. (1961), 'The Provo Experiment in Delinquency Rehabilitation', *Amer. Sociol. Rev.*, vol. 26, October, 679-95.

Empey, LT. (1967), 'Delinquency Theory and Recent Research', *J. Research in Crime and Delinq.*, vol. 4, no.1, 28-41.

Erikson, EH. (1965), 'Identity versus Identity Diffusion'. In Mussen, PH., Conger, JJ & Kagan, J. (eds.), *Readings in Child Development and Personality*, New York: Harper and Row.

(1965), *Childhood and Society*, Harmondsworth: Penguin Books.

Evans, KM. (1962), *Sociometry and Education*, London: Routledge & Kegan Paul

Eysenck, HJ. (1970), *Crime and Personality*, London: Paladin Edition, Granada Publishing.

Farrant, MR. (1965), 'The Nature and Structure of Groups in an Adolescent Society', Exeter University, MA thesis.

Farrant, MR & Marchant, H. (1970), *Making Contact with Unreached Youth*, Manchester: Youth Development Trust.

Ferguson, T. (1952), *The Young Delinquent in his Social Setting*, London: Oxford University Press.

Ferguson, T & Pettigrew, MG. (1954), 'A Study of 718 Slum Families Rehoused for upwards of Ten Years', *Glasgow Medical J.*, vol. 35, no.8.

Festinger, L., Riecken HW & Schachter S. (1956). *When Prophecy Fails*, Minneapolis: University of Minnesota Press.

Fisher, S. (1962), 'Varieties of Juvenile Delinquency', *Brit. J. Crimin.*, vol. 2, no.3, 251-61.

Fletcher, C. (1964), 'Beat and Gangs on Merseyside'. In Raison, T. (ed.) 1966, *Youth in New Society*, London: Rupert Hart-Davis.

Franklyn, J. (1960), *A Dictionary of Rhyming Slang*, London: Routledge & Kegan Paul.

Freud, S. (1922), *Group Psychology and the Analysis of the Ego*, London: Hogarth Press.

Friedlander, K. (1947), *The Psycho-Analytical Approach to Juvenile Delinquency*, London: Routledge & Kegan Paul.

Fyvel, TR. (1963), *The Insecure Offenders*, Harmondsworth: Penguin Books.

Gannon, TM. (1967), 'Dimensions of Current Gang Delinquency', *J. Research in Crime and Delinq.*, vol. 4, no.1, 119-31.

Geis, G. (1965), 'Juvenile Gangs', President's Committee on Juvenile Delinquency and Youth Crime, Washington.

Gerrard NL. (1964), 'The Core Member of the Gang', *Brit. J. Crimin.*, vol. 4, no.4, 361-71.

Gillambordo, R. (ed.) (1966), *Juvenile Delinquency*, New York: John Wiley.

Gibbens, TCN, Pond DA & Stafford-Clerk, D. (1959), 'A Follow-up Study of Criminal Psychopaths', *J. Mental Science*, vol. 105, no.438, 108-15.
(1970), 'How Should We Treat Violent Offenders?', *New Society*, no.414, 3 September, 408-10.

Gibbens, TCN & Ahrenfeldt RH. (eds.) (1966), *Cultural Factors in Delinquency*, London: Tavistock.

Gibson HB & Hanson, R. (1969), 'Peer Ratings as Predictors of School Behaviour and Delinquency', *Brit. J. Soc. Clin. Psychol.*, vol. 8, 313-22.

Glueck S & Glueck, ET. (1950), *Unraveling Juvenile Delinquency*, New York: Commonwealth Fund.
(1959), *Predicting Delinquency and Crime*, Cambridge, Mass.: Harvard University Press.
(ed.) (1959), *The Problem of Delinquency*, Cambridge Mass.: Riverside Press.

Glueck, ET. (1966), 'Identification of Potential Delinquents at 2-3 Years of Age', *Internat. J. Soc. Psychiatry*, 1966, vol. 12, 5-16.

Goetschius, GW & Tash, MJ. (1967), *Working with Unattached Youth*, London: Routledge & Kegan Paul.

Gold, RL. (1958), 'Roles in Sociological Field Observations', *Social Forces*, vol. 36, no.3, 217-23.

Gordon RA. (1967), 'Social Level, Social Disability, and Gang Interaction', *Amer. J. Sociol.*, vol. 73, 42-62.

Grieve, R & Robertson DJ. (1964), *The City and the Region*, University of Glasgow Social and Economic Studies, Occasional Papers No. 2, Edinburgh: Oliver & Boyd.

Halsey, AH. (1972), 'British Action – The E.P.A. and After', Speech to Conference on Social Deprivation and Change in Education, York University, 7 March.

Hanson, K. (1964), *Rebels In The Streets*, New York: Tower Publications.

Hardman, DG. (1967), 'Historical Perspectives of Gang Research', *J. Research in Crime and Delinq.*, vol. 4, no.1, 5-27.

Hargreaves, DH. (1967), *Social Relations in a Secondary School*, London: Routledge & Kegan Paul.

Hindelang, MJ. (1970), 'The Commitment of Delinquents to their Misdeeds: Do Delinquents Drift?', *Social Problems*, vol. 17, no.4, 502-509.

Hood, R & Sparks, R. (1970), *Key Issues in Criminology*, London: World University Library.

House, J. (1965), *The Heart of Glasgow*, London: Hutchinson.

Institute for the Study and Treatment of Delinquency, Scottish Branch, Glasgow Working Party (1970), 'The Carrying of Offensive Weapons', *Brit. J. Crimin.*, vol. 10, no. 3, July, 255-69.

Jansyn, LR. (1966), 'Solidarity and Delinquency in a Street Corner Group', *Amer. Sociol. Rev.*, October, 600-13.

Jephcott, P. (1967), *Time of One's Own*, Edinburgh: Oliver & Boyd.

Jones H. (1960), *Reluctant Rebels*, London: Tavistock.

(1965), 'The Approved School: A Theoretical Model', *Sociol. Rev.*, no.9, June, 99-110.

(1967), *Crime in a Changing Society*, Harmondsworth: Penguin Books.

Jones, M. (1968), *Social Psychiatry in Practice*, Harmondsworth: Penguin Books.

JKantor, D & Bennett, WI. (1968), 'Orientations of Street-Corner Workers and Their Effect on Gangs'. In Wheeler, S. (ed.), *Controlling Delinquents*, New York: John Wiley.

Keiser, RL. (1969), *The Vice Lords: Warriors of the Streets*, New York: Holt, Rinehart & Winston.

Kitsuse, JI & Dietrick, DC. (1959), 'Delinquent Boys: A Critique', *Amer. Sociol. Rev.*, vol. 24, no.2, 208-15.

Klein, MW. (ed.) (1967), *Juvenile Gangs in Context*, New Jersey: Prentice-Hall.

Bibliography

Klein, MW & Crawford, LY. (1967), 'Groups, Gangs, and Cohesiveness', *J. Research in Crime and Delinq.*, vol. 4, no.1, 63-75.

Klein, MW. (1971), *Street Gangs and Street Workers*, Englewood Cliffs, New Jersey: Prentice-Hall.

Kluckhohn, FR. (1940), 'The Participant Observer Technique in Small Communities', *Amer. J. Sociol.*, 1940, vol. XLVI, no.3, 331-43.

Kobrin, S. (1951), 'The Conflict of Values in Delinquency Areas', *Amer. Sociol. Rev.*, vol. 16, 656-61.

(1959), 'The Chicago Area Project - A Twenty-five-year Assessment', *Annals*, vol. 322, March, 20-9.

(1961), 'Sociological Aspects of the Development of a Street Corner Group: An Exploratory Study', *Amer. J. Orthopsych.*, vol. 31, no.4, 685-702.

(1962), 'The Impact of Cultural Factors on Selected Problems of Adolescent Development in the Middle and Lower Class', *Amer. J. Orthopsych.*, vol. 32, no.3, 387-90.

Laurie, P. (1965), *Teenage Revolution*, London: Anthony Blond.

Liebow, E. (1967), *Tally's Corner*, London: Routledge & Kegan Paul.

Lindsay, C. (1970), *School and Community*, Edinburgh: Pergamon Press.

Lorenz, K. (1966), *On Aggression*, London: Methuen.

McArthur, A & Long, K. (1964), *No Mean City*, London: Transworld Publishers, Corgi Edition.

McArthur, A & Watts, P. (1969), *No Bad Money*, London: Transworld Publishers, Corgi Edition.

McClintock, FH. (1963), *Crimes of Violence*, London: Macmillan.

McCord, J & McCord, W. (1959), 'A Follow-up Report on the Cambridge-Somerville Youth Study', *Annals*, no. 321-3, 89-96.

(1964), *The Psychopath*, Princeton, New Jersey: Van Nostrand.

McGhee, B. (1963), *Cut and Run*, London: Transworld Publishers, Corgi Edition.

McKay, HD. (1959), 'The Neighbourhood and Child Conduct'. In Glueck, S. (ed.), *The Problem of Delinquency*, Cambridge, Mass.: Riverside Press.

McQuaid, J. (1968), 'An Inquiry into the Personality Structure of the Scot', *Brit. Med. Students' J.*, Autumn, vol. 23, 43-5.

(1970), 'A Personality Profile of Delinquent Boys in Scottish Approved Schools', *Brit. J. Crimin.*, vol. 10, no.2, April, 147-57.

Mack, JA. (1957), 'The Scarred Page', *Scotland*, March, 11-13.

(1958), 'Crime in Glasgow'. In Cunnison, J & Gilfillan, JBS (eds.), *The Third Statistical Account of Scotland*, vol. 5, The City of Glasgow, Glasgow: Collins.

(1963), 'Police Juvenile Liaison Schemes', *Brit. J. Crimin.*, April, 361-75.
(1964), 'Full-time Miscreants, Delinquent Neighbourhoods, and Criminal Networks', *Brit. J. Sociol.*, 38-53.
(1968), 'Police Juvenile Liaison – Practice and Evaluation', Glasgow: School of Social Study.
(1968), 'Crime and Violence: a statistical note'. Article in *Glasgow Herald*, 15 November.

Makarenko, AS. (1951), *The Road to Life*, Moscow: Foreign Languages Publishing House. Translated in three parts by I. and T. Litvinov.

Mannheim, H. (1965), *Comparative Criminology*, vol. 2, London: Routledge & Kegan Paul.

Martin, JM. (1961), *Juvenile Vandalism*, Springfield, Ill.: Charles C. Thomas.

Mattick, HW & Caplan, NS. (1967), 'Stake Animals, Loud-Talking, and Leadership in Do-Nothing and Do-Something Situations'. In Klein, MW. (ed.), *Juvenile Gangs in Context*, New Jersey: Prentice-Hall.

Matza, D & Sykes, GM. (1957), 'Techniques of Neutralization: A Theory of Delinquency', *Amer. Sociol. Rev.*, vol. 22, 664-70.
(1961), 'Juvenile Delinquency and Subterranean Values', *Amer. Sociol. Rev.*, vol. 26, 712-19.

Matza, D. (1964), *Delinquency and Drift*, New York: John Wiley.
(1969), *Becoming Deviant*, New Jersey: Prentice-Hall.

May, D. (1971), 'Delinquency Control and the Treatment Model: Some Implications of Recent Legislation', *Brit. J. Crimin.*, vol. 11, no.4, October, 359-70.

Mays, JB. (1954), *Growing Up in the City*, Liverpool: Liverpool University Press.
(1959), *On the Threshold of Delinquency*, Liverpool: Liverpool University Press.
(1963), 'Delinquency Areas – A Re-assessment', *Brit. J. Crimin.*, January, 216-30.
(1965), *The Young Pretenders*, London: Michael Joseph.
(1965), 'The Liverpool Police Liaison Officer Scheme', *Sociol. Rev.*, no.9, June, 185-200.
(1967), *Crime and the Social Structure*, London: Faber & Faber.
(1968), 'Crime and the Urban Pattern', *Sociol. Rev.*, vol. 16, no.2, 241-55.

Merton, RK. (1957), *Social Theory and Social Structure*, New York: Free Press of Glencoe.

Meyerhoff, HL & Meyerhoff, BG. (1964), 'Field Observations of Middle Class "Gangs"', *Social Forces*, March, vol. 42, no.3, 328-36.

Miller, SM & Riessman, F. (1961), 'The Working Class Subculture: A New

View', *Social Problems*, vol. 9, no.1, 86-97.
Miller, WB. (1957), 'The Impact of a Community Group Work Program on Delinquent Corner Groups', *Social Service Rev.*, vol. 31, 390-406.
(1958), 'Lower Class Culture as a Generating Milieu of Gang Delinquency', *J. Social Issues*, vol. 14, Summer, 5-19.
(1962), 'The Impact of a Total-Community Delinquency Control Project', *Social Problems*, vol. 10, no.2, Autumn, 168-91.
(1966), 'Violent Crimes in City Gangs', *Annals*, 364, March, 96-112.
Miller, WB, Geertz, H & Cutter, HSG. (1961), 'Aggression in a Boys' Street-Corner Group', *Psychiatry*, vol. 24, November, 283-98.
Monod, J. (1967), 'Juvenile Gangs in Paris: Towards a Structural Analysis', *J. Research in Crime and Delinq.*, vol. 4, no.1, 142-65.
Morris, T. (1957), *The Criminal Area*, London: Routledge & Kegan Paul.
Morse, M. (1965), *The Unattached*, Harmondsworth: Penguin Books.
New York City Youth Board (1958), *Reaching The Unreached Family*, New York: New York City Youth Board.
(1960), *Reaching The Fighting Gang*, New York: New York City Youth Board.
Oakley, CA. (1967), *The Second City*, Glasgow: Blackie.
Pfautz, H. (1961), 'Group Theory and Collective Behavior', *Social Problems*, vol. 9, no.2, 167-74.
Phillipson, CM. (1971), 'Juvenile Delinquency and the School'. In Carson, WG & Wiles, P. (eds.), *Crime and Delinquency in Britain*, London: Martin Robertson.
Piliavin, I & Briar, S. (1964), 'Police Encounters with Juveniles', *Amer. J. Sociol*, vol. 70, no.2, 206-14.
Polsky, HW. (1962), *Cottage Six*, New York: John Wiley for Russell Sage Foundation.
Power, MJ, Alderson, MR, Phillipson, CM, Shoenberg, E & Morris, JN. (1967), 'Delinquent Schools?', *New Society*, 19 October, 542-3.
Power, MJ, Benn, RT & Morris, JN (1972), 'Neighbourhood, School, and Juveniles before the Court', *Brit. J. Crimin.*, vol. 12, no.2, 111-32.
Powers, E & Witmer, H. (1950), *An Experiment in the Prevention of Delinquency*, New York: Columbia University Press.
Reckless, WC, Dinitz, S & Murray, E. (1956), 'Self-Concept as an Insulator against Delinquency', *Amer. Sociol. Rev.*, 21, 744-6.
Redl, F. (1945), 'The Psychology of Gang Formation and the Treatment of Juvenile Delinquents'. In *The Psychoanalytic Study of the Child*, vol. I, 367-77.
(1956), Article in Witmer, HL & Kotinsky, R. (eds.), *New Perspectives*

for Research on Juvenile Delinquency, Washington: Government Printing Office.

Redl, F & Wineman, D. (1957), *The Aggressive Child*, New York: Free Press of Glencoe.

Report by a Joint Working Party on Community Problems, appointed by the Corporation of the City of Glasgow and the Secretary of State for Scotland, 1969.

Rivera, RJ & Short, JF., jnr. (1967), 'Occupational Goals: A Comparative Analysis'. In Klein, MW. (ed.), *Juvenile Gangs in Context*, New Jersey: Prentice-Hall.

Robertson, DJ. (1958), 'Population, Past and Present'. In Cunnison, J & Gilfillian, JBS, *Glasgow*, Third Statistical Account of Scotland.

Robison, SM. (1964), 'Why Juvenile Delinquency Preventive Programs are Ineffective'. In Dressier, D. (ed.), *Readings in Criminology and Penology*, New York: Columbia University Press.

Rose, G. (1959), 'Status and Grouping in a Borstal Institution', *Brit. J. Delinq.*, vol. IX, no.4, 258-75.

(1967), *Schools for Young Offenders*, London: Tavistock.

Rose, G & Hamilton, RA. (1970), 'Effects of a Juvenile Liaison Scheme', *Brit. J. Crimin.*, vol. 10, no.1, 2-20.

Rutter, M, Tizard, J & Whitmore, K. (1970), *Education, Health, and Behaviour*, London: Longmans.

Salisbury, HE. (1959), *The Shook-up Generation*, London: Michael Joseph.

Scarpitti, FR, Murray, E, Dinitz, S & Reckless, WC. (1960), 'The "Good" Boy in a High Delinquency Area: Four Years Later', *Amer. Sociol. Rev.*, vol. 25, 555-8.

Schwartz, MS & Schwartz, CG. (1955), 'Problems in Participant Observation', *Amer. J. Sociol.*, vol. 60, 343-53.

Schwendinger, H & Schwendinger, J. (1967), 'Delinquent Stereotypes of Probable Victims'. In Klein, MW. (ed.), *Juvenile Gangs in Context*, New Jersey: Prentice-Hall.

Schwitzgebel, R. (1965), *Streetcorner Research*, Cambridge, Mass.: Harvard University Press.

Scott, P. (1956), 'Gangs and Delinquent Groups in London', *Brit. J. Delinq.*, vol. 7, no.1, 4-24.

(1964), 'Approved School Success Rates', *Brit. J. Crimin.*, vol. 4, 525-56.

Scottish Housing Advisory Committee (1967), *Scotland's Older Houses – Report of the Sub-Committee on Unfit Housing*, Edinburgh: HMSO.

Sherif, M & Sherif, CW. (1964), *Reference Groups*, New York: Harper & Row.

(1967), 'Group Processes and Collective Interaction in Delinquent

Activities', *J. Research in Crime and Delinq.*, vol. 4, no.1, 43-62.
Shields, JVM & Duncan, JA. (1964), *The State of Crime in Scotland*, London: Tavistock.
Shields, R. (1962), *A Cure of Delinquents*, London: Heinemann.
Short, JF, jnr. (1963), Introduction to abridged edition of Thrasher, FM, *The Gang*, Chicago: University of Chicago Press.
Short, JF, jnr. & Strodtbeck, FL. (1965), *Group Process and Gang Delinquency*, Chicago: University of Chicago Press.
Short, JF, jnr. (ed.) (1968), *Gang Delinquency and Delinquent Subcultures*, New York: Harper and Row.
Sillitoe, P. (1955), *Cloak without Dagger*, London: Cassell.
Smith, C. (1966), 'The Youth Service and Delinquency Prevention', *Howard J.*, June, 42-51.
Smith, C, Farrant, M & Marchant, H. (1972), *The Wincroft Youth Project*, London: Tavistock.
Sparks, RF & Hood, RG. (eds.) (1968), *The Residential Treatment of Disturbed and Delinquent Boys*, Cambridge: Institute of Criminology.
Spencer, JC. (1950), 'The Unclubbable Adolescent', *Brit. J. Delinq.*, vol. I, no.1, October, 113-24.
— (1964), *Stress and Release in an Urban Estate*, London: Tavistock.
Spergel, I. (1964), *Racketville, Slumtown, Haulburg*, Chicago: University of Chicago Press.
— (1966), *Street Gang Work: Theory and Practice*, Reading, Mass.: Addison, Wesley.
Spinley, BM. (1953), *The Deprived and the Privileged*, London: Routledge & Kegan Paul.
Stalker, CG. (1966), 'Stabbings', *J. Law Soc. of Scotland*, vol. XI, no.1, January, 12-15.
Storr, A. (1968), *Human Aggression*, London: Allen Lane, The Penguin Press.
Stott, DH. (1960), 'The Prediction of Delinquency from Non-delinquent Behaviour', *Brit. J. Delinq.*, vol. 10, no.3, 195-210.
— (1961), 'Glasgow Survey of Boys Put on Probation During 1957', University of Glasgow.
— (1964), *Thirty-Three Troublesome Children*, London: National Children's Home.
— (1966), *Studies of Troublesome Children*, London: Tavistock.
— (1971), *The Social Adjustment of Children*, Manual of the Bristol Social Adjustment Guides, Fourth Edition, London: University of London Press.
Stürup, GK. (1952), 'The Treatment of Criminal Psychopaths in

Herstedvester', *Brit. J. Med. Psychol.*, 25, 31, 31-8.
  (1968), *Treating the 'Untreatable': Chronic Criminals at Herstedvester*, Baltimore: John Hopkins Press.
Sullivan, MA, jnr., Queen, ST & Patrick, RC, jnr. (1958), 'Participant Observation as employed in the Study of a Military Training Program', *Amer. Sociol. Rev.*, vol. 23, 660-7.
Suttles, CD. (1968), *The Social Order of the Slum*, Chicago: University of Chicago Press.
Taylor, LJ. (1968), 'Alienation, Anomie and Delinquency', *Brit. J. Soc. Clin. Psychol.*, 7, 93-105.
  (1971), *Deviance and Society*, London: Michael Joseph.
Taylor, M. (1971), *Study of the Juvenile Liaison Scheme in West Ham 1961-1965*, London: HMSO.
Tennent, TG. (1971), 'School Non-Attendance and Delinquency', *Educ. Res.*, vol. 13, no.3, 185-190.
Thomson, A. (1895), 'Random Notes on Maryhill, 1750-1894', Glasgow.
Thrasher, FM. (1927), *The Gang*, Chicago: University of Chicago Press.
Toby, J. (1966), 'Violence and the Masculine Ideal: Some Qualitative Data', *Annals*, 364, March 1966, 19-27.
Toch, H. (1969), *Violent Men*, Chicago: Aldine.
Turner, ML. (1953), *Ship without Sails*, London: University of London Press.
Turner, ML & Spencer, JC (1955), 'Spontaneous Youth Groups and Gangs'. In Kuenstler, P. H. K. (ed.), *Spontaneous Youth Groups*, London: University of London Press.
Truxal, AG. (1929), *Outdoor Recreation Legislation and its Effectiveness*, New York: Columbia University Press.
Tyerman, MJ. (1968), *Truancy*, London: University of London Press.
Valentine, CA. (1968), *Culture and Poverty*, Chicago: University of Chicago Press.
Vaz, EW. (1962), 'Juvenile Gang Delinquency in Paris,' *Social Problems*, vol. 10, no.1, Summer, 23-31.
Veness, T. (1962), *School Leavers: Their Aspirations and Expectations*, London: Methuen.
Vidich, AJ. (1955), 'Participant Observation and the Collection and Interpretation of Data', *Amer. J. Sociol.*, vol. 60, 354-60.
Walker, N, Hammond, W, Steer, D & Carr-Hill, R. (1970), 'The Violent Offender - Reality or Illusion?', Oxford University Penal Research Unit, Occasional Paper Number One, Oxford: Basil Blackwell.
Ward, C. (1970), *Violence: Its Nature, Causes and Remedies*, Harmondsworth: Penguin Education, Connexions Series.

Webb, J. (1962), 'The Sociology of a School', *Brit. J. Sociol.*, vol. 13, no.3, September, 264-72.
Werthman, C & Piliavin, I. (1967), 'Gang Members and the Police'. In Bordua, D. (ed.), *The Police: Six Sociological Essays*, New York: John Wiley.
West, DJ. (1967), *The Young Offender*, Harmondsworth: Penguin Books.
(1969), Present Conduct and Future Delinquency, London: Heinemann.
West, DJ & Gibson, HB. (1970), 'Social and Intellectual Handicaps as Precursors of Early Delinquency', *Brit. J. Crimin.*, vol. 10, no.1, 21-32.
West, DJ & Farrington, DR. (1971), 'A Comparison Between Early Delinquents and Young Aggressivcs', *Brit. J. Crimin.*, vol. 11, no.4, 341-58.
Whiteley, JS. (1968), 'The Treatment of Delinquents in a Therapeutic Community', *Howard J.*, vol. XII, no.3, 183-90.
Whyte, WF. (1943), 'A Slum Sex Code', *Amer. J. Sociol.*, vol. XLIX, July, 24-31.
(1955), *Street Corner Society*, Second Edition, Chicago: University of Chicago Press.
Wilkins, LT. (1961), 'Crime, Cause and Treatment: Recent Research and Theory', *Educ. Res.*, vol. IV, no.1, November, 18-33.
(1963), 'Juvenile Delinquency: A Critical Review of Research and Theory', *Educ. Res.*, vol. V, no.2, 104-19.
(1964), *Social Deviance*, London: Tavistock.
Wilkinson, CJ. (1964), 'The Decline of a Success Rate?', *Approved Schools Gazette*, vol. 57, no.10, 391-3.
Willmott, P. (1966), *Adolescent Boys of East London*, London: Routledge & Kegan Paul.
Wills, WD. (1971), *Spare the Child*, Harmondsworth: Penguin Books.
Wolfgang, ME. (1966), 'A Preface to Violence', *Annals*, 346, March, 1-7.
Wolfgang, ME & Ferracuti, F. (1967), *The Subculture of Violence*, London: Tavistock.
Wolman, B. (1951), 'Spontaneous Groups of Children and Adolescents in Israel', *J. Social Psych.*, 34, 171-82.
Wootton, B. (1959), *Social Science and Social Pathology*, London: Allen & Unwin.
Yablonsky, L. (1959), 'The Delinquent Gang as a Near-Group', *Social Problems*, vol. 7, no.2, 108-17.
– (1962), *The Violent Gang*, London: Collier-Macmillan; (1967) Harmondsworth: Penguin Books.
– (1965), *The Tunnel Back: Synanon*, New York: Macmillan.
Yinger, JM. (1960), 'Contraculture and Subculture', *Amer. Social. Rev.*, vol. 25, no.5, 625-35.
Young, M. (1965), *Innovation and Research in Education*, London: Routledge & Kegan Paul.

Index

Adams, S, cost of detached workers, 194

Aichhorn, August, idea of therapeutic communities (*Wayward Youth*), 191

Approved schools, boys on leave, 1, 15 and n1, 120-2, 215; abscondings, 5, 25-6, 36, 81, 114, 188; group counselling, 37; declining success rate, 187-8; institutional practices, 188-9; psychiatric and psychological staff, 189; use of corporal punishment, 189; after-care, 189; conditions of employment, 189-90; staff-pupil ratio, 190; change of name, 190; subordination of treatment to containment, 190; subterranean peer group culture, 190-1; history of truancy among inmates, 200

Armstrong, Gail, interim reports on Glasgow gangs, 148

Arneil, GC, 'Rickets returns in British children', 150

— and Crosbie, JC, 'Infantile Rickets returns to Glasgow', 150

Auld, MH, 'Attaching Social Workers to Schools', 201

Australia, pre-adolescent gangs, 141

Barker, Paul, and community's punitive reaction, 145 ('The Margate Offenders')

Batey, NR and MacBain, GC, ages of victims and weapon used, 147 ('Injury by Stabbing')

Becker, HS, pathological explanations of deviance, 178; typology of deviant behaviour, 180 (*The Outsiders*)

Beeley, AL, 'A Sociopsychological Theory of Crime and Delinquency', 198

Bermant, Chaim I, *Jericho Sleep Alone*, 128

Bernstein, Basil, on 'selection', 116

Bernstein, Saul, problem of the 'gang psycho', 183; and recent gang activity, 184; and street-corner workers, 194 (*Youth on the Streets*)

Bernstein, Walter, 'The Cherubs are Rumbling', n9.

Bettleheim, B, 'Violence: A Neglected Mode of Behaviour', 200

Bibb, M, 'Gang-Related Services of Mobilization for Youth', 201

Bloch, HA, and Niederhoffer, A, 68, 71, 78, 138; and leadership, 162; and education, 171; and psychopathic disturbance in deviants, 183 (*The Gang*)

Bloom, B, the school as a predictor of delinquency, 197 (*Stability and Change in Human Characteristics*)

Bolitho, William, on Glasgow, 128

Bordua, DJ, 'Delinquent Sub-cultures', 172

Borstal institutions, 188-9; failure rates, 188

Boston R, 'The Glasgow Gangs', 148, 187

Brennan, T, *Reshaping a City*, 136

Briggs, DL, 'A Transitional Therapeutic Community for Young Violent Offenders', 191

Bristol, housing estate and the 'Espressos', 142; Social Adjustment guide, 197

Bulletin, and a 'reign of terror', 150, 151

Burt, Sir Cyril, 220; and teachers as predictors of delinquency, 222 (*The Young Delinquent*)

Cadogan Committee, and effect of corporal punishment, 209

Cambridge-Somerville Youth Study, 209

Cambridge Study in Delinquent Development, 133

Carson, WG and Wiles, P, evaluation of Matza, 156 (*Crime and Delinquency in Britain*)

Cavan, RS, specialised vocabulary, 173 (*Juvenile Delinquency*)

Chicago Area Project, 193

Chicago School, and remedial action for delinquent gangs, 203

Clark, DH, 'The Therapeutic Community', 181

Index

Cloward, RA, 202-3
— and Ohlin, LE, 12, 184; theoretical writings, 137, 150, 152-3; and gangs in slum clearance projects, 148; sources of gang violence, 170; delinquent response to social injustice, 152; theory of delinquent subcultures, 152-3, 156, 158; *criminal, conflict* and *retreatist* types, 153; and psychopathological explanations of deviance, 182; and the detached worker, 193; target for preventive action, 195 (*Delinquency and Opportunity: A Theory of Delinquent Gangs*)

Cohen, AK, 171-2, 183; and recreational facilities, 115; and repudiation of middle-class standards, 116, 152-3, 171, 176; theoretical writings 137, 152-3; theory of status frustration, 144 and n31, 153; characteristics of delinquent subculture, 152; and group autonomy, 163; short-run hedonism, 175; non-utilitarian gang activities, 176 (*Delinquent Boys: The Culture of the Gang*)
— and Short, JF, 'Research in Delinquent Sub-Cultures', 177

Cohen, Stan, xi; 'Mods, Rockers, and the Rest', 145; 'Research into group violence and vandalism among adolescents', 169, 178; 'Who are the Vandals?', 177; *Images of Deviance*, 148, 197

Cooper, CN, 'The Chicago YMCA Detached Workers', 193

Craft, M, and therapeutic communities, 191 ('A Follow-up Study of Disturbed Juvenile Delinquents')

Crane, AR, pre-adolescent gangs and moral development, 141 ('The Development of Moral Values in Children')

Crawford, PL, *et alii*, 182-3, 193; and club leadership, 160; role allocation, 162 (*Working with Teenage Gangs*)

Cressey, Donald, and group therapy, 192, 193 ('Changing Criminals')

Cullingworth, JB, *A Profile of Glasgow Housing* (1965), 128

Daily Record, Pat Roller column, 51

Darner, S, and an urban research centre, 203 ('Missing facts on life in Glasgow')

Defoe, Daniel, on Glasgow, 128 (*A Journey through Scotland*)

Delaney, LT, and role allocation, 162 ('Establishing Relations with Anti-Social Groups')

Downes, David, xi; 139, 145, 154 and n33, 156, n34, 171, 175, 203; and Teddy boys, 141; delinquency in Stepney and Poplar, 144-5, 175, 177; and conformity to working-class value systems 156; delinquent reaction to school, 171; and short-run hedonism, 175; and poverty as a force for crime, 177, 203 (*The Delinquent Solution*); 'The Gang Myth', 139, 194

Edinburgh, gang names 10; 131; crime rate, 149

Empey, LT, and group cohesion, 166; and episodic delinquent acts, 166 ('Delinquency Theory and Recent Research')
— and Rabow, J, criterion for treatment and release, 191, 195 ('The Provo Experiment in Delinquency Rehabilitation')

England, absence of structural gangs in the 50s and 60s, 141-2, 145-6, 172; Mods and Rockers disturbances, 73, 145; official crime statistics, 149; differentiated from US, 156; research into psychological factors in gang members, 183-4; police juvenile liaison schemes, 201

Evans, KM, characteristics of leadership, 160 (*Sociometry and Education*)

Eysenck, HJ, characteristics of psychopaths, 175 (*Crime and Personality*)

Farrant, Michael, housing estate study, 143, 146; power of the peer group, 171 (The Nature and Structure of Groups in an Adolescent Society')

Ferguson, T, juvenile delinquency in Glasgow, 146-7, 202 (*The Young Delinquent in his Social Setting*)
— and Pettigrew, MG, rehousing of slum families, 171 ('A Study of 718 Slum Families Rehoused for upwards of Ten Years')

Index

Festinger, L, *et alii*, *When Prophecy Fails*, 77
Fisher, S, and group membership, 157 ('Varieties of Juvenile Delinquency')
Fletcher, Colin, 'Beat and Gangs on Merseyside', 143, 145
Fleur, LB de, 'Delinquent Gangs in Cross-Cultural Perspective', 154
Franklyn, J, *Dictionary of Rhyming Slang*, n7, n22.
Freud, S, 175; *Group Psychology and the Analysis of the Ego*, 163
Friedlander, K, delinquent failure to defer gratification, 175; prediction of anti-social behaviour, 196-7 (*Psychoanalytical Approach to Juvenile Delinquency*)
Fyvel, TR, Teddy boys and acts of violence, 141 (*The Insecure Offenders*)

Gannon, TM, and group cohesion, 165; recent gang developments, 184 ('Dimensions of Current Gang Delinquency')
Geis, G, and psychopathology of deviance, 198; and recent gang activity, 184; and the detached worker, 193, 194 ('Juvenile Gangs')
Gerrard, NL, 'The Core Member of the Gang', 165
Gibbens, TCN, and brain surgery, 192 ('How Should We Treat Violent Offenders?')
— and Ahrenfeldt, RH, and the gang myth, 146 (*Cultural Factors in Delinquency*)
Gibson, HB and Hanson, R, 'Peer-Ratings as Predictors of School Behaviour and Delinquency', 196
Glasgow, awareness of juvenile violence, 7-8; crime figures for 1965, 8; gang names and territories, 8-11 and n4, 22; background of delinquency, 11-2; reputation for slums and violence, 128, 132, 150-1, 173; monumental housing problem, 128; objects of local pride, 129-30; population increase, 131-2; unemployment, 132, 149; return of juvenile gangs, 139; compared with England (gangs), 139-46 *passim*; (cities), 145; fusion of 'teenage' and 'gang' culture, 143; research into the modern gang, 146-9; rate for alcoholic dependence, 149; juvenile drunkenness, 149; network of inequalities, 150; UCS 'work-in', 150; subculture of violence, 172-4, 195; suggested use of detached workers, 192, 193-4; target for preventive action, 195; resilience of its gang culture, 198; part-time education of schoolchildren, 199-200; use of school social workers, 200; ignorance of its social problems, 203
Glasgow Council on Alcoholism, 149
Glasgow Evening Citizen, gang names, 10-11, and gang history, 135
Glasgow Herald, on background to juvenile delinquency, 11; and gang violence (1916), 134
Glasgow Report on Community Problems (1969), 129 and n25
Glueck, ET, 'Identification of Potential Delinquents at 2-3 Years of Age', 222
Glueck, Sheldon, *The Problem of Delinquency*, 182
Goetschius, GW and Tash, MJ, *Working with Unattached Youth*, 193
Gordon, RA, personality disturbances, 172, 183 ('Social Level, Social Disability, and Gang Interaction')
Grieve, R and Robertson, DJ, on the Gorbals, 129 (*The City and the Region*)

Halsey, AH, 'British Action — The EPA and After', 199
Hardman, DG, and US small town gangs, 137; delinquency and violence-dominated gangs, 172 ('Historical Perspectives of Gang Research')
Hargreaves, DH, 156; and norms of a group, 166; and function of social researchers, 185 (*Social Relations in a Secondary School*)
Hindelang, Michael, 'The Commitment of Delinquents to their Misdeeds', 156

Inner London Education Authority, attitude to research into juvenile delinquency, 198
Institute for the Study and Treatment of Delinquency (ISTD), and carrying offensive weapons, 148; and relationship bet-

Index

ween truancy and delinquency, 200

Jansyn, LR, US gangs, 138; and leadership, 160; and gang solidarity, 164 ('Solidarity and Delinquency in a Street Corner Group')

Jephcott, P, and imbalance in population age structure, 147; Drumchapel Bucks, 166; identification of future gang leaders, 196; nursery schools in Drumchapel, 199 (*Time of One's Own*)

Jones, Howard, on importance of clothes, 98 (*Crime in a Changing Society*); Reluctant Rebels, 190

Jones, Maxwell, *Social Psychiatry in Practice*, 191

Juvenile gangs, preoccupation with clothes, 3, 14, 21, 30, 97-8, 168, 169; position of the police, 7-8, 19, 24-5, 37-43 *passim*, 55 and n11, 108-12, 192; unimportance of religion, 20, 168; relations with girls, 17, 37-8, 45, 62, 86-91, 92-6, 169-70, 201; leadership, 21, 24ff, 83-4, 158-62; drug-taking, 37-8, 45, 95, 106-8, 168; importance of territory, 21-2, 77, 168; tattooing, 67; concern with toughness, 69, 168; desire for status, 78, 98, 168-9; nicknames, 78; desire for notoriety, 80, 169; internal organisation and hierarchy, 81-2, 157-8; violations of 'no-grassing' rule, 84-5; sexual behaviour, 86-92, 119, 144, 168, 169; graffiti, 101-03; research literature, 158-60; lack of remorse, 159, 181; lack of group cohesion, 162-6; main norms, 166-7, 173-4; values, 168-9; use of 'patter', 169; educational, occupational and social background, 170ff.; short-run hedonism, 175-7; wanton and vindictive vandalism, 177; evidence of psychopathological disturbance, 178-84; irrational acts of violence, 179, 180; anxieties about their mental health, 179-80, 180-3; suggested forms of treatment, 185ff; effect of corporal punishment, 185

Kantor, D and Bennett, WI, 'Orientations of Street-Corner Workers and their Effect on Gangs', 193

Keiser, RL, gangs studied, 138; and leadership, 160; role allocation, 162; ideology of brotherhood, 164; use of weapons, 166; irrational violence, 179; recent developments, 184 (*The Vice Lords*)

Kitsuse, JI and Dietrick, DC, and utilitarian behaviour, 177 ('Delinquent Boys: A Critique')

Klein, MW, *Juvenile Gangs in Context*, 138; *Street Gangs and Street Workers*, 193

— and Crawford, LY, and group norms, 166, 167 ('Groups, Gangs and Cohesiveness')

Kobrin, S, 138; use of the detached worker, 217; 'The Impact of Cultural Factors on ... Adolescent Development in the Middle and Lower Classes', 158; 'Sociological Aspects of the ... Street Corner Group', 162, 168, 169, 171, 196

Lane, Homer, and the therapeutic communities, 191

Liebow, E, 137; and short-run hedonism, 176 (*Tally's Corner*)

Little, Alan, teacher-pupil ratios, 199

Lindsay, Catherine, n24; and truancy-delinquency relationship, 200 (*School and Community*)

Liverpool, Merseyside gangs, 143; influence of rock n' roll music, 143; marginal delinquents, 183-4; police juvenile liaison scheme, 201

London, slum gangs of the 1950s, 139; three categories of delinquent groups, 140-41; Teddy boys, 141; East End delinquency, 144; peer groups, 144; Tower Hamlets research, 154, 198

McArthur, A. and Long, K, Razor Kings, 101; and a 'fair fight', 106; *No Mean City*, 73, 101, 106, n30

McClintock, FH, *Crimes of Violence*, 142

McCord, J & W, Follow-up Report on the Cambridge-Somerville Youth Study, 186, 197

McGhee, Bill, gang activity in Glasgow, n6, 136 (*Cut and Run*)

Index

McKay, HD, 'The Neighbourhood and Child Conduct', 115

McQuaid, J, sociopathic singularity of south-west Scotland, 150 ('Personality Structure of the Scot', 'Personality Profile of Delinquent Boys')

Mack, JA, and girls in gangs, 87; and birth of the gangs, 132 ('Crime in Glasgow'); and crime rates by ages, 148-9, 201 ('Crime and Violence'); and gang battles, 134; 'Police Juvenile Liaison Schemes', 201-2

Makarenko, AS, and therapeutic communities, 191 (*The Road to Life*)

Mannheim, H, utilitarian and non-utilitarian acts, 177 (*Comparative Criminology*)

Martin, JM, *Juvenile Vandalism*, 177

Mass media, television programmes, 7, 9, 82; and Glasgow gang violence, 8, 132-5, 191-2; and gang notoriety, 80 and n18; 141-2; exaggeration of malicious damage, 145; and new housing estates, 148

Mattick, HW and Caplan, NS, 'Stake Animals, Loud-Talking, and Leadership in Do-Nothing and Do-Something Situations', 161

Matza, D, xi, 9, 152, 192, 207; pathological explanations of deviance, 111, 116, 178, 180; sense of desperation, 150-1; similarity of delinquents to other youths, 155; theory of delinquency, 155-6; and loyalty, 167 (*Delinquency and Drift, Becoming Deviant*)

— and Sykes, GM, justifications of delinquent behaviour, 111-2 ('Techniques of Neutralization'); similarity between 'delinquent' and 'gentleman' values, 155 ('Juvenile Delinquency and Subterranean Values')

May, D, 'Delinquency Control and the Treatment Model', 190

Mays, JB, 'Crime and the Urban Pattern', 156; 'Delinquency Areas', 183; *Growing up in the City*, 181, 185, 200; 'The Liverpool Police Liaison Scheme', 201

Merton, RK, and empirical research, 137 (*Social Theory and Social Structure*)

Meyerhoff, HL and BG, and Yablonsky's 'near-group' concept, 165; and the detached worker, 194 ('Field Observations of Middle Class "Gangs"')

Midwinter, Eric, Liverpool EPA, 199

Miller, WB, 100, 138, 152, 156, 172, 183; 'Aggression in a Boys' Street-Corner Group', 163-4, 182; 'The Impact of a Community Group Work Program on Delinquent Corner Groups', 159, 186, 193-4, 194; 'The Impact of Total-Community Delinquency Control Project ('synergism' concept), 198; 'Lower Class Culture as a Generating Milieu of Gang Delinquency', 100, 154, 156, 163, 168-9; 'Violent Crimes in City Gangs', 119, 138, 177

Miller, SM. and Reissman, F, and middle-class 'acting-out', 175-6 ('The Working Class Subculture')

Monod, J, 154; and 'argot', 169 ('Juvenile Gangs in Paris')

Morris, J, and 'psychiatric delinquency', 183; (*The Criminal Area*)

Morse, Mary, differing fields of care, 192; short-run hedonism, 175 and the street-corner worker, 193, 194; identification of future troublemakers, 196; and youth clubs, 202 (*The Unattached*)

New York, gang invasion, n4; baseball project, 47; Pirate gang, 68, 138, 162; a 'fair fight', 106; gang differences, 138; close parallel to Glasgow gangs, 156; Easterhouse gangs amnesty, 187; Mobilization for Youth project, 201

New York City Youth Board, 106, 160, 165, 183 (*Reaching the Fighting Gang*); and street-corner workers, 193-4

Oakley, CA, *The Second City*, 131

Ohlin, Lloyd, 152; see Cloward, RA.

Paris, research into gang subcultures, 154; and gang 'argot', 169

People's Journal, and Glasgow gangs, 133

Pfautz, H, 'Group Theory and Collective Behavior', 165, 173, 195

Phillipson, CM, 'Juvenile Delinquency and

233

Index

the School', 197-9, 201
Piliavin, I and Briar, S, 'Police Encounters with Juveniles', 108, n10
Plowden Committee, viability of EPA's, 199; effect of pre-schooling, 199
Polsky, Howard, analysis of peer group culture (*Cottage Six*), 160 and n34; and delinquent leadership, 161; psychotic behaviour in gang members, 183; staff-pupil ratios and relations, 190; subordination of therapy to containment, 190; acceptance of boys' system of values, 190-1
Power, M. *et alii*, 'Delinquent Schools?', 154, 198; 'Neighbourhood, School, and Juveniles before the Court', 154, 198
Powers, E. and Witmer, H, *An Experiment in the Prevention of Delinquency*, 186

Presley, Elvis, 73

Redl, F, 182; 'The Psychology of Gang Formation and the Treatment of Juvenile Delinquents', 189
Rhyming slang, 19, 61, 73, 100, n7, n22
Robertson, DJ, 'Population, Past and Present', 131
Robison, SM, 'Why Juvenile Delinquency Preventive Programs are Ineffective', 115
Rose, G, *Schools for Young Offenders*, 187, 195; 'Status and Grouping in a Borstal Institution', 188
— and Hamilton, RA, 'Effects of a Juvenile Liaison Scheme', 201-2
Rutter, M, *et alii*, *Education, Health and Behaviour*, 181

Salisbury, Harrison, 'mother swearing', 100; definition of 'heart', 168; and gang mental disturbance, 183; police, hot-rod clubs, 202; and the will to prevent gangs, 203 (*The Shook up Generation*)
Schools, pupil violence, 20-1 and n8, 63-4; gang burglaries, 171; as predictors of delinquency, 196-7; variation in delinquent characteristics, 196; redeployment of resources 199-200; and the attack on delinquency, 199-203

Schwendinger, H & J, 'Delinquent Stereotypes of Probable Victims', 163
Schwitzgebel, R, self-help movements, 192 (*Streetcorner Research*)
Scott, P, three categories of delinquent groups, 139-41, 143; and psychological factors in gang leaders, 183; and 'breaking-up' the gang, 187 ('Gangs and Delinquent groups in London'); 'Approved School Success Rates', 188
Scottish Housing Advisory Committee, *Scotland's Older Houses*, n28
Shanas, E, investigation into recreation and delinquency, 115
Sherif, M & CW, 183, 199; and gang leaders, 160; and norms, 166, 168; psychopathological explanations of deviance, 178, 182; aloofness of academic researchers, 186; results of dispersing gangs, 186 (*Reference Groups*)
Shields, R, and therapeutic communities, 191 (*A Cure of Delinquents*)
Shields, VTM, and Duncan, JA, *The State of Crime in Scotland*, 12, 149
Short, JF, Jr., n9; 153, 160, 183; and gang notoriety, n17; and Thrasher's *The Gang*, 157, 159; and leadership, 159; status hierarchy, 169 (*Gang Delinquency and Delinquent Subcultures*)
— and Strodtbeck, FL, 153, 154, 160; social disability of gangs, n21; non-existence of full-blown criminal gang, 154; and group membership, 157; and gang leadership, 159-60; influence of group norms, 167; study of parenthood, 170; and factors contributing to job failure, 171, and short-run hedonism, 176; and the detached worker, 193 (*Group Process and Gang Delinquency*)
Sillitoe, Sir Percy, and Glasgow Gangs of the 30s, 87, 132, 134-5; and alcoholism, 149 (*Cloak without Dagger*)
Smith, C, 'The Youth Service and Delinquency Prevention', 193
Southern Press, on juvenile gang violence (1916), 134
Spencer, JC, and Barge Boys' Club, 139, 202; and group loyalty, 164, ('The

Index

Unclubbable Adolescent'); and eliminating the gang, 210; *Stress and Release in an Urban Estate*, 142, 172-3, 183, 187

Spergel, I, role of the girlfriend, 87 (*Racketville, Slumtown, Haulburg*)

Spinley, BM, on London adolescent gangs, 139, 145, 183 (*The Deprived and the Privileged*)

Stalker, CG, 'Stabbings', 147

Stott, DH, 'Glasgow Survey of Boys Put on Probation during 1957', 146 (*Troublesome Children*); Bristol Social Adjustment Guide, 197

Stürup, Dr GK., 'The Treatment of Criminal Psychopaths in Herstedvester', 191

Sunday Chronicle, on gang violence in Glasgow, 133

Suttles, GD, *The Social Order of the Slum*, 12

Taylor, LJ, and acts of vandalism, 170 ('Alienation, Anomie and Delinquency')

Taylor, M, *Study of Juvenile Liaison Scheme in West Ham, 1961-1965*, 201

Tennent, TG, 'School Non-Attendance and Delinquency', 200

Thomson, Alexander, *Random Notes on Maryhill*, 22

Thrasher, FM, 152, 157, 159, 171, 172, 182, 183, 196; origin of the Tongs, n15.; and 'goofy guys', 79; 'Sex in the Gang', 88-9; and leadership, 158-9; and characteristics of a gang, 163; and the destruction of the gang, 186; treatment and prevention, 196 (*The Gang*)

Times, The, on Glasgow gangs, 132

Toch, Hans, and ritualized insults, 101; subculturally induced violence, 180; self-help movements, 191-2, 200 (*Violent Men*)

Truxal, AG, *Outdoor Recreation Legislation*, 115

Turner, ML, and Barge Boys' Club, 139 (*Ship without Sails*)

— and Spencer, JC, and Hoxton juvenile gangs, 139, 160; and gang solidarity, 164-5 ('Spontaneous Youth Groups and Gangs')

Tyerman, MJ, *Truancy*, 200

United States, origin of Chinese gangs (Tongs), n4; social disability of gangs, n21; negro boys and the police, 111; gang differences, 137-8; research into gangs, 152-6; position of lower working-class boys, 152, 153; drug taking, 153-4, 184; importance of status, 156; contrasted with England, 156; subculture of violence, 174; recent gang activity, 184; staff-pupil ratios in custodial institutions, 190; use of detached workers, 193; Group Guidance Project, Los Angeles, 193-4

Valentine, CA, *Culture and Poverty*, 154-5

Veness, T, *School Leavers*, 156

Vaughan, Frankie, 187

Ward, Colin, *Violence*, 200

Webb, J, 'The Sociology of a School', 171

Werthman, C, 169

— and Piliavin, I, 'Gang Members and the Police', n10

West, DJ, and detached worker, 124-5 (*The Young Offender*); *Present Conduct and Future Delinquency*, 196; 'Precursors of Early Delinquency', 196; 'A Comparison Between Early Delinquency and Young Aggressives', 196

Whiteley, JS, 'The Treatment of Delinquents in a Therapeutic Community', 191

Whyte, WF, 183; and gang leaders, 159; and gang co-operativeness, 165; sex code, 170; and social disability, 172 (*Street Corner Society*)

Wilkins, LT, Crime, Cause and Treatment', 169

Wilkinson, CJ, 'The Decline of a Success Rate?' (approved schools), 211

Willmott, P, gangs in Bethnal Green, 144, 156 (*Adolescent Boys of East London*)

Wilson, Mary, report on Glasgow gangs, 148

Wolfgang, ME & Ferracuti, F, 172, 173-4; transference of subculture from one generation to another, 174; location, 174; and the detached worker, 195 (*The Subculture of Violence*)

Wolman, B, and maladjustment in gang

235

Index

members, 183 ('Spontaneous Groups of Children and Adolescents in Israel')

Wootton, B, and recidivism after reformative institutions, 188 (*Social Science and Social Pathology*)

Yablonsky, L, n4, 138, 182-3; baseball project, 47; 'gang bangs', 89; 'mother-swearing', 100-1; social gangs, 141, 156; three types of gangs, 156, 157, 165; and group membership, 157; illusionary numbers, 158; and gang leaders, 159, 160, 161, 187; concept of the 'near group', 165; and sex for the violent boy, 169; part played by violence, 173; profile of the sociopath, 181; marginal delinquents, 183; concept of the gang as a 'pathological entity', 187; and effect of peace meetings, 187; his 'group-fulfilling prophecy', 194 (*The Violent Gang*); therapeutic practice at Synanon, 191 (*The Tunnel Back*)

Young, Kimball, 178

Young, M, *Innovation and Research in Education*, 2